D1598011

'This wonderfully clearly written book shows professional and trainee social workers how they can greatly improve their practice by becoming practical sociologists. It also demonstrates to sociologists how their ideas can inspire concrete activities that are socially beneficial and positively transformative.'

—**David Inglis**, *University of Helsinki, Finland*

'A rich meditation on the intersection between social theory and social work. Christopher Thorpe's excellent contribution brings into focus the importance of ideas and concepts for social work. Wonderful to see the inclusion of Norbert Elias who reflects on the emergence of new forms of "civilized" life mirrored by much of social work's front-line engineering.'

—**Stephen A. Webb**, *Glasgow Caledonian University, Scotland*

'*Social Theory for Social Work* by Chris Thorpe provides a very good foundation for sociological social work approaches to professional practice that many of us have been advocating. It covers crucial sociological perspectives from Durkheim to Bourdieu and applies them to social work, using a critical reflective stance. Moreover, its approach to theory is one that students and practitioners can easily follow.'

—**Lena Dominelli**, *Co-Director, Institute of Hazard, Risk and Resilience, Durham University, UK*

SOCIAL THEORY FOR SOCIAL WORK

Trying to understand what the world looks through the eyes of individuals and groups and how it shapes the ways they think and act is something social workers do all the time. It is what social theorists do too. This book identifies and explains in a highly accessible manner the absolute value of social theory for social work. Drawing on the theoretical ideas and perspectives of a wide range of classical and modern social theorists, the book demonstrates the insights their work can bring to bear on social work practice scenarios, issues and debates.

Departing with the work of the classical theorists, the book covers a diverse range of theoretical traditions including phenomenology, symbolic interactionism, Norbert Elias, Michel Foucault, Pierre Bourdieu, feminism and globalization theory. Putting to work ideas from these different perspectives, a range of social work scenarios, issues and debates are opened up and explored. The final chapter brings together the various theoretical strands, and critically considers the contribution they can make towards realizing core social work values in a rapidly globalizing world.

Demonstrating exactly how and in what ways social theory can make important and enduring contributions to social work, *Social Theory for Social Work* is essential reading for social work students, practitioners and professionals alike.

Christopher Thorpe is a lecturer in sociology at the University of Exeter. His areas of expertise include classical and modern social theory, cultural sociology and social justice. Previously he was at the Robert Gordon University, Aberdeen, where he taught sociology and social theory to social work students. Together with David Inglis, he is author of *An Invitation to Social Theory* (2012).

Student Social Work

www.routledge.com/Student-Social-Work/book-series/SSW
   This exciting new textbook series is ideal for all students studying to be qualified social workers, whether at undergraduate or masters level. Covering key elements of the social work curriculum, the books are accessible, interactive and thought-provoking.

New titles

Human Growth and Development
John Sudbery

Social Work Placements
Mark Doel

Social Work
A Reader
Viviene E. Cree

Sociology for Social Workers and Probation Officers
Viviene E. Cree

Integrating Social Work Theory and Practice
A Practical Skills Guide
Pam Green Lister

Social Work, Law and Ethics
Jonathan Dickens

Becoming a Social Worker, 2nd ed.
Global Narratives
Viviene E. Cree

Social Work and Social Policy, 2nd ed.
An Introduction
Jonathan Dickens

Mental Health Social Work in Context, 2nd ed.
Nick Gould

Forthcoming title

Social Work with Children and Young People, Their Families and Carers
Janet Warren

SOCIAL THEORY FOR SOCIAL WORK

Ideas and Applications

Christopher Thorpe

Routledge
Taylor & Francis Group

LONDON AND NEW YORK

First published 2018
by Routledge
2 Park Square, Milton Park, Abingdon, Oxon OX14 4RN

and by Routledge
711 Third Avenue, New York, NY 10017

Routledge is an imprint of the Taylor & Francis Group, an informa business

© 2018 Christopher Thorpe

British Library Cataloguing-in-Publication Data
A catalogue record for this book is available from the British Library

Library of Congress Cataloging-in-Publication Data
A catalogue record for this book has been requested

ISBN: 978-0-415-82639-6 (hbk)
ISBN: 978-0-415-82640-2 (pbk)
ISBN: 978-0-203-52963-8 (ebk)

Typeset in Bembo
by Apex CoVantage, LLC

Printed in the United Kingdom
by Henry Ling Limited

For Oscar, Marcus-Anthony and Samantha.

CONTENTS

List of tables   x

1 Why social theory matters for social work   1

2 Classical social theory and modern social problems   16

3 Phenomenology and social theory: exploring the lifeworld
   of the service-user   35

4 Symbolic interactionism and the social self   53

5 Norbert Elias: emotions, rationality and self-restraint   71

6 Michel Foucault: social work and professional power   89

7 Pierre Bourdieu: symbolic violence and self-exclusion   107

8 Feminist social theory and social work   124

9 Globalization and social work   143

10 The future of social theory and social work   162

Index   178

TABLES

1.1	What social theory can *do* for social work	10
1.2	Composition of social theoretical knowledge	12
1.3	Structure versus agency debate	13
2.1	Summary of Durkheim	20
2.2	Summary of Marx	26
2.3	Summary of Weber	31
3.1	Summary of Schutz	40
3.2	Summary of Berger and Luckmann	41
3.3	Summary of Bernstein	42
3.4	Summary of Merleau-Ponty	44
4.1	Summary of Mead	57
4.2	Summary of Blumer	58
4.3	Summary of Cooley	59
4.4	Summary of Goffman	60
5.1	Summary of socio-genesis and psycho-genesis	72
5.2	Summary of the civilizing process	76
5.3	Summary of social habitus	77
6.1	Summary of discourse	92
6.2	Summary of governmentality	95
6.3	Summary of surveillance society	96
7.1	Summary of habitus	109
7.2	Summary of types of capital	110
7.3	Summary of fields	112
7.4	Summary of distinction games	115
8.1	Summary of liberal feminist theory	127
8.2	Summary of Marxist-socialist feminist theory	130
8.3	Summary of radical feminist theory	131
8.4	Summary of post-structuralist and post-modernist feminist theory	132

9.1   Summary of Wallerstein   146
9.2   Summary of Beck   148
9.3   Summary of Castells   150
9.4   Summary of the cultural dimensions of globalization   152

1

WHY SOCIAL THEORY MATTERS FOR SOCIAL WORK

> Philosophy and the study of the real world have the same relation to one another as onanism and sexual love.
>
> *– Karl Marx (1998 [1845–46]: 253)*

Of all the quotations you might expect a book about social theory and social work to open with, one that makes reference to 'sexual love' and 'onanism' (masturbation) might not strike you as the most likely. The questions ensue: why was the decision taken to use *that* quote to open *this* book? What was the purpose of doing so? How does it relate to the theoretical ideas, concepts and discussions that fill the ensuing pages? These questions may well be in the forefront of your mind. The idea the quotation is intended to express is certainly a provocative one! Why use it to open a book about social theory and social work? Let us begin by taking a moment to explain why the decision was taken to use *that* quotation and how it relates to the relationship between social theory and social work in the present day.

Born in 1815, in Trier, Germany, Karl Marx was a foundational figure in the development of social theory. As a young philosophy student at the University of Berlin, Marx quickly established a reputation as a highly critical and provocative thinker. Surveying the philosophical scene of the day, Marx was convinced his contemporaries had lost sight of the true purpose of philosophy. Up until now, proclaimed Marx (1998 [1845–46]), 'philosophers have only interpreted the world in various ways – the point, however, is to change it!' Marx was despairing of what he regarded as the overly abstract questions and debates posed by academic philosophers. In his view, philosophy had become little more than self-indulgent mental stimulation – mental masturbation as he likens it – an activity he considered even more reprehensible because it was divorced from people in the real world, whose lives it did little to serve or positively change.

That philosophy had come so far off course, claimed Marx, was because philosophers had lost sight of the fact that for any kind of speculation about human life to take place at all, certain real world factors already had to be in place. These include cultural factors e.g. the normative ideals and values out of which philosophical speculation and debate arise; social factors e.g.

the relationships between individuals and groups that unify and divide different communities; and material factors e.g. certain basic needs such as food and shelter. Furthermore, how these factors interact with one another, Marx claimed, directly shapes the types of questions posed by philosophers and the ideas they develop in response to them. It was clear to Marx that to understand how and why human agents think and behave as they do – this includes philosophers no less – analysis needed to be trained back onto the real world, not away from it. Taking real people in the real world as his starting point, the body of work left by Marx played a definitive role in laying down the conceptual foundations of a new and distinct approach to the analysis of human social life. That form of analysis is social theory.

Fine. But why choose *that* quotation by Karl Marx for *this* book? What does it have to do with social theory and social work? Marx claimed that philosophy had become little more than a form of self-indulgent abstract speculation. In recent years, a similar conception of social theory has begun to take hold among social work professionals, lecturers and students with the result that social theory has come to seem much like the kind of abstract speculation Marx intended it to replace. Social theory appears overly abstract, esoteric and inapplicable to social work. As a generation of social workers whose careers spanned the social and political activism of the 1960s and '70s enters retirement, recognition of the importance of social theory for social work is going with them. For the current generation of social work students and professionals alike, the value of social theory for what they do requires to be identified, explained and demonstrably applied. This book aims to do exactly this.

Social workers have not always held such an uninspired view of social theory. In 1902, attempts to formalize the education of social workers led to the founding of the School of Sociology at the London School of Economics. Sociology and social theory were central to the education of social workers (Jones, 1996, 1983). More than half a century later in 1964, the highly influential social worker and co-founder of the Council for Training in Social Work, Dame Eileen Younghusband (1964: 39), defined social work as centring 'around social problems arising from the interrelation between man and his social environment'. As part of government changes to social work education led by the Younghusband Report (1957), sociology was established as one of the cognate disciplines within social work together with social policy and psychology. During the social and political unrest of the 1960s and '70s, social theory provided the intellectual underpinnings behind the radical social work movement, in particular feminist and Marxist-inspired streams of social work. Grounded in the critical impulses and emancipatory politics of the 'radical turn', the emergence of community-based, anti-oppressive and anti-discriminatory social work began to take root and develop (Langan, 2002). These different but related streams of social work continue to inform mainstream social work theory and practice in the present day.

Since the late 1980s, the perceived value of social theory within social work has steadily declined. This is evident in the progressively fewer, narrow-ranging and sporadic ways social theoretical ideas feature in the social work curriculum, textbooks, monographs and academic journals. Today, social work theory and practice draw far more on individual-centred conceptual paradigms and forms of analysis e.g. psychological, psychoanalytic and existential models and modes of reasoning (Houston, 2014; Levin, Haldar and Picot, 2015). This is particularly true of social work in many parts of Western Europe, North America and Australia. The shift in thinking and practice away from *social* towards *individual* factors is the result of the complex interplay of a number of wider changes to modern society of which the most significant include: the spread of neo-liberal economic ideology and policy; increasing bureaucratization and managerialism; advancing governmentality and surveillance; and the intensification and acceleration of globalization. Understanding exactly how these developments have impacted on social work forms the subject matter of this book.

The social and cultural context in which the relationship between social work and social theory is positioned has changed radically. As both cause and effect of these changes, the rise and rise of individualism is particularly significant in accounting for the negative light in which social theory has come to be cast. The advanced capitalist societies of modern Western Europe and beyond are characterised by very high levels of individualism (Durkheim, 1964 [1893]; Elias, 2001 [1981]; Beck and Beck-Gernsheim, 2002). Individualism refers to a cultural condition that emphasises the moral sanctity and autonomy of the individual. In a culture of individualism, our individuality, uniqueness and autonomy strike as a social fact – as something natural, self-evident and, therefore, for the most part, beyond question. As counter-intuitive as it may seem, however, there is nothing natural or necessary when we conceive of ourselves and others in this way – as individuals. Our individuality is sociological not ontological. Prior to modernity, and in more collectively based cultures still today, the self-conception and identity of individuals was, and continues to be, rooted in wider social collectives such as the family unit and community.

Far from being an inevitable aspect of what it means to be human, individualism is a direct consequence of changes to the organisation and structure of modern society. The classical social theorist Emile Durkheim (Chapter 2) regarded the rising individuality characteristic of modern society as a fundamentally positive development. At the same time he was wary of it too. A situation in which members of society are insufficiently integrated with one another can become pathological (Durkheim, 1964 [1893]). In a culture of pathological individualism, the ways and extent to which social factors shape individual behaviour are (mis)understood and (mis)represented in ways that fail to grasp the significance of the former for explaining the latter. Instead, social factors appear of secondary importance for understanding how individuals think, act and interact. As we shall explore in greater depth, many of the issues and problems faced by social workers and service-users can be seen as having their roots in the excessive, if not already pathological, levels of individualism characteristic of modern society.

In a culture of pathological individualism notions of the social and society are understood in increasingly narrow and constricted terms. The fact that as human beings we are biologically 'individuated' – quite literally, that each of us has our own mind and body – leads us to think that society is something outside of us, something aside from and external to the individual we imagine ourselves to be. In contrast to this view, a far more instructive way of understanding the relationship between the social and the individual involves reimagining society as comprising two forms: on the one hand, organisations, institutions and material artefacts such as books, technology, consumer goods and so on; and on the other, the culturally learned and socially patterned dispositions all human agents come to embody through socialization. In short, the socialized body, what we refer to as the individual, 'is not opposed to society: it is one of its forms of existence' (Bourdieu, 1993: 15).

Since the mid to late 1980s, social work theory, policy and practice have increasingly been (re)organised around the individual at the expense of the social. Individual social workers draw increasingly on individual-centred concepts and theories to assist individual service-users. The 'rising' individualism within social work has not gone unnoticed. Social work academics, professionals and service-user groups have all voiced critical concerns about the rising levels of individualism permeating the profession (Jones, 1996; Kahn and Dominelli, 2000; Ferguson, 2001; Ferguson, 2009; Ferguson and Lavalette, 2004). They are critical of this tendency which they claim has led to a number of negative and unintended consequences, including:

- the tendency within social work in the U.K. since the late 1970s towards the 'theoretical stripping out of the social work curriculum'

  (Jones, 1996)

- the increasing trend among social work academics to 'pull away from seeing what contemporary developments in social theory have to offer practitioners'

  (Singh and Cowden, 2009: 480)

- the narrowing and reduction of social work education and training to a concern with 'practical competencies'

  (Dominelli, 1997)

- an over-emphasis on individual reflexive practice which 'does little to equip social work students with the critical analytic skills they need to address the multi-layered complexity of their clients' problems'

  (Applegate, 2004: 33)

Attempts to resist the ideological individualism at the heart of contemporary social work have met with limited success. Furthermore, as the organisation and delivery of social work around the individual first and foremost continue, a danger exists that it becomes normalized, taken-for-granted, and passes unchallenged by future generations of social workers. This book seeks to interrupt and intervene in this process, which it aims to do by realizing the following aims and objectives:

- to examine how and why changes within modern society have led to a culture of individualism and rationality
- to explain how these changes have led to the rising dominance of individual-centred forms of theory and practice within social work
- to identify and critically appraise the limits of individual-centred theoretical paradigms and knowledge

This book will achieve these aims by:

- identifying how and demonstrating why social theory is an essential accompaniment to social work theory and practice
- demonstrating the relevance and applicability of social theoretical ideas across a range of social work practice scenarios, issues and debates
- drawing attention to the possibilities and limits contained within different social theoretical paradigms and concepts
- explaining social theory in a way that is current, applied and devoid of academic jargon

Defining social theory

In a general sense, social theory is a body of knowledge aimed at making sense of human life, both from a broad historical perspective and specifically too in the forms it takes in society today. Social theory is made up of concepts from, as well as supplying ideas and concepts to, a range of academic disciplines. Of these disciplines, social theory is aligned most closely with sociology. Many of the concepts dealt with in this book were developed by sociologists. But this is not the whole story. Social theory is an intellectually inclusive and versatile body of ideas. Social theory draws on and informs a wide range of academic disciplines including philosophy, psychoanalytic theory, anthropology, history, economics, education studies, literary theory cultural studies and so on. A good example of how social theory has shaped and been shaped by ideas from adjacently positioned disciplines is captured by the ideas of the Austrian psychoanalyst and thinker Sigmund Freud (1856–1939). It would be hard to overestimate the influence Freud's ideas have had on the development of modern social theory. (Freud's ideas have strongly influenced social work theory and practice too.) Freud emphasised the unconscious dimensions of the human mind as crucial for understanding how individuals think, feel and interact. His model of the human psyche draws attention to the formative role social and cultural processes play in shaping the mind in ways that for the most part bypass the conscious awareness of individuals. The idea that social and cultural factors influence how human agents think and act in only partially conscious ways is a recurrent one within modern social theory as we shall see.

Aside from the intellectual content of his ideas, Freud's work is instructive in another important way. Freud's account of the human mind draws on ideas and themes taken from what are now considered different academic disciplines e.g. psychology, sociology, philosophy, etc. The same is true of social theory. Social theory draws on ideas and concepts taken from a wide range of academic disciplines. The points at which those ideas intersect provide many of the analytical constructs used by social theorists to organise their ideas and theories. These include individual and society; structure and agency; objective and subjective; natural and cultural; conscious and unconscious; intended and unintended; and so on. It is important to understand something about how these analytical categories influence the way social theorists try to make sense of human social life before progressing any further.

Modern societies are highly complex entities. From the late eighteenth century onwards, the structure of modern society has come to be divided up into an increasingly wide range of functionally different parts, or spheres. This is what social theorists mean when they refer to modern societies being organised around a highly differentiated, complex division of labour. Within each sphere, individuals perform a specialized and narrow range of activities. No less than any other sphere of society, the intellectual sphere (e.g. universities and academic departments) has been subject to increasing differentiation and specialization, with each discipline and sub-discipline having developed its own conceptual ideas and distinct ways of thinking which the people working within it use to make sense of and construct the objects they study. Over time, the people working within these different disciplines no longer fully recognise that the ideas they use shape how they see the world. Instead, it just seems natural that the ideas they use are in fact the way the world really is. Rather than reflecting how the world actually is, the ideas are in fact conceptual artefacts, the structure of which refracts how the intellectual division of labour is carved up and organised in the present (these ideas are explored in greater detail in Chapter 6). The increasing differentiation of intellectual life in modern society impacts directly on the ways social workers learn to see and construct the world.

Throughout their training, social work students learn to see the world through conceptual lenses taken from a wide range of disciplines e.g. sociology, law, psychology, social policy, etc. Different disciplines provide different ways of seeing, which social workers use to perform the roles they play. In a university context, the dividing line between the different disciplines seems relatively clear and straight-forward. In the messy reality that is the real world, however, where exactly the applicability of ideas belonging to a particular discipline e.g. sociology can be said to stop, and the applicability of ideas from another e.g. psychology can be said to begin, can be very difficult to discern – just ask any social worker! This is an important point to make. It is *not* the aim of this book to suggest that the kinds of individual-centred concepts and theories characteristic of the 'psych-' disciplines social workers increasingly draw on are inherently flawed, or require to be replaced by social theory. The division between the individual and the social and the psychological and the social theoretical, for example, should not be understood as requiring you to make a choice about which to side with, nor is one necessarily superior to the other. Rather, different disciplines 'construct' the world in different ways. As it happens, social theory is very good at explaining how particular social processes, such as the differentiation of intellectual life into a range of academic disciplines, enable us to construct and see the world in certain ways, while constraining our capacity to construct and see it in others.

Developing an awareness of the ways wider social change influences how different academic disciplines carve up the world is important for social workers, connecting directly with various issues to do with power and truth. At different stages in the development of Western society, different academic disciplines have stressed the importance of certain types of knowledge e.g. psychoanalytic, economic, social theoretical, etc. for explaining how people think and act. As part of its concern with power, certain forms of social theory seek to explain how the structure and organisation of power relations shape knowledge about human agents. In the work of French theorist Michel Foucault (Chapter 6), for example, this has meant trying to identify how power works to define certain ways of thinking as offering the 'truth' about human agents, at the same time as devaluing other forms of knowledge as less important and illegitimate. As we shall see in the work of the classical theorists Karl Marx and Max Weber (Chapter 2), the work of Pierre Bourdieu (Chapter 7) and certain strands of feminist thought (Chapter 8), one of the main aims of social theory is to unveil the social and cultural mechanisms by which power is exerted. This often occurs in ways that are less than fully consciously grasped by those wielding the power, no less those under its sway.

Dispelling myths about social theory

Social theory and social work are united by a shared concern with and interest in people. Yet mention of the words 'social theory' to social work students often evokes feelings of bewilderment and unease. This is almost entirely due to a number of the unhelpful myths that have grown up around social theory within social work. In recent times, social theory has come to be (re)presented and (mis)understood as knowledge that is dry and uninteresting, difficult because it is abstract, and of little use to a profession that deals with 'real world situations . . . and practical, social and emotional problems' (Singh and Cowden, 2009: 479). It is worth trying to penetrate and explore these myths with a view to dispelling them once and for all.

Whether or not social theory is boring is in part a matter of opinion, but consider this: if your intention is to become a social worker, or you already are a social worker, then your job will involve dealing with people from a broad range of backgrounds and experiences. To be able to assist them as well as you can, it is important you know something about those people, the relationships they have with others, how they experience and are shaped by their relationships, and the situation that has brought you into contact with them. This may require you either alone or in dialogue with the service-user to think about and try to provide answers to the following questions: from what kind of social background does this person come? How does it inform their sense of selfhood and identity? How do they relate to themselves and act towards other people? Is the person negatively perceived and marginalized by others, or are they positively integrated with the people around them? How do your background and experiences shape your relationship and interactions with service-users? As a social work professional you will take an interest in all of these questions and the wider issues they raise. As it happens, many of the very same questions and issues comprise the subject matter of social theory. Far from engaging in abstract questions and debates, social theory provides answers to many of the same questions posed by social workers.

But social theory is difficult?! This is a view many social work students have of social theory. On closer scrutiny, however, it appears far from convincing, not least because theorizing about social life is something you already know a lot about. Theorizing about people and the situations around you is something that you already *do* all of the time. Note the very deliberate wording of the last sentence, in particular the use of the verb 'to do'. Social theory is not something people *think* about so much as something they *do*. Social theory is more like an activity than a mental exercise, one we all do throughout the day, every day – social workers more than most! But because much of what we think and do takes place at an only semi-conscious level – at the level of 'practical consciousness' (Chapter 3) – we often fail to notice that we are doing a version of social theory all the time. Considered in this way, the myth that social theory is *necessarily* difficult is simply untrue because we are all doing a version of it all of the time. This is why as you read through this book many of the ideas and issues will be recognisable to you – because they involve raising questions about people and situations that you already know a lot about. In a general sense, social work and social theory are bound by a shared interest in people, as well as overlapping in a number of more specific ways, which we will now identify and explore in greater depth.

What social theory can *do* for social work

Power and empowerment

Power is of fundamental concern to both social work and social theory. This is true generally, but more specifically too as power relates to values and notions such as empowerment, oppression, control, emancipation, self-realization, social justice and so on. Social theorists examine issues of power at various levels and from a range of different perspectives. These include understanding power from a micro perspective, between individuals and in small-group settings; at a 'mezzo' level in the form of institutions, organisations and collectives; and at a macro level, in the organisation and relations between different social spheres, and increasingly whole societies. A concern with power is more or less explicit in all social theory. Social theory is an inherently political form of knowledge, a point dealt with in different ways by different think-ers, as we shall see. Through identifying and explaining the nature and operation of power within modern society, social theoretical knowledge is rooted in and forms part of those strug-gles. One way this is true concerns the empowering nature of social theoretical knowledge itself, whereby those who possess it are better equipped to grasp the dynamics and structures of power they are shaped by as well using it to shape the people and situations around them.

De-familiarize the familiar

It can be very difficult to see how the effects of power shape the ways we think and act in a relationship or situation we are so familiar with that we rarely think to question it. The term *de-familiarize* denotes the importance social theorists place on trying to step back from people, relationships and situations with which we are overly familiar, and instead try to see them as if they were unfamiliar and alien to us. It involves posing questions about the underlying values, assumptions and common sense ways of thinking people use in take-for-granted ways in their everyday lives and interactions. The ideas and methods characteristic of phenomenological forms of social theory seek to do exactly this (Chapter 3). By re-examining familiar ideas and assumptions as if they were totally unfamiliar, it becomes possible to adopt a more detached, value-free and objective perspective from which to view them. Doing so allows us to see that the taken-for-granted 'feel' characteristic of many of the ways in which we think and act on a daily basis is not naturally occurring or inevitable. It is instead the result of being socialized into a particular social and cultural context.

Trying to adopt a detached and objective perspective towards the people and situations around us plays an important part in bringing to light the relations and structures of power embedded within them. It can also open up a space in which to imagine how different social life could be. Had we been born into a different society and culture at another point in human history, how we see and experience the world would be very different indeed. The fact that how we think and act over time comes to strike us as natural and inevitable, often in ways that we feel powerless to change, is captured by Marx's concept of 'alienation' (Chapter 2). Being aware that so much of how we see and act towards others is not in fact natural but the result of learning to operate within a particular social context can be an incredibly empowering experi-ence. Why? Because it presents us with an opportunity for making a choice: to ignore our new found awareness and carry on as before, or to use it to cultivate new ways of engaging with the people and world around us.

Connect the private and the public

Understanding how the actions of individuals shape and are shaped by wider social processes is central to social theory. Social theory does this by making connections with and between the *private* and *personal* consequences of wider *public* and *social* processes, and vice versa (Wright, 1959). Many of the most intimate and private aspects of our own identity and experiences cannot be understood without reference to wider social and cultural processes. The decision to become a social worker, for example, is a highly personal one. Nevertheless, the decision will have been structured by a range of social factors, many of which you will not be aware of, such as your class background and the ideals, attitudes and values of the group you belong to. A considerable part of doing social theory involves identifying and making connections between wider social dynamics and processes and the influence these have for shaping how individuals act and interact. Pierre Bourdieu's concept of 'habitus', for example (Chapter 7), demonstrates how a range of social and cultural factors actively dispose individuals to think and act in ways that tend to reproduce their social status, typically in ways they are unaware of.

How the actions and interactions of individuals shape and are shaped by wider social processes is of primary concern to social theorists. Not only is this true for thinking about social life in the present, but historically too. Many of the social processes that shape our lives today have their roots at particular points in history which we may know very little about, or are unaware of altogether. The work of Norbert Elias (Chapter 5) demonstrates how and why changes to the behavioural standards of people in the late medieval period impact on the ways people act and interact in the present day. A key point here is that these changes largely came about for reasons that were not planned or intended. Elias regards the tendency of individuals to act with greater levels of self-restraint and foresight as an unintended consequence of long-term historical changes to the configuration of modern social relations. These changes were not consciously intended by anyone and developed in ways that were largely unforeseen.

The concept of unintended consequences relates closely to the notion that what are often regarded as individual problems are typically rooted in much wider and seemingly unrelated developments in society. One of the main objectives of this book is to explain and demonstrate how and why this is the case in relation to the issues and problems faced by both social workers and service-users. Modern social theory abounds with examples of the ways impersonal social factors shape the personal experiences and lives of individuals. Feminist social theory (Chapter 8) is expressly concerned with demonstrating and explaining the social causes of the oppressed status of women in patriarchal society. The work of Michel Foucault (Chapter 6) explains how struggles for power between the state and professions such as psychiatry and social work have led to certain identities and behaviours being classified as problematic and deviant. His work focusses on the ways scientific forms of knowledge and discourse are used to construct certain social identities e.g. 'gay', 'black', 'mentally ill', etc. as deviant and a threat to social order.

Raise reflexive awareness

Learning to think 'reflexively' is an important part of social work and social theory (Houston, 2015). Reflexivity refers to the process by which individuals actively reflect on the part played by their own perceptions and actions in shaping situations. Adopting a reflexive stance towards your own thoughts and actions is an integral part of good social work practice. Similarly with social theory, thinking reflexively about the nature of your engagement with the ideas you encounter throughout this book will make reading it a more meaningful and transformative experience. This is true on a number of levels. Social theoretical ideas and concepts can be brought to bear on your own self, allowing you to grasp how your self-identity is and has been shaped by a range of impersonal social and cultural forces. These insights will be of value to you in your interactions with service-users and colleagues across a wide range of professional scenarios. In many ways, this is *social theory at its best* – providing those who engage with it with a vocabulary for putting into words what they intuitively know and feel but find difficult to articulate. Using social theory in self-directed and reflexive ways also allows you to gain a greater understanding of those aspects of yourself that are not necessarily yours.

TABLE 1.1 What social theory can *do* for social work

Identify power and empower	Identify relations, structures and mechanisms of power – learning to see power is empowering
De-familiarize the familiar	Provide new ways of seeing and thinking about people, situations and events
Connect the private with the public	Identify the relationship between wider social processes and changes and actions and interactions of individuals, and vice versa
Raise reflexive awareness	Heighten capacity to reflect on the role our own ideals, ideas and actions play in shaping situations and events

Another way of saying this is that particular forms of social theory can help you to identify those aspects of your own self-identity that derive from the wider social environment. Rather than being 'determined' by social forces of which you were not necessarily (fully) aware, you will be able to reclaim a sense of agency and control over those processes. Going forward, this self-awareness can serve as the basis for developing and enhancing your professional practice.

Thinking reflexively about your own self-identity and values can lead to valuable self-knowledge, but it will take you only so far (Bourdieu and Wacquant, 1992). Just as important is learning to use social theoretical concepts to think reflexively about the organisational contexts and relations into which you enter. Depending on the area of social work you go into, or are already in, you will be required to assume certain professional roles, attitudes and responsibilities. Using social theory to reflect on these roles and responsibilities will allow you to think more clearly about how they enable you to think and act in certain ways, while simultaneously constraining you to think and act in others. The third level of reflexivity concerns the historical development and position of social work in society, specifically how it relates to other public professions such as the police, the criminal justice system, the National Health Service and so on. Thinking reflexively about the development of social work from an historical perspective will allow you to de-familiarize how social work is organised and practiced in the present day. It will also highlight how the activities of social workers are increasingly shaped by events taking place in other parts of society, as well as in other parts of the world more broadly (Chapter 9).

Anatomy of social theory

Social theory makes claims about the nature of human life and society. Embedded within those claims are two further inter-related dimensions of knowledge. The first relates to ontology, and the second concerns epistemology. Ontology refers to ideas about what social reality is, what it consists of and what the nature of the things it is made up of are like. All social theoretical concepts contain an ontological dimension, which is to say they contain assumptions about what social reality consists of and what it is like. Depending on the theoretical ideas you are dealing with, the ontological assumptions contained within them will be more or less explicit. Different theoretical ideas and traditions are premised on different ontological assumptions about what social reality consists of and how it works. This is why social theory comprises such a wide range of different perspectives. One of the main ontological positions within social theory is 'social structuralism'. Structuralist thinkers regard social reality as consisting primarily of social structures, such as 'class', 'religion', 'family', etc. For structuralist thinkers such as Durkheim and Foucault, social structures operate in ways that are largely independent of individuals. Social structures have a life of their own and therefore are real. Structuralists regard social structures as exerting causal power over individuals. They constrain individuals to think and act in structured and patterned ways. A key premise for structuralist thinkers is that changes to the organisation of society result in changes to the way people think about and interact with one another. This is why structuralist thinkers prioritise social structures and the nature of their organisation ahead of the individuals whose actions and interactions they shape.

Individual-centred theories such as phenomenology and symbolic interactionism view social reality very differently (Chapters 3 and 4). For thinkers in these traditions, society consists primarily of individuals and their actions. From this perspective, social structures either do not exist at all or are merely the product of aggregates of individuals acting and interacting in patterned ways. Moreover, individual-centred paradigms conceive of social reality as an ongoing process, or event. Society does not precede concrete individuals, but instead arises out of the actions, interactions and reactions of aggregates of individuals. In the case of relational thinkers such as Norbert Elias and Pierre Bourdieu (Chapters 5 and 7), the issue of whether or not to prioritise social structures ahead of individuals is rejected altogether. Elias and Bourdieu regard the nature and type of social relations binding individuals and groups – as opposed to the individual per se or the structure of the group – as more important for understanding social reality. The work of these thinkers is regarded as taking up a 'relational' perspective on social life.

Questions about the nature of social reality and what it consists of directly inform the epistemological dimensions of social theory. Epistemology involves asking questions about how we can arrive at knowledge of reality e.g. social structures, individual actions, social processes, etc. Epistemology concerns trying to understand what counts as knowledge about social reality, as well as investigating the status of different types of knowledge e.g. common sense ideas, religion, scientific knowledge, etc. As we shall see, what comes to be understood and defined as knowledge in society, and the status attributed to different types of knowledge, is of fundamental concern within certain strands of social theory. An important point to make here is that certain types of knowledge (epistemology) are more appropriate than others for trying to get to grips with and understand social reality.

Broadly speaking, the epistemological orientation of social theory falls into one of two camps. For some theoretical traditions e.g. phenomenology, interactionism and certain variations of feminist social theory, knowledge about social reality is derived using interpretative (also known as qualitative) methods, such as interviews, ethnographic studies and participant observation, as well as more textually based forms of research such as document analysis and historiographical data. For theorists working within the interpretative traditions, this means actively trying to interpret the values and meanings inculcated in the minds of individuals, as it is these which shape how individuals think, feel and interact. Culture implants ideas, values and beliefs in the minds of individuals, which interpretative research methods are intended to gain access to and capture. An alternative epistemological position is that of 'positivism'. Positivism holds that social theory, and the social science that it guides, should aspire to search for law like generalizations about human behaviour in ways that

TABLE 1.2 Composition of social theoretical knowledge

Concepts and ideas	Ways of thinking about and grasping social phenomena e.g. structures, selfhood, power, estrangement, discourse, etc.
Ontological dimension	Assumptions about what social reality consists of e.g. individuals, structures, processes, networks, etc.
Epistemological dimension	Orientation of theory towards certain types of knowledge: quantitative e.g. facts and statistics; qualitative e.g. interviews, participant observation and historical documents
Normative dimension	Ideals and values embedded in theoretical ideas e.g. empowerment, social-determination, self-determination, etc.

emulate the natural sciences. The structuralist thinking of Marx and Durkheim, for example, operates within a largely positivistic framework. A central assumption underlying positivist methods is that human nature is uniform everywhere, and for this reason the same procedures characteristic of the natural sciences can be used to study people in any context. Positivism is closely associated with quantitative research methods and data such as statistics, facts and numerical data.

An important point to make about both interpretative and positivist epistemologies, and the corresponding methods they give rise to, is that they are not mutually exclusive. To qualify as legitimate knowledge, the concepts social theorists develop must be able to withstand logical and rational scrutiny. This holds true regardless of whether or not the data they use to substantiate their arguments employ qualitative or quantitative methods, or a combination of both. It is not the case, for example, that facts and statistical data are more real or legitimate than textual and historical forms of data. Simply, certain types of data are more suitable than others for grasping different aspects of social reality. As we shall see with regard to the work of Foucault, the view within Western culture that scientific forms of knowledge are superior is often used by professional groups to advance their own claims to power and expertise.

Structure and agency

A key issue for social theorists is what is commonly referred to as the 'structure versus agency' debate. Recent developments in social theory tend to replace the term *action* with *agency*, the term *agency* forming part of a wider shift away from thinking about structures as wholly external to and separate from the actions of individuals. In essence, this debate concerns the ideas about ontology we have just dealt with, in particular whether or not actions or social structures are more important for understanding what reality consists of and how it works. A key point here is that social theorists reject philosophical debates that regard human agents either as possessed of free will or as somehow 'determined'. Social theorists focus instead on the ways social structures shape the minds and actions of individuals, as well as the extent and ways individuals are able to respond creatively to and influence social structures. Capturing these ideas very clearly, Marx (2009 [1851]: 1) stated the social theoretical view that people 'make history but not in conditions of their own choosing'. This is the idea that individuals are free to act in self-selected ways but always in contexts shaped to varying degrees by social-structural factors and processes they had little if any involvement in or control over. How individuals act and

TABLE 1.3 Structure versus agency debate

Social structures
Patterned ways of thinking, acting and interacting e.g. social class, gender, ethnicity, age, etc.
Agency
Capacity of social actors to react creatively to and influence social structures

interact serves either to remake, alter or transform those processes over time. The notion of social life as an ongoing process is an important one here along with the dialectical view that structure and agency feed into and inform one another in different ways to varying extents. As we shall see, social theorists have developed a wide range of theoretical perspectives to try to make sense of the dialectical nature of these processes.

Society: past, present and future

Like social work, social theory was born of the great social and political transformations of the nineteenth century. This was the century in which modern society – also known as 'modernity' – began to take shape and gain momentum. In the broadest sense, social theory is concerned with modernity. This was a term that appeared in the work of the classical theorists and was used to designate the kind of society to emerge in Western Europe out of a series of developments and changes extending back in time to approximately the sixteenth century. Culminating in the late eighteenth and nineteenth centuries, these developments led to the changes that replaced the previous type of social organisation characteristic of medieval feudalism. Originating in Western Europe, those changes have increasingly spread across the world, for the most part in ways that were unintended and are ever more global in reach and consequence. In the present day, a general consensus has arisen among social theorists that how we understand modernity has changed in various and significant ways. A significant aspect of social theory since the 1990s has involved trying to identify and explain the principal characteristics of modernity as it is developing and changing now. As we shall see (Chapter 9), social theorists have developed a range of terms to refer to the current stage of modernity, including *late modernity*, *risk society*, *network society*, *light modernity*, *global modernity* and so on. These terms have been introduced by social theorists to try to capture the distinctive nature of the changes they claim have taken place in recent years and that continue in the present day.

Conclusion

This book attempts to bring together social work and social theory in a systematic and engaging way by *applying* social theory to a wide range of social work practice scenarios, issues and debates. As will become clear, social theory can be used to think about a broad range of aspects of social work including the organisational contexts in which social workers are embedded, the nature of the relations between social workers and the state, the types of relations between social workers and service-users, and so on and so forth. There really is no limit to the different ways social theory can be applied to social work. Precisely because of this, perhaps the best way to think about this book is to imagine it as something akin to a conceptual toolkit, one that provides a range of theoretical tools to be taken up and applied within the professional scenarios and settings you go into. Once you have learned more about the thinkers and ideas featured in this book, you should find that the theorizing you do in both your professional and everyday life becomes more sophisticated and far more alert to the subtleties and nuances of the social world around you. You will become more sensitive and attuned to certain interpersonal processes and dynamics which you may have been aware of in the past, but are now able to see more clearly and talk about in ways that you found difficult before.

Before proceeding, it is important to acknowledge one final thing. The biggest difficulty in writing this book concerned the application of the ideas, but not that it was difficult to see how the concepts and ideas were of use or could be applied to social work. Whenever I have taught social theory to social work students, it has always struck me – no less the students – as abundantly obvious how the concepts can be used to inform and relate to what social workers do. Rather, the difficulty came from deciding which aspects of social work to apply the ideas at the cost of leaving out so many equally viable others. It is important to acknowledge this. It points to the fact that how the ideas have been applied throughout the various chapters could have been done many different ways. This is why I hope that once you have developed a better understanding of and feel more confident with the theoretical ideas we cover, they inspire, are taken up and are incorporated into the ways of seeing and interacting you bring to the people and, relationships around you. For this is the spirit in which social theory was intended to be read. Not as a static and stuffy body of knowledge whose insights are reserved for an intellectually privileged few, but one intended to be used by and empower real human beings as they act and interact with one another in the real world.

References

Applegate, J. S. (2004) 'Full Circle: Returning Psychoanalytic Theory to Social Work Education', *Psychoanalytic Social Work*, 11(1): 23–36.

Beck, U. and Beck-Gernsheim, E. (2002) *Individualization: Institutionalised Individualism and Its Social and Political Consequences*. London: Sage.

Bourdieu, P. (1993) *Sociology in Question*. Cambridge: Polity Press.

Bourdieu, P. and Wacquant, L. (1992) *An Invitation to Reflexive Sociology*. Cambridge: Polity Press.

Dominelli, L. (1997) *Sociology for Social Work*. Oxford: Palgrave.

Durkheim, E. (1964 [1893]) *The Division of Labour in Society*. New York: Free Press.

Elias, N. (2001 [1981]) *The Society of Individuals*. London: Continuum.

Ferguson, H. (2001) 'Social Work, Individualization and Life Politics', *British Journal of Social Work*, 31(1): 41–55.

Ferguson, I. (2009) 'Another Social Work Is Possible! Reclaiming the Radical Tradition', in Leskosek, V. (ed.) *Theories and Methods of Social Work: Exploring Different Perspectives*. Ljubljana: University of Ljubljana, pp. 81–98.

Ferguson, I. and Lavalette, M. (2004) 'Beyond Power Discourse: Alienation and Social Work', *British Journal of Social Work*, 34(3): 297–312.

Houston, S. (2014) 'Beyond Individualism: Social Work and Social Identity', *The British Journal of Social Work*, 46(2): 532–548.

Houston, S. (2015) 'Enabling Others in Social Work: Reflexivity and the Theory of Social Domains', *Critical and Radical Social Work*, 3(2): 245–260.

Jones, C. (1983) *State Social Work and the Working Class*. London: MacMillan.

Jones, C. (1996) 'Anti-Intellectualism and Social Work Education', in Parton, N. (ed.) *Social Theory, Social Change and Social Work*. London: Routledge, pp. 190–210.

Kahn, P. and Dominelli, L. (2000) 'The Impact of Globalization on Social Work in the UK', *European Journal of Social Work*, 3(2): 95–108.

Langan, M. (2002) 'The Legacy of Radical Social Work', in Adams, R., Dominelli, L. and Payne, M. (eds.) (2002) *Social Work: Themes, Issues and Critical Debates*. Basingstoke: Palgrave, pp. 209–218.

Levin, I., Haldar, M. and Picot, A. (2015) 'Social Work and Sociology: Historical Separation and Current Challenges', *Nordic Social Work Research*, 5(1): 1–6.

Marx, K. (1998 [1845–46]) *The German Ideology: Including Theses on Feurbach and Introduction to the Critique of Political Economy*. New York: Prometheus Books.

Marx, K. (2009 [1851]) *The Eighteenth Brumaire of Louis Bonaparte*. Gloucester: Dodo Press.

Singh, G. and Cowden, S. (2009) 'The Social Worker as Intellectual', *European Journal of Social Work*, 12(4): 479–493.

Wright, C. M. (1959) *The Sociological Imagination*. Oxford: Oxford University Press.

Younghusband, E. (1957) *Report on the Employment and Training of Social Workers*. Edinburgh: Constable.

Younghusband, E. (1964) *Social Work and Social Change*. London: George Allen & Unwin.

2

CLASSICAL SOCIAL THEORY
AND MODERN SOCIAL PROBLEMS

The theoretical concepts and perspectives dealt with in this book belong to modern social theory. To understand modern social theory it is essential to know something about classical social theory. The distinction between *modern* and *classical* theory is an important one, denoting significant transformations to the intellectual and social conditions out of which the related but distinct bodies of knowledge emerged. An important part of the process by which social theorists today try to understand society involves entering into a dialogue with the ideas and intellectual formulations of the classical theorists. Irrespective of whether or not modern theorists elect to take up and elaborate, modify and adapt, or reject altogether the ideas of the classical theorists, the legacy of classical theory continues to exert a powerful influence over the ideas and exchanges between social theorists in the present day. Classical social theory denotes the work of three thinkers in particular: Emile Durkheim, Karl Marx and Max Weber.

What exactly is 'classical' about classical theory? One way of answering this question involves thinking about what the classical theorists are understood to have achieved and how this relates to the different directions in which modern social theory has developed. First, classical theory provides the analytical parameters and concerns that distinguish social theory from other academic disciplines. Second, classical theory attempts to grasp the uniqueness of modernity, both on its own terms as well as in relation to what came before and what lies ahead. Third, the theoretical concepts developed by the classical theorists continue to cast a powerful light on contemporary social and cultural phenomena. A useful way of summarizing the relationship between classical and modern social theory is this: classical theory comprises the intellectual questions and provocations that subsequent generations of social theorists have sought and continue to try to answer. This chapter does two things: it identifies and explains the main conceptual ideas of the classical theorists and applies them to a number of aspects of contemporary social work; and it identifies the influence of those ideas on the work of the modern social theorists covered throughout the rest of the book. The chapter concludes by reflecting on the relevance of classical theory today for getting to grips with contemporary social work issues and problems, and its continuing importance for understanding the directions in which modern social theory has developed.

Emile Durkheim: control and consensus

Emile Durkheim (1858–1917) was a French sociologist and the first university-based professor in sociology. Durkheim's vision of the purpose of social theory resonates strongly with that of social work: to play an active part in resolving individual and social problems (Marske, 1987). The view that individual problems are fundamentally rooted in the structure and organisation of society is central to Durkheim's thought. Durkheim adopted a 'functionalist' approach to the analysis of social life. This involves trying to understand the various functions social structures play in the harmonious functioning of the social 'whole'. Durkheim regarded social structures as existing independently of any particular individual. Moreover, social structures exert a coercive force over the individual, constraining them to think and act in socially patterned ways. Examples of social structures include gender, social class, ethnicity and religion, each of which involves people acting and interacting in patterned ways which can be studied independently of them.

The coercive power of social structures is essential for ensuring social life proceeds in orderly and predictable ways. Whereas Karl Marx (discussed later in this chapter) regarded social structures as negatively constraining, Durkheim held that they are essential to the orderly functioning of society. If the coercive power of social structures were to break down, the patterned and predictable basis of social life would be threatened. The idea that human agents need to be coerced and regulated derives from Durkheim's (2005 [1914]) conception of human nature known as 'homo duplex'. Homo duplex is the idea that human subjectivity is rooted in a kind of double existence:

> . . . on the one hand is our individuality – and, more particularly, our body in which it
> is based; on the other is everything in us that expresses something other than ourselves.
> *(Durkheim, 2005 [1914]: 37)*

Durkheim's entire conception of society leads out from the concept of homo-duplex. Prefiguring Freud's ideas about the human psyche as rooted in the conflict between the id and super-ego, Durkheim conceived the human psyche as characterised by, on the one hand, egoistic and insatiable primal drives and desires, and, on the other, the moral regulations and normative values instilled by society. On this view, society comprises a range of morally coercive structures e.g. norms, class, culture, etc. the function of which is to regulate the destructive and anti-social desires and impulses of the individual in their pre-social state. That for the most part social life proceeds in relatively predictable and structured ways is not something that occurs naturally. It is because social structures function to regulate and integrate individuals in uniform, and patterned ways.

Culture and socialization

The function of culture is to ensure that social patterns are maintained. From the moment a baby is born, socialization begins. Socialization refers to the socially shaped processes by which individuals are integrated into the culture of the group. In different ways and to varying degrees, socialization continues throughout the life of the individual. One of the main functions of culture is that it works to tame nature. It is through culture that we learn to regulate and restrain our natural impulses and desires. The period of socialization spanning the earliest years of a child's life is referred to as 'primary socialization'. This is widely understood as a formative period in the development of the individual.

During primary socialization, children are encouraged to think, feel, act and interact with others in ways that conform to the normative ideals and values of the group. Not to conform to these ideals is liable to result in the child being told off, such as when a parent reprimands a child because they refuse to share their toys. Secondary socialization involves children learning to participate in wider social life, with members of the community and formal institutions such as school. A significant part of secondary socialization involves children internalizing the interpersonal rules and norms necessary for interacting with a much wider range of types of people and institutions.

Aside from regulating how individuals interact, culture provides ways of interpreting and attributing meaning to the world. Elaborating on ideas about the human mind developed by the German philosopher Immanuel Kant (Chapter 3), Durkheim drew attention to the socially shaped nature of human understanding. Socialization involves learning to make sense of situations and events in socially patterned ways. Durkheim claimed that the capacity to organise and make sense of reality is rooted not in the minds of individuals, but in the classifying structures – 'collective representations' – implanted in the mind through socialization (Durkheim and Mauss, 1969 [1903]). These are the ways reality is made intelligible collectively by the members of the group. Collective representations (or classifications) are the socially created lenses through which people make sense of reality and the world around them.

During socialization the mind of the individual is shaped through and by culture. Collective representations comprise the normative and cognitive frameworks through which people think and the bases on which they act. Crucially, how people interpret the world around them is not only made possible by collective representations, but actively constituted by them. In other words, there is nothing natural or inevitable about how the members of a group organise and construct their experience of reality. Rather, their experience is actively shaped and constructed by the ideas and categories contained within the culture of the group. Implicit in this idea is the view that were you to have been born into a different culture, the collective representations socialized into your mind would lead you to construct and experience social reality in very different ways. Culture does not just mediate our experience of reality; it actively creates and shapes it.

Solidarity and integration

In addition to regulating how individuals interact, culture integrates and binds people too. Culture forms the basis for social cohesion and solidarity between individuals. In traditional society, members of rural communities were bound to one another through and by the culture of the group. Life in traditional communities was characterised by a narrow range of tasks and activities around which shared morals and values grew up. These shared values oriented individuals actions and interactions towards one another and the attainment of wider collective goals. Durkheim (1964 [1893]) referred to these ideals and values as the 'collective conscience'. Implanted in the mind of group members through socialization, the collective conscience exerted a powerful, morally coercive force, disposing individuals to think and act in ways oriented towards conforming to, as opposed to deviating from, the group. In traditional society, the collective conscience generated solidarity between group members, ensuring that the moral outlook and actions of individuals positively aligned them towards one another and the wider community.

Under the conditions of mechanical solidarity, social cohesion and unity derive from the culture of the group. By contrast, the basis for social cohesion in modern society involves changes to the types of *social relations* binding individuals. In modern society, structured by a complex division of labour, individuals are bound by 'organic solidarity' (Durkheim, 1964 [1893]). As the division of labour advances, mechanical solidarity is replaced by organic solidarity. Different social groups e.g. working-class communities, ethnic and religious groups, middle-class professionals, etc. give rise to their own distinct cultural formations, each of which contains the particular moral ideals and values which differentiate them from other groups. The complex division of labour in modern society gives rise to a correspondingly diverse range of moral outlooks and perspectives.

Social groups are no longer bound primarily by shared cultural ideals and values in modern society. They are bound instead through social relations of *dependency*. As the nature of the work people perform has become increasingly specialized, so in turn the extent to which we depend on others to perform the roles and tasks allocated to them has increased. For example, as a university lecturer, while I am at work I depend upon other people to perform the roles they are tasked to do e.g. bakers are baking bread, the mechanic is fixing my car and the school teacher is teaching my children. For my life to proceed in an orderly and predictable manner, I *depend* on other people to fulfil their respective roles in the social division of labour, and vice versa. By emphasising the declining role played by culture as the basis for collective solidarity, Durkheim was not suggesting that the collective conscience disappears entirely in modern society. Certain core ideals and values that all members of society are committed to upholding must exist. Rather, the values at the heart of the collective conscience change. Instead of the minds and actions of individuals being oriented towards conformity and consensus, a sense of unity and cohesion derives from the values of individuality, respect for difference and individual moral autonomy.

Durkheim on social pathology

Durkheim regarded the declining power of the collective conscience as a positive outcome of the transition to modernity (Marske, 1987). He positively embraced the rising individuality and moral autonomy to which a situation of organic solidarity gives rise. At the same time, however, he was wary of excessive levels of individuality, a situation he referred to as 'pathological individualism' (Durkheim (2002 [1897]). If the power of social structures to regulate the desires and impulses of the ego is insufficient, the consequences can be individually and collectively destructive. Durkheim's classic study *Suicide* (2002 [1897]) demonstrates exactly this. Durkheim reasoned that the decision to end one's own life by committing suicide represents the single greatest expression of individual autonomy. But even then, the decision to commit suicide is one thoroughly shaped by social reasons. This is why suicide rates demonstrate markedly patterned features over time and across different societies. The patterned nature of suicide levels corresponds directly with wider changes to the structure of society, albeit in ways that those who commit suicide are typically unaware of.

Durkheim (2002 [1897]) used a range of data and statistics to demonstrate that certain social types are more likely than others to commit suicide. Women, for example, are less likely than men to commit suicide, as is also true more generally for people who are married as opposed to those who are single. In both cases, even more so if the individual is female and married, the decision to commit suicide or not can be explained with reference to the concepts of regulation and integration. In modern societies, the most prevalent types of suicide are 'egoistic' and 'anomic' (Durkheim, 2002 [1897]). Egoistic suicide is associated with pathologically high levels of individualization and correspondingly low levels of social integration. Egoistic suicide is likely to occur when individuals are poorly integrated into society. A single, unemployed, young male, for example, is more likely to commit suicide than a married woman with children. Without the sense of purpose a professional status and intimate relationship provide, the young male is more susceptible to feelings of isolation, a sense of purposelessness and a lack of meaning to his life. At times of emotional distress he is more likely to feel overwhelmed by the intensity of his feelings because he is denied the kinds of close and personally meaningful relationships people normally use to discharge and disperse those feelings. By contrast, as a 'mother' and 'wife', the self-identity of the woman is rooted in the solidarity provided by the family unit. A powerful pressure to go on in spite of emotional turmoil is exerted over the woman through the conjugal and maternal roles and relationships that bind her to her husband and children respectively.

Anomic suicide is likely to occur in the event of sudden and/or rapid social change. Durkheim developed the term *anomie* to refer to a temporary condition of insufficient moral regulation,

TABLE 2.1 Summary of Durkheim

Social structures

- exist independently of individuals e.g. class, gender, ethnicity
- comprise patterned ways of acting and interacting
- function to integrate and regulate individuals

Forms of solidarity

Mechanical

- typically found in traditional forms of community
- characterised by simple division of labour
- strong collective culture organised around shared norms and values
- morally coercive collective conscience

Organic

- emerges out of mechanical solidarity
- characterised by complex social division of labour
- gives rise to culture of individualism
- binds individuals through social relations of (inter)dependency
- weak collective conscience

Anomie

- condition of insufficient moral regulation
- breakdown in normative rules, expectations and codes of conduct
- occurs during periods of sudden and rapid social change
- disorientating and destabilizing for individual

and the ensuing breakdown in the normative rules and boundaries regulating egoistic desires and aspirations. Following a sudden and unexpected crash in the global financial market, a businessman is suddenly made redundant. Quite literally, overnight, the main source of his self-identity and social status collapses. In modern society, the social and professional roles we fulfil provide us with a powerful sense of personal identity as well as what we can reasonably hope to achieve and expect from life. The normative ideals and professional identities we assume play an important role in regulating the potentially endless wants and desires of the ego. If those normative structures and boundaries suddenly fall away, the individual becomes highly vulnerable to the unregulated demands of the ego. Stripped of his identity and the lifestyle in which his innermost self-understanding is rooted, the businessman is more likely to commit suicide.

Applying Durkheim to social work

Applying Durkheim's functional perspective to social work involves considering the function social work plays in relation to the smooth running of the wider social 'whole'. Social workers provide assistance to service-users, often helping them to reintegrate their lives back into the wider community and society. In this sense, social work plays a conservative social function, because it contributes to conserving and reproducing the prevailing social order. As we shall see in relation to the work of Karl Marx (discussed later in this chapter) the effort of social workers to integrate people back into rather than fundamentally trying to change society is a highly problematic one. From a Marxist perspective, the cause of the vast majority of service-users' difficulties derives directly from the structure of capitalist society and the various injustices and forms of inequality to which this gives rise.

The view of social work as a socially conservative form of activity is a matter of perspective. Viewed from the perspective of society as a whole, the unintended or latent consequence of much of what social workers do serves to conserve prevailing social structures and values. Different strands of social work, however, such as anti-discriminatory, anti-oppressive and feminist social work practice, actively seek to challenge structural tensions and the inequalities they perpetuate. In short, social workers are committed to challenging and trying to reform normative, institutional and legal structures, wherever they work to contribute to inequality and injustice. At the level of concrete individuals, the primary goal of social work is to assist service-users to confront and address the issues facing them. How or to what extent social work can be said to work to conserve, rather than bring about, changes to prevailing social structures is contingent along a number of lines. In many cases, providing assistance to service-users means working within the existing structures of society. In others, social workers actively work to try to identify and challenge the social-structural causes of oppression within society.

Socialization

To become part of society all individuals must undergo a degree of socialization. The concept of socialization is implicit in all social theory, although the extent to which different thinkers explicitly address the mechanisms by which it takes place, and the ways and extent to which it is understood to shape the individual, varies considerably. Durkheim's account of social-ization arises out of the concept of homo duplex. Homo duplex is Durkheim's account of the duality of human nature. In their natural state, human agents are driven by primal and egotistical desires which can be regulated and constrained only by society. This leads to the paradoxical situation whereby human beings cannot be 'free' without internalizing the moral boundaries and normative values necessary for overcoming the primal desires that threaten to enslave them. Put another way, freedom is possible only in a context whereby individuals are sufficiently constrained.

Durkheim's conception of homo duplex and the vision of socialization leading out from it raises important questions. They invite us to consider how and to what extent socialization shapes the person we become. The distinction between primary and secondary socialization is an important one here. This distinction rests on the notion that primary socialization is forma-tive and, as the term suggests, primary for understanding our subsequent development. As we shall see, however, such a view is one social theorists have called into question and challenge as overly fixed and static. More generally, social theory tends to operate on the premise that how human agents act and interact cannot be separated out from the organisation and types of relations in which they are embedded. On this view, the notion of human nature tends to be regarded as little more than an abstraction (Abbott, 2016). Who we are and how we act are not so much 'determined' by the unfolding of inner mental processes as we develop in a pre-determined or definitive way, but instead change as the organisation and type of social relations binding human agents change over time.

As we shall see, socialization is a central concept in the work of a number of modern theo-rists. Pierre Bourdieu's work (Chapter 7) pays close attention to socialization as a key moment in the intergenerational transmission of different forms of capital, which play an influential role in shaping the life chances of the individual. Feminist social theorists (Chapter 8) iden-tify socialization as a key moment in the production of gender roles and the role these play in perpetuating forms of sexual inequality and oppression. Norbert Elias (Chapter 5) adopts an historical perspective to demonstrate the increasing complexity of Western socialization practices from the medieval period onward, focussing in particular on the uneven distribution of emotional and behavioural dispositions across different social groups. The work of Michel Foucault (Chapter 6) highlights how powerful forms of discourse are socialized into the minds of individuals, in ways that are only partially consciously grasped and contribute to wider and enduring structures of power.

More generally, the concept of socialization is an important one because it allows us to explain how and why what we regard as our most *personal* characteristics and traits are shaped by a range of impersonal *social* processes. As biological organisms we may be hardwired to seek out the company of others, procreate, fight and defend ourselves when necessary, but how these fundamental human traits develop cannot be grasped without an understanding of the myriad social and cultural processes with which they intersect and are played out. A key part of social work training involves learning to develop an awareness of and reflect on the social and cultural processes shaping your own selfhood (Beckett and Maynard, 2005). The same is true of service-users. Understanding how the ideas, attitudes and actions of service-users are informed by a range of socially and culturally shaped processes is a key part of learning to become a social worker.

Socialization is also useful for thinking about a number of the issues faced by social workers operating in an increasingly multicultural society (Chapter 9). Social work today involves responding to the needs and problems of service-users from a wide range of cultural, religious and ethnic backgrounds. Differences in the value systems and belief structures of different ethnic groups and communities raise complex issues and debates for social work. Working with service-users from ethnically diverse backgrounds and communities often involves trying to negotiate the cultural and religious traditions in which their identities are rooted. Learning to understand how culture shapes the identities, beliefs and experiences of different groups (the focus of phenomenologically inspired theories; see Chapter 3) forms an important part of the contemporary social worker's knowledge base.

Social pathologies and individual problems

Durkheim's study of suicide demonstrates in the most literal sense how the life of the individual is directly conditioned by changes to the organisation and structure of society. If individuals are insufficiently integrated and regulated by social structures the likelihood increases that suicide becomes a viable course of action. While suicide patterns remain markedly consistent, the vast majority of people who experience isolation, redundancy and other challenging circumstances do not choose to commit suicide. Nonetheless, Durkheim's emphasis on the importance of social integration and regulation for shaping individual behaviour can be extended to think about a much wider range of issues relevant for social work.

A society whose members are insufficiently integrated and regulated gives rise to pathological levels of individualism, the consequences of which impact heavily on not only the individual, but wider society too. From a Durkheimian perspective, many of the problems of the advanced capitalist societies of Western Europe and North America can be seen as deriving from the declining power of social structures to regulate and constrain the individual. This is the social cause of the anomic tendencies of modern culture. Anomie refers to a cultural condition in which individuals are insufficiently normatively regulated and bound. Traditional forms of association and stability such as the family, religion, community, etc. no longer bind people in the ways they did even thirty years ago. Towns and cities are made up of a wide variety of people from an increasingly diverse range of backgrounds, ethnic groups and professions. The transient nature of modern work prevents many people from forming meaningful attachments to the areas where they live, either because they were compelled to move there in pursuit of work, or because they know that they may have to leave again soon if and when their circumstances change.

The lack of shared values and beliefs characteristic of modern culture fails to regulate people's experiences through imposing clear moral boundaries, normative rules and shared codes of conduct. In the absence of these, the tacit moral guidelines underpinning social interaction, become poorly defined and uncertain. Much of modern culture fails to provide the kinds of shared value basis necessary for ordering the actions and interactions of individuals. As the coercive power of culture becomes weaker, the tendency towards deviance and novel forms of criminality increases. New expressions of collective disunity and inter-group hostilities arise in the form of rising levels of interpersonal crimes such as racism, terrorism, hate crime and cyberbullying (Aas, 2013).

Compounding the lack of integration and regulation of modern society is the pervasive sense of uncertainty and unpredictability life in a globalizing world entails. Globalization (Chapter 9) complicates and destabilizes the social and cultural configurations of early modernity, in new and unprecedented ways. What happens in another part of the world increasingly impacts on local happenings, such that the decision of a multinational corporation to relocate to another country can have drastic consequences for members of a local community e.g. in the sudden decline of employment opportunities in an area. The lack of job stability, the high-paced nature of social and political change, the threat of terrorism at home and abroad, and the proliferation of news and information via internet-based technologies all undermine the stability, predictability and ordering of everyday life. Life in a globalizing world is increasingly unpredictable, characterised by rapid social change and rising levels of uncertainty about the future (Furedi, 1997, 2005).

The pathological individualism of modern culture provides a robust challenge to the well-being and mental health of modern individuals. Research undertaken by Mind, a U.K.-based national charity, suggests that one in four people experiences mental health problems, and that one in ten suffers from anxiety disorders (Mind, 2013). On the whole, people are far less likely to get married, with those who do more likely to end up getting divorced (Office for National Statistics, 2014). The number of alcohol-related hospital admissions and people seeking help for substance misuse issues is steadily rising as people try to cope with the isolation, disorientation and anxiety characteristic of everyday life (Mann, 2014). More than 50 per cent of the victims of violent crimes believed that the offender was under the influence of alcohol (Office for National Statistics, 2015). Cast in the Durkheimian terms of 'integration' and 'regulation', the tendency to see the cause of these problematic conditions and behaviours as explicable in individual terms seems highly naïve. Yet the steady shift towards individual-centred ways of conceptualising and responding to these problems continues to predominate across an ever greater range of social spheres including social work.

Karl Marx: conflict and capitalism

Karl Marx (1818–1883) was a German philosopher and social theorist. His work draws extensively on the ideas of the German philosopher Georg Hegel (1770–1831), specifically his method of dialectics and the concept of alienation. The notion of dialectics carries various meanings, but in its elementary form refers to processes of movement and change – in particular, situations where opposing forces come into contact and clash with each other. As these opposing forces clash, both the situation and the nature of the conflicting forces are transformed. The clash transforms both forces, each being reconfigured by the other, such that they come to have new natures, comprising elements of each other. The new situation now contains elements from each of the opposing forces, as well as elements that are entirely new. The clash of opposing forces is dialectical, and the clash creates new forces and situations that are also dialectical in nature.

Marx uses Hegel's abstract ideas about the dialectical nature of change as the basis for this 'materialist' theory of human history (Cohen, 1978). Herein, human society is understood as having developed dialectically through a number of historical stages, each of which contains parts of the old society while simultaneously containing new structures that form the basis for the next stage in the process. The motor driving historical and social change is conflict. Conflict in society derives primarily from the economic sphere. Marx regards the economy as the most important part of society. The role of the economy is to ensure that basic material needs are met. Marx's work focusses primarily on economic factors to explain all the other parts of society. This is because in all societies basic material needs e.g. food, clothing, shelter, etc. must be met if social life is to persist.

Marx invoked the metaphors of 'base' and 'superstructure' to emphasise the importance economic factors play in shaping all other parts of society. The base comprises the economic foundations of society. How the economic base of society is organised determines the 'social relations of production' through which different groups are joined. How these social relations are organised concerns property relations centring on ownership: of raw materials (e.g. wood, oil) which are turned into goods; of the means (e.g. tools, industrial machines); and of the finished objects themselves. The group which owns the property, factories and raw materials i.e. the means of production is the ruling class. The ruling class controls the class of people who make the products i.e. the workers. In modern capitalist society, the social relations of production are divided into two main class groups: the class of capitalists – the bourgeoisie (e.g. the factory owners); and the working class – the proletariat (e.g. the factory workers).

The class that controls the economic base controls every other area of society. All the other parts of society e.g. the legal system, government, culture, education, family life, etc. comprise the 'superstructure'. Social order is like a building. The foundations comprise the economy, and the upper storeys comprise all the other parts of society. The economic base generates, shapes and over time controls the different parts of society that make up the superstructure. Marx used his 'base/superstructure' model to claim that culture in capitalist society is ideological. Capitalist culture is ideological because it does not reflect the ideals, beliefs and values of the vast majority of the population – the workers; instead, in capitalist society the dominant ideals, morals and values derive from the culture of dominant social groups – the bourgeoisie. In capitalist society, 'culture functions as a veil', the purpose of which is to conceal the social causes of people's exploitation and oppression (Marx, 1988 [1865]: 84).

Marx was not claiming that capitalist society is run along the lines of an organised conspiracy. Just as the ideals and values of capitalist culture refract and serve the interests of socially dominant groups in ways that for the most part pass unnoticed, so too can the same be said for the ruling class. Marx claimed that, no less than the workers, the ruling capitalist class is dominated by the ideals and values it regards as its own, but that in actuality have their origins in the very structure of society. In capitalist society *all* social groups, from the most rich and powerful to the poorest and most oppressed, are dominated by the ideals and values of the wider social system, even if this does serve to benefit some groups more than others as a consequence.

For Marx, modernity had given rise to a society defined by conflict and alienation. The concept of alienation is one Marx took over from Hegel, who had already begun to use it in his analysis of modern society (Liebersohn, 1988). As elaborated by Marx, alienation refers to a process whereby human agents create relationships, situations and material objects, which they subsequently lose control of and are dominated by. Hegel regarded alienation as an intrinsic part of human life because almost all human actions have wider consequences that cannot be entirely anticipated or controlled. For Marx, however, alienation is the defining feature of life in modern capitalist society because the economy dominates all aspects of society and culture:

> Modern bourgeois society with its relations of production, of exchange and of property, a society that has conjured up such gigantic means of production and exchange, is like

the sorcerer who is no longer able to control the powers of the nether world that he has called up by his spells.

(Marx and Engels, 2002: 136)

Alienation refers to a situation of estrangement and loss of control affecting all human groups in capitalist society. But as with all social phenomena, the extent to which *specific* individuals and groups experience alienation is highly unevenly distributed:

> . . . the propertied class and the class of the proletariat present the same human self-estrangement. But the former class feels at ease and strengthened in this self-estrangement . . . the class of the proletariat feels annihilated in its estrangement.
>
> *(Marx, 2016 [1845]: 49)*

Marx claimed that *all* human groups are alienated in capitalist society. But a situation of alienation is most acute for the workers whose jobs are lowly paid, menial and exploitative. This is because capitalism transforms the nature of human labour – work – in ways that are neither personally nor collectively fulfilling. Workers feel estranged because the work they perform is work they are compelled to do to earn money, and not something they would choose to do under different circumstances. Moreover, not only are workers estranged from the goods and services they produce because they cannot afford to buy them, they are estranged from themselves and others too. Work in capitalist society ceases to be an enjoyable and life-affirming activity rooted in and of benefit to the wider community. Instead, work is something people do to survive, albeit at the cost of exacerbating their own self-estrangement as well as that of others at the same time.

TABLE 2.2 Summary of Marx

Social superstructure

- government, legal system, family, culture, education

Economic base

- means of production e.g. property, factories, material goods
- social relations of production e.g. ruling class who controls the means of production and working class who produces goods

Ideology

- imposition of ruling class culture e.g. ideas, beliefs and values on the working class

Alienation

- loss of control over human products e.g. relationships, institutions, material artefacts
- individuals and groups are estranged from and oppressed by the (unintended) consequences of their and others' actions and interactions
- characteristic of social relations in capitalist society e.g. organisation of society into opposing social classes

Applying Marx to social work

Marx's highly critical account of capitalism has strongly influenced social work thinking and practice, particularly in the U.K. (Langan and Lee, 1989). This is hardly surprising given that his work addresses social work values such as emancipation, oppression, inequality and social justice. During the 1960s and '70s in Britain, Marxist thinking provided a key intellectual resource in the rise of the radical social work movement (Bailey and Brake, 1981; Ferguson, 2001; Ferguson and Lavalette, 1999, 2004; Lavalette, 2011; Jones, 2001). A seminal text in the formulation of radical Marxist social work was Roy Bailey and Mike Brake's *Radical Social Work* published in 1975. From its earliest beginnings, the authors argue, social work has failed to acknowledge sufficiently the 'position of the oppressed in the context of the social and economic structures they live in' (Bailey and Brake, 1975: 9). As the radical social work movement developed throughout the 1960s and '70s in a number of directions, the emphasis on identifying the social-structural causes of service-users' problems formed the unifying theme. Advocates of radical Marxist social work argue that the families and communities hit hardest by social and economic problems should be the main focus for the profession, and not service-users as they are dealt with on an individual basis (Garrett, 2009).

From a Marxist perspective social work was born of the wider class-based struggles and contradictions rooted in the organisation and structure of capitalist society. As a result, those same tensions are refracted in and structure the relations between social workers and the state on the one hand, and social workers and service-users on the other. Considered in this light, social work in a capitalist society necessarily comes to occupy a contradictory and ultimately self-defeating role. In this view, the efforts of social workers to address the needs of service-users are both heroic and tragic at the same time. Social workers are heroic because they are committed to trying to empower people whose lives are worst affected by the inequalities and injustice inherent in a capitalist society. At a collective level, however, social work is tragic because the unintended consequence of assisting service-users to carry on involves integrating them back into the exploitative capitalist system which created the very need for social work in the first place.

Social class and social exclusion

Social work is and always has been a class-based activity. The vast majority of the recipients of social work services come from economically impoverished and working-class backgrounds. In Britain, 80 per cent of social work problems can be classified as income related (Jones, 1983, 2011). As social work has developed it has attempted to 'play down this class-specificity' for fear of contributing to the stigmatization and negative stereotyping of working-class people generally (Jones, 1998: 42). In place of the ideologically charged terms of *class* and *class relations*, the depoliticized terms of *inclusion* and *exclusion* have come to dominate political and welfare discourse (Giddens, 2007). Nevertheless, that the vast majority of social work service-users come from socially marginalized backgrounds cannot be conjured away by semantics. In a capitalist society, lack of financial resources leads to exclusion, and exclusion gives rise to social inequality, conflict and a range of social problems. These problems are felt most keenly by the members of socio-economically marginalized groups and communities, the social basis of the majority of service-users.

Social exclusion and alienation

Alienation is central to Marx's account of life in capitalist society. Social exclusion and alienation are closely bound up with and mutually inform one another. Exclusion leads to alienation, and alienation increases the likelihood of exclusion. Social exclusion occurs when individuals and groups are systematically excluded from participating in mainstream society (Sheppard, 2006). Prolonged exclusion from mainstream social relations and institutions impacts negatively on individuals in multiple ways (Byrne, 1999). Lack of money is the primary cause of social exclusion in modern capitalist society. Service-users living in poverty, or with little disposable income, find it very difficult to take part in even the most mundane social activities. Long-term unemployment due to lack of job opportunities, an absence of marketable skills and formal education, health problems, low pension levels in the case of elderly people and an absence of childcare for single-parent families are all factors which make it harder for people to enter mainstream society.

Having very little money impacts heavily on the capacity of people to construct and assert their identity. Spending money on consumer goods and services has become a form of social activity in and of its own right. Consumer practices such as shopping are an integral part of the way people construct and express their personal and social identity. In a society organised increasingly around the consumption of material goods, the acquisition of consumer goods and services has come to be read as an expression of our innermost selfhood (Miller, 1998; Schor and Holt, 2000). Having only enough money to pay for the bare essentials such as food and heating renders vast swathes of modern life obsolete, as well as denying people the means to realize and express a sense of personal identity and social status (Sassatelli, 2007).

While the majority of social exclusion occurs primarily for economic reasons, the consequences of exclusion can extend well beyond a material level. Social exclusion can negatively impact on service-users' most intimate sense of self-identity. The work of symbolic interactionist thinkers (Chapter 4) focusses on the importance of interactions and relationships with others in the formation of selfhood. The person we imagine ourselves to be cannot be separated out from the interpersonal exchanges and interactions we have with others. This is particularly true in the way wider society reacts to and confirms the marginalized identity of individuals and groups. For service-users living in poverty, the range of material and symbolic resources available to them for constructing their identity is very narrow and constraining, as well as being read by others as a signifier of their socially marginalized status. As a result, the identity they are constrained to adopt is something they experience as having played very little part in constructing. Rather than serving as an accurate portrayal of the person they imagine themselves to be, their identity confronts them as something oppressive and in many cases 'alien'. This can lead to service-users experiencing further forms of exclusion, such as stigmatization and discrimination.

Penetrating even deeper than the material and symbolic levels, long-term exclusion from mainstream society results in people being denied the kinds of relationships and experiences underpinning a range of 'pro-social' dispositions and traits. Byrne (1999: 55) defines those who are socially excluded as 'those parts of the population who have been actively under developed'. As we shall see with regard to the work of Norbert Elias (Chapter 5), individuals and communities cut off from mainstream society are far less likely to be embedded in the kinds of social networks necessary for developing a range of psychological, emotional and behavioural dispositions. As we shall explore in greater detail, Elias's work casts a discerning light on the ways inequalities come to be inscribed on the bodies of marginalized individuals and groups.

Max Weber and rationality

Similar to Marx, the German historian and social theorist Max Weber (1864–1920) regarded modern society as characterised by a condition of profound alienation. Marx regarded capitalist society as alienating because it gives rise to opposing social classes whose material interests bring them into conflict with one another and estrangement from themselves. Weber agreed with Marx that *material* factors are important for explaining the development of society, but he did not believe that they are more important than *ideal* factors. Ideal factors – culturally specific ideas, beliefs and values – are just as important for shaping how human agents think and act. A concern with ideal factors formed part of the wider focus on culture characteristic of German intellectual life during Weber's lifetime. Of particular influence was the view of culture as the collective expression of the spirit of a group or nation, unique to and distinguishing it from all others. The culture of a group is permeated by the mental patterns, attitudes, emotions and ways of doing things characteristic of that group. Focussing on ideal factors means trying to understand how those mental patterns and values give rise to culturally specific forms of consciousness, or culturally shaped mindsets. How a specific cultural mindset shapes the way members of a group act and interact was of central concern to Weber.

Weber adopted a hermeneutic method to the study of social action. Hermeneutics involves the study and interpretation of meaning. Social action refers to any action or course of actions to which meaning is attributed, either by the person undertaking the action or by those attributing meaning to it (Turner, 1999). Weber employed a hermeneutic method to understand the relationship between meaning and action, specifically how meaning shapes the subjectivity of the individuals who form part of a particular culture, and how in turn this disposes them to think and act. Weber's hermeneutic method of 'verstehen' involves the analyst trying to sympathetically imagine what it is like to see and experience the world through the eyes of the typical member of a culture (Freund, 1968: 99). Using a range of qualitative data including historical documents, interviews, letters and so on, the task of the analyst is to interpretatively reconstruct how the typical individual brought up in the culture of the group thinks and feels. For Marx and Durkheim, social-structural factors are central to understanding how social agents think and act. By contrast, Weber (1978) focussed on how the ideas and values implanted in agents' minds through culture shape social action and change over time.

Much of Weber's work concentrates on the subject of rationalization. Weber regarded the increasing rationalization of Western culture as the defining feature of modernity. In his classic study *The Protestant Ethic and the Spirit of Capitalism* (1930), Weber identified changes in the interpretation of Calvinist religious ideals and values as closely implicated in the development of capitalism. The steady rationalization of modern culture compounded the alienating tendencies of modern society described by Marx, as well as giving rise to a wider and pervasive sense of cultural and spiritual disenchantment. A culture of rationality erodes the affective and spiritual dimensions of social relations, as emotions come to be regarded as unruly, unpredictable obstacles to achieving specific ends. Weber was deeply concerned about the rationalizing tendencies of modern culture, which he regarded as leaching social relations of their life-affirming and spiritual qualities:

> The peculiarity of modern culture, and specifically its technical and economic basis, demands th[e] calculability of success . . . it develops this peculiarity the more perfectly . . . the more successfully it is able to 'dehumanize' itself, to eliminate love, hate and all purely personal – or generally all irrational – emotions, which are obstacles to calculability . . .
>
> *(Weber in Schroeder, 1992: 117)*

In modern society, value-oriented behaviour e.g. acting and interacting in ways that have no other aim than the realization of a particular normative value such as kindness or friendship is replaced with 'purely formal or technical calculations' to achieve a given end by the most efficient means (Schroeder, 1992: 115). A culture of rationality involves fundamental changes to the organisation of society and the affective aspects of social relations. In this sense, both material *and* ideal factors feed into and change one another dialectically, in ways that perpetuate the tendency towards increasing rationality. To this end, Weber regarded the rise of bureaucracy as the most significant development driving the increasingly rational and routinized character of modern life.

Rationalization and bureaucracy

Weber wanted to investigate the alienating effects of bureaucracy on human experience and relationships. Bureaucratic organisations are organised around the values of rationality and efficiency. The hierarchically arranged positions occupied by people in bureaucracies are called 'roles'. Attached to roles are specific tasks and duties. Individuals contribute to bureaucratic organisations by performing the tasks and duties assigned to those roles. Roles call forth certain aspects of the individual self, at the same time as requiring others to be bracketed off and suppressed. To think and act in emotionally led ways or on the basis of personally held moral convictions, for example, is not relevant to the roles individuals play. To import these aspects of oneself into roles and relationships with others is considered unprofessional. It is considered inappropriate to act and interact in ways other than those prescribed by the role the individual plays.

Bureaucratically organised institutions are made up of different roles, attached to which are delimited amounts of power. Limiting the amount of power and influence attached to roles prevents any one individual from acquiring too much power, using it to advance their personal interests ahead of those of the organisation. But the unintended consequence is that it severely limits the capacity for individuals to instigate meaningful change, either to the role they perform or the wider organisation. The result is that the organisation confronts the individual as an autonomous, all-powerful entity possessed of a will of its own, largely resistant to change or influence by the individuals who belong to it. People in bureaucracies typically have very little input in shaping the roles they play or the aims and values of the wider organisation. Instead, they are just expected to play and adhere to them. In the face of the impersonal and faceless bureaucratic institutions they work for, individuals experience themselves as akin to cogs in a giant machine, the aims and direction of which they are relatively powerless to change.

TABLE 2.3 Summary of Weber

Verstehen
• interpretative method • involves sympathetic reconstruction of culturally shaped mindset of individuals and groups

Culture of rationality
• ideal aspects e.g. dominant cultural ideals and values organised around rationality, efficiency and instrumentalism • material aspects e.g. instrumental actions, interactions and bureaucratic institutions and organisations • leads to a situation of social estrangement, alienation and spiritual disenchantment

Applying Weber to social work

Verstehen

Weber's method of verstehen is instructive for thinking about social worker/service-user relations. It draws attention to the role ideal factors such as attitudes, feelings and values play in shaping the actions and interactions of service-users. It also highlights how important it is to adopt an empathetic approach towards service-users. Trying to understanding how service-users interpret, feel and make sense of the situation they are in involves trying to suspend your own personal beliefs and values. It means working with service-users to sympathetically reconstruct how the world looks inside the culturally-shaped mindset they embody. Building up a detailed understanding of the mindset of the service-user makes it possible to reconstruct what from their particular point of view are viable courses of action, as well as allowing you to understand how and why they think and feel the ways they do. How exactly the socially shaped nature of human subjectivity disposes individuals and groups to think and act in particular ways is a subject we shall explore in greater depth in Chapter 3.

Social work, bureaucracy and alienation

The increasing rationalization of an ever greater range of spheres of human life forms a central plank in Weber's gloomy diagnosis of modernity. Social work is typically regarded as an organisational profession because most of the roles and activities undertaken by social workers take place in formal agency settings. It would be very difficult today to think of any of those settings that are not organised bureaucratically. Regardless of which area of practice you go in to, all social workers are required to operate in some kind of bureaucratic capacity. From a Weberian perspective, a significant part of being a social worker involves working in the capacity of a state bureaucrat. From the1980s, the organisation and delivery of social work services have been subject to increasing rationalization and bureaucratization (Lymbery, 2001; Harris, 1998). In the U.K. and North America, the spread of economic models and techniques of service delivery such as New Public Management has rapidly accelerated this process (Jones and Novak, 1993). Instead of increasing efficiency, many social work professionals feel increasingly frustrated and constrained by the bureaucratic organisations in which they work (Van Heugten, 2011).

The increasing bureaucratization of social work is regarded by many social workers as posing significant challenges to the task of assisting service-users (Evans and Harris,

2004). Many social workers express difficultly in exercising professional effectiveness and competency in the bureaucratically organised settings in which they practice (Dioum et al., 2012). A recurrent tension concerns the conflicting demands placed on social workers with regard to professional authority and control. Social workers are often answerable to a number of different 'actors', including the profession, the organisation they belong to, the service-user and the wider community (Green, 1966). This means trying to reconcile the uniqueness of service-users situations with the demand for standardized and formal procedures and protocol. Bureaucratic procedures often impede the task of meeting the needs of and delivering assistance to service-users (Basw.co.uk, 2017). The codification of bureaucratic rules and procedures makes it very difficult to address the issues of service-users whose particular situation falls outside of the predetermined and standardized categories used to classify them (Lipsky, 2010 [1980]). Working with the 'whole' service-user, as opposed to those parts strictly relevant to resolving their issues, is also reported as being difficult within bureaucratic relations (Ruch, 2005, 2011).

As the bureaucratization of social work has intensified, the amount of time social workers devote to administrative tasks and duties has increased dramatically. Evidence from social work surveys demonstrates that many social workers feel that the person-centred nature of their work is compromised by the proliferation of administrative legislation (Dioum et al., 2012). Evidence of rising stress levels amongst social work staff and managers is a recurrent theme within social work departments, the pages of journal articles and union-led surveys (Balloch et al., 1997; Jones, 2001). Many social workers experience this situation as confusing and difficult to reconcile. On the one hand social workers feel torn between trying to practice in ways that 'they believed were in the bests interests of their clients', at the same time as being stifled by rising levels of bureaucratic policy and procedure (Ferguson, 2009: 90).

Conclusion

Since Max Weber's death in 1920, Western societies have undergone profound transformation and change. Yet many of the theoretical ideas and concepts contained in the works of the classical theorists remain as illuminating and relevant today as they ever did. In many instances, particularly in the case of Durkheim's concept of anomie, Marx's concept of alienation and Weber's concerns about the increasing rationalization of Western culture, the ideas of the classical theorists are more boldly exemplified by developments to the contemporary social terrain. Rather than losing their capacity to explain vast tracts of modern society with the passing of time, the analytical prowess of the classical theorists continues to be affirmed and reaffirmed, particularly for understanding many of the issues facing contemporary social workers and service-users.

As we will see throughout the book, modern social theorists owe a considerable intellectual debt to the classical theorists. Much of modern social theory has involved adapting, synthesizing and refining classical social theoretical ideas in light of subsequent developments and changes to society. Even when modern social theorists explicitly reject the ideas of the classical theorists, the questions they pose and the conceptual ideas they develop form part of an intellectual universe that bears a strong imprint of the influence of Durkheim, Marx and Weber. As society has developed and changed, so too has social theory as it has attempted to update and refine the ideas of the classical theorists so that they remain as analytically insightful and current as they once did.

Further reading

Bailey, R. and Brake, M. (eds.) (1981) *Radical Social Work and Practice*. London: Sage.
Durkheim, E. (2002 [1897]) *Suicide*. New York: Routledge.
Marx, K. and Engels, F. (2002) *The Communist Manifesto*. London: Penguin Books.
Turner, B. S. (1999) *Classical Sociology*. London: Sage.

References

Aas, K. F. (2013) *Globalization and Crime*. London: Sage.
Abbott, A. (2016) *Processual Sociology*. Chicago: The University of Chicago Press.
Allen, K. (2004) *Max Weber: A Critical Introduction*. London: Pluto Press.
Bailey, R. and Brake, M. (eds.) (1975) *Radical Social Work*. London: Edward Arnold.
Bailey, R. and Brake, M. (eds.) (1981) *Radical Social Work and Practice*. London: Sage.
Balloch, S. (1999) *Social Services: Working Under Pressure*. Bristol: Policy Press.
Balloch, S., Pahl, J. and Mclean, J. (1997) 'Working in the Social Services: Job Satisfaction, Stress and Violence', *British Journal of Social Work*, 28(3): 329–350.
Basw.co.uk. (2017) *Voices from the frontline | BASW Resources*. [ONLINE] Available at: www.basw.co.uk/resource/?id=499 [Accessed 7 April 2017].
Beckett, C. and Maynard, A. (2005) *Values and Ethics in Social Work: An Introduction*. London: Sage Publications.
Byrne, D. (1999) *Social Exclusion*. Buckingham: Open University Press.
Cohen, G. A. (1978) *Karl Marx's Theory of History: A Defence*. Oxford: Oxford University Press.
Dioum, M., Yorath, S., Chatfield, G., Lennon, L., McClaren, P. and Sreenan, C. (2012) *Voices from the frontline: Supporting our social workers in the delivery of quality services to children*. [ONLINE] Available at: http://cdn.basw.co.uk/upload/basw_115256-9.pdf [Accessed 29 January 2017].
Durkheim, E. (1964 [1893]) *The Division of Labour in Society*. New York: Free Press.
Durkheim, E. (2002 [1897]) *Suicide*. New York: Routledge.
Durkheim, E. (2005 [1914]) 'The Duality of Human Nature and Its Social Conditions', *Durkheimian Studies*, 11: 35–45.
Durkheim, E. and Mauss, M. (1969 [1903]) *Primitive Classification*. London: Cohen and West.
Evans, T. and Harris, J. (2004) 'Street-Level Bureaucracy, Social Work and the (Exaggerated) Death of Discretion', *British Journal of Social Work*, 34(6): 871–895.
Ferguson, H. (2001) 'Social Work, Individualization and Life Politics', *British Journal of Social Work*, 31(1): 41–55.
Ferguson, I. (2009) 'Another Social Work Is Possible! Reclaiming the Radical Tradition', in Leskosek, V. (ed.) *Theories and Methods of Social Work: Exploring Different Perspectives*. Ljubljana: University of Ljubljana, pp. 81–98.
Ferguson, I. and Lavalette, M. (1999) 'Social Work, Postmodernism and Marxism', *European Journal of Social Work*, 2(1): 27–40.
Ferguson, I. and Lavalette, M. (2004) 'Beyond Power Discourse: Alienation and Social Work', *British Journal of Social Work*, 34(3): 297–312.
Freund, J. 1968. *The Sociology of Max Weber*. Aylesbury, Bucks: The Penguin Press.
Furedi, F. (1997) *Culture of Fear: Risk Taking and the Morality of Low Expectation*. London: Continuum International Publishing Group.
Furedi, F. (2005) *Politics of Fear: Beyond Left and Right*. London: Continuum International Publishing Group.

Garrett, P. M. (2009) 'Marx and "Modernization": Reading Capital as Social Critique and Inspiration for Social Work Resistance to Neoliberalization', *Journal of Social Work*, 9(2): 199–221.

Giddens, A. (2007) *Over to You Mr Brown: How Labour Can Win Again*. Cambridge: Polity Press.

Green, A. (1966) 'The Professional Social Worker in the Bureaucracy', *Social Service Review*, 40(1): 71–83.

Harris, J. (1998) 'Scientific Management, Bureau-Professionalism and New Managerialism: The Labour Process of State Social Work', *British Journal of Social Work*, 28(6): 839–862.

Jones, C. (1983) *State Social Work and the Working Class*. London: The MacMillan Press Ltd.

Jones, C. (1998) 'Social Work and Society', in Adams, R., Dominelli, L. and Payne, M. (eds.) *Social Work: Themes, Issues and Critical Debates*. Hampshire: Palgrave, pp. 41–49.

Jones, C. (2001) 'Voices from the Front Line: State Social Workers and New Labour', *British Journal of Social Work*, 31(4): 547–562.

Jones, C. and Novak, T. (1993) 'Social Work Today', *British Journal of Social Work*, 23(3): 195–212.

Jones, O. (2011) *Chavs: The Demonization of the Working Class*. London: Verso.

Langan, M. and Lee, P. (eds.) (1989) *Radical Social Work Today*. London: Routledge.

Lavalette, M. (ed.) (2011) *Radical Social Work Today: Social Work at the Crossroads*. Bristol: Policy Press.

Liebersohn, H. (1988) *Fate and Utopia in German Sociology, 1870–1923*. Cambridge, MA: MIT Press.

Lipsky, M. (2010 [1980]) *Street Level Bureaucracies: Dilemmas of the Individual in Public Service*. 2nd ed. New York: Russel Sage Foundation.

Lymbery, M. (2001) 'Social Work at the Crossroads', *British Journal of Social Work*, 31(3): 369–384.

Mann, J. (2014) *British Drugs Survey 2014: Drug use is rising in the U.K. but we are not addicted*. [ONLINE] Available at: www.theguardian.com/society/2014/oct/05/-sp-drug-use-is-rising-in-the-uk-but-were-not-addicted. [Accessed 3 February 2017].

Marske, C. (1987) 'Durkheim's Cult of the Individual and the Moral Reconstitution of Society', *Sociological Theory*, 5(1): 1–14.

Marx, K. (2016 [1845]) *The Holy Family: Or Critique of Critical Criticism*. Leopard Books.

Marx, K. (1988 [1865]) *Capital*. Vol. 1. Harmondsworth: Penguin.

Marx, K. and Engels, F. (2002) *The Communist Manifesto*. London: Penguin Books.

Miller, D. (1998) *A Theory of Shopping*. Cambridge: Polity Press.

Mind. (2013) *How common are mental health problems*. [ONLINE] Available at: www.mind.org.uk/information-support/types-of-mental-health-problems/statistics-and-facts-about-mental-health/how-common-are-mental-health-problems/. [Accessed 3 February 2017].

Office for National Statistics. (2014) *Divorce*. [ONLINE] Available at: www.ons.gov.uk/peoplepopulation andcommunity/birthsdeathsandmarriages/divorce. [Accessed 3 February 2017].

Office for National Statistics. (2015) *Overview of violent crime and sexual offences*. [ONLINE] Available at: www.ons.gov.uk/peoplepopulationandcommunity/crimeandjustice/compendium/focusonviolent crimeandsexualoffences/yearendingmarch2015/chapter1overviewofviolentcrimeandsexualoffences# additional-information-on-violent-crime-from-the-csew. [Accessed 3 February 2017].

Ruch, G. (2005) 'Relationship-Based Practice and Reflective Practice: Holistic Approaches to Contemporary Child Care Social Work', *Child and Family Social Work*, 10(2): 111–123.

Ruch, G. (2011) 'Where Have All the Feelings Gone?', *British Journal of Social Work*, 42(7): 1315–1332.

Sassatelli, R. (2007) *Consumer Culture: History, Theory and Politics*. London: Sage.

Schor, J. and Holt, R. (2000) *The Consumer Society Reader*. New York: The New Press.

Schroeder, R. (1992) *Max Weber and the Sociology of Culture*. London: Sage.

Sheppard, M. (2006) *Social Work and Social Exclusion: The Idea of Practice*. Hampshire: Ashgate.

Turner, B. (1999) *Classical Sociology*. London: Sage.

Van Heugten, K. (2011) *Social Work under Pressure: How to Overcome Stress, Fatigue and Burnout in the Work Place*. London: Jessica Kingsley Publishers.

Weber, M. (1930) *The Protestant Ethic and the Spirit of Capitalism*. London: Methuen.

Weber, M. (1978) *Max Weber: Selections in Translation*, Runciman, W. G. (ed.). Cambridge: Cambridge University Press.

3

PHENOMENOLOGY AND SOCIAL THEORY

Exploring the lifeworld of the service-user

As a social worker a significant part of your job will involve working with service-users to identify how best to deal with the issues confronting them. With this in mind, picture the following scenario: having assessed the needs of Ryan, a 39-year-old service-user who is out of work, together you decide that the best course of action for him is to attend the local job centre. Having agreed that this is the best way to proceed, you arrange to meet up with him a few days later to see how he got on. On meeting, you notice that Ryan seems agitated and upset. You mention this to him, and he explains how the trip to the job centre went. This is what he says:

> ' . . . Ah went intae thi' job centre yisterday . . . there was like tables an' a chair and some space next to this posh cow, ya know, fit, well-dressed an' middle class, an' I didnae want tae sit near her, I didnae feel I could like, I got all conscious of ma weight, I felt over-weight, so I started swettin', I started getting a' agitated, shufflin' ma feet, I kept thinkin' "na! I'm no' gonnae sit there, I dinae want tae dee her heid in". It disnae make me feel good, and I could tell she wiz uncomfortable an' a' . . . it's like I am too gross to look at . . . you can see it on their faces . . . folk look at ya like yer invadin' their space . . . like you shouldnae be there . . . it makes me no' wanna go oot . . . It stresses me right out, it's exhausting . . . It never stops either . . . everytime I'm oot in public I feel it . . . I just wanted tae run oot. I felt embarrassed just standing there . . . the thing is she doesnae know that that's nae me. I do, but she doesnae. . . . stuck-up cow . . . just because shes got time fae the gym, the body the clothes . . . that's why she can hae tha' confidence and tha' attitude . . . that's no' my fault tho' is it . . .'

Now that you have read the service-user's account of his experience at the job centre consider the following questions: why do you think that he experienced waiting in the job centre in this way? What were the reasons for him reacting so strongly to the situation? Did he over-react? How easy was it to understand what he said? In what ways was his perception of the situation shaped by social factors? How might understanding why he (re)acted the way he did inform the kind of assistance you would provide to him? How could an understanding of his experience be of use for assisting service-users in the future?

This chapter attempts to provide answers to these questions and more by drawing on the ideas and concepts contained within phenomenological ways of thinking. Phenomenological approaches to social life occupy a central role in modern social theory. This is because they enable us to understand how the world is perceived and understood from the points of view of particular individuals and groups. The word *phenomenology* derives from Greek and is made up of two words: 'ology', which means 'the study of', and 'phenomenon', which means 'observable occurrences'. How the world is understood and experienced from the point of view of the people being studied is a key concern of phenomenological thinkers. More broadly, this involves focusing on differences in the ways particular individuals and groups interpret and make sense of their experiences – namely by trying to understand how they see, perceive, understand, feel, experience, make sense of and respond to themselves, other people and the wider social environment. Phenomenological ways of thinking are often described as being 'actor-centred'. In some ways this is true, but it is more accurate to say that they are concerned with the consciousness of individuals acting, reacting and interacting with one another. How consciousness influences and makes interaction possible between individuals and groups is of central importance to phenomenological thinkers.

Given that phenomenology is concerned to understand how and why people see and experience the world in particular ways, it is surprising that social work has not drawn more extensively on phenomenological ideas and methods (Black and Enos, 1981; Houston, 2003). Social work academics such as Webb (2006) claim that phenomenological ideas have yet to be fully embraced and utilised by social work (McCormick, 2011; Houston and Mullan-Jensen, 2012). Where they have been, the aim has tended towards rethinking and challenging conventional understandings of the lived experiences of particular service-user groups, such as survivors of cancer and young and old people (Houston, 2003; Pascal, 2010; Thompson, 1992; Thompson, 2016). The concept of 'person-centred planning', a highly prominent one within social work, is founded on the phenomenological concept of 'lifeworld', for example. Yet the concept tends to be used implicitly rather than explicitly, with the result that it has failed to be taken up by others and developed further.

This chapter demonstrates the value of a range of core phenomenological concepts and themes. We begin by outlining the philosophical origins of phenomenology, before examining how these ideas were taken up and imported into social theory in the work of sociologist Alfred Schutz. Following on from this we turn to examine the work of Berger and Luckmann and Bernstein, focussing in particular on their respective accounts of the relationship between language and subjectivity. The first part of the chapter draws to a close by sketching-out the existential-phenomenological account of embodiment developed by Merleau-Ponty, in particular his emphasis on the centrality of the body in shaping human subjectivity.

The applied section of the chapter uses phenomenological concepts to think closely about the social dynamics structuring the communication between social workers and service-users. In addressing these themes, we identify a number of the difficulties language poses to the social work relationship and the active part social workers can play in overcoming these difficulties. The final part of the applied section applies the ideas of Merleau-Ponty to critically appraise the service-user scenario depicted at the start of the chapter. The chapter concludes by reflecting on the strengths and weaknesses of phenomenological ideas and concepts for social work.

Phenomenology and social theory

Phenomenological ideas and methods have their origins in philosophy, in particular the ideas of the German philosopher Immanuel Kant (1724–1804). Questions to do with the nature of the human mind and consciousness are central to Kant's thought. In essence, Kant regarded the human mind as a kind of synthesizing machine – knowledge of the world arrives through the sensory faculties whereupon it is transformed by a number of innate 'categories of mind'. These mental categories play an important role in organising and classifying the sensory data inputted into the mind. Without them, information received by the senses would not be intelligible to us. Kant wanted to reject the view of the mind as akin to a blank slate – tabula rasa – passively receiving sensory information about the world. Rather, he saw the mind as actively shaping that information. The mind actively constitutes how we perceive and experience the objects of consciousness.

Sensory information about the world (epistemology) is actively transformed and classified by mental categories. This is the world as it appears to us in consciousness. Kant referred to this as the world of 'phenomena'. This is different from the world as it is 'in-itself' i.e. as it exists outside of human consciousness, which he referred to as 'noumena'. The distinction between the world of phenomena and noumena is a central one in the work of Kant and social theory more generally. The world of noumena can never be known or directly perceived by the human mind. To understand how the mind shapes our perception and experience of reality it is necessary to study phenomena e.g. mental representations as they are constructed and appear to us in consciousness. This is what phenomenology tries to do. Phenomenology is about examining the objects of consciousness with a view to understanding the active role the mind plays in constructing those objects. As phenomenology developed over the course of the twentieth century it was taken up by thinkers in the social sciences (Pressler and Dasilva, 1996). This led to a shift towards focussing on the role culture plays in shaping the mental representations generated by the human mind.

As we saw in the work of Durkheim (Chapter 2), human agents learn to make sense of people and situations through socialization. Phenomenological sociology, therefore, is concerned to unpack how and in what ways the shared ideas and beliefs contained within the culture of human groups shape individual experience. Within philosophy, phenomenology had tended to focus on understanding human consciousness in a very abstract sense. Within social theory phenomenological methods and ideas have been used to try to examine the *social* and *cultural* conditions of inter-subjectivity (Roche, 1973). This means concentrating on how the world is perceived by *specific* individuals and social groups, as opposed to human beings in the most *general* sense.

A key figure in adapting phenomenological ideas and methods for the study of social life was Alfred Schutz (1899–1959). Schutz's work brings together Weber's ideas about social action (Chapter 2) with certain key ideas, such as the concept of 'lifeworld', taken from the work of the German philosopher Edmund Husserl (1815–1938). Schutz focussed his attention on what he referred to as the 'lifeworld' (*lebenswelt*). The lifeworld is the mundane, everyday world in which people operate. The lifeworld is created by the culture of the group to which the individual belongs. Culture creates the common sense ways in which people experience the lifeworld (Heeren, 1971). The individuals immersed within the lifeworld learn to make sense of one another and the (life)world around them by drawing on the common sense ways of thinking contained within it (culture). Individuals in the lifeworld experience these ways of thinking and acting as common sense, and so they tend to regard them as self-evident and natural. For the most part, the ways of thinking and acting within the lifeworld are taken-for-granted, with the result that people only very rarely bring them into question.

Schutz (1967) referred to the habitual common sense understandings used by people in the lifeworld as the 'natural attitude'. The natural attitude is the mental disposition people adopt most of the time because it provides them with a set of tried and tested ways of responding to one another and events. The natural attitude allows people to operate in their everyday lives (lifeworld). They tend not to subject it to rational criticism or scrutiny; rather, they use it without ever questioning why or from where it came. For the majority of the time, people are largely unaware of the ways the natural attitude shapes their thoughts and actions. It is only when something extraordinary happens, like if they were to discover they had been adopted, for example, that they would be forced to call into question the ideas and assumptions rooted in the natural attitude. Even then, they may try to conceal from themselves and others what they have learned in order to maintain a sense of normality (Laing, 1960). The natural attitude is the mode of consciousness individuals adopt as they negotiate their daily lives and the practical exigencies of the lifeworld.

The natural attitude operates at the level of 'practical consciousness'. This is the level of consciousness people operate with most of the time, as they negotiate the *practicalities* of everyday life. Practical consciousness is knowledge that we take for granted and only rarely think to question because it enables us to function in practical ways. The mental disposition we adopt when we focus our attention and are actively concentrating on what we are doing is referred to as 'discursive consciousness'. As I write this book, for example, I am operating at the level of discursive consciousness. This is because I am actively thinking about and focussing on what it is I am trying to say, how best to say it and how it relates to what will follow. When I take a break from writing to make a cup of coffee, this involves me slipping back into practical consciousness. I need to make the transition from discursive to practical consciousness if I am to perform the succession of tasks that making a cup of coffee involves. Because making a cup of coffee is something I have done many times, I know how to do it without devoting much conscious thought to doing so. Practical consciousness enables people to act in practical ways, without having to concentrate on or think about how it is they know to do what they are doing.

Schutz wanted to provide a vocabulary for thinking about how practical consciousness both shapes and is shaped by the lifeworld. It is important to understand the nature of the lifeworld because it forms the basis for all social life. Operating in the lifeworld involves adopting the natural attitude. The natural attitude is made up of what Schutz (1967) refers to as 'first-order categories'. First-order categories are rooted in practical consciousness, and used habitually in practical ways. In my lifeworld, for example, a first-order category is that of *car*, because I know what it means and how to drive one. The idea of *car* is one I use without thinking about or experiencing it as a category for me. I am likely to consciously reflect on the category of *car* implanted in practical consciousness only when my car breaks down. Then the category is elevated from the level of a taken-for-granted first-order category, to one I require to consciously reflect on if I am to construct a course of action which results in getting the car fixed.

For a social worker trying to understand the lifeworld of a service-user, this would mean trying to build up an accurate picture of how the world looks through their eyes, along with the other people who share that lifeworld. The social worker would need to try to unpack and understand the meanings and feelings attached to certain mental categories, along with how these relate to other categories. In trying to understand what the first-order category *job centre* means to a service-user, the social worker would have to ask the service-user to try to depict what this means to them in their own words. If the social worker were then to try to communicate to other social workers what the service-user had said, the social worker would be using her own language i.e. 'second-order categories' to describe the first-order category of *job centre* as it is understood and used by the service-user. Phenomenological analysis involves using second-order categories to try to understand the first-order categories of the lifeworld in which an individual, or group, exists.

First-order categories comprise and are constructed from typifications. Schutz (1970) draws attention to the role played by typifications for making sense of the lifeworld. Typifications are 'ideal-typical' aspects of the object, person or situation which first-order categories depict (Schutz, 1971). So while a great number of job centres exist across the U.K., typically all *job centres* have members of staff who work in them. Furthermore, many of those job centres differ in shape, size and look. Nevertheless, all job centres are job-centre-like in that how they are run and the purpose they serve demonstrate a significant number of shared ideal-typical features. In other words, there is no job centre that has the size, shape or look of, say, a clothes shop. If there were, it would not be a job centre but instead the kind of retail outlet depicted by the first-order category of *clothes shop*. First-order categories are substantiated by unique combinations of typifications. The typifications contained in first-order categories are practically enabling, because they allow individuals in the lifeworld to make sense of their experience and take action. They also enable us to interact with other people. This is because the categories of my lifeworld were not devised by me in isolation. They are collectively created and shared entities rooted in the culture of the wider group. The categories that exist in my lifeworld are at the same time categories used by the vast majority of people who exist in the lifeworld with me. This is why I am able to communicate with them and they are with me. The categories that make up the lifeworld do not belong to individuals, but instead are rooted in the shared culture of the group.

Schutz's work draws on phenomenological ideas and concepts to highlight the social and cultural dimensions of intersubjective communication within the lifeworld. Elaborating on Kant's view that the world as it exists outside of the human mind – noumena – can never be known, Schutz explains how agents' experience of reality is constructed by the collectively produced categories and typifications of the lifeworld. Within the lifeworld, individuals are socialized into the natural attitude, which provides them with a practical orientation towards the people, objects and situations around them. A key point to draw attention to here is that while much of what people think and do within the lifeworld appears natural and taken-for-granted, in actuality it is constructed from the collectively produced meanings contained within the culture of the group. As individuals go about their everyday lives, they remain largely unaware of the ways culture shapes their experience of the lifeworld. Instead, how they see and experience the world becomes ever more habitualized and taken-for-granted over time.

TABLE 3.1 Summary of Schutz

Theoretical concepts	
Lifeworld	Everyday, common sense ways of thinking, feeling and acting supplied by the culture of the group
Natural attitude	Culturally shaped mode of consciousness adopted by individuals in the lifeworld
Practical consciousness	Knowledge that is semi-consciously grasped and practically enacted; different to discursive knowledge which can be articulated and objectified e.g. through oral and written forms of communication
First- and second-order categories	Categories supplied by the lifeworld, used by actors; and categories used by analysts to understand actors' categories

Berger and Luckmann: socially constructing reality

The idea that social phenomena are rooted primarily in human consciousness was taken up and developed in a number of ways to try to understand the nature of meaning in modern society. In their landmark text *The Social Construction of Reality*, Berger and Luckmann (1991 [1966]) connect and develop Schutz's ideas about the lifeworld and practical consciousness with Marx's concept of alienation (Chapter 2). They argue that in modern society the meanings people use to make sense of social reality derive increasingly from outside of the lifeworld, originating instead in wider social institutions and objectified structures of meaning such as language (Berger and Luckmann, 1991 [1966]). In modernity, the categories of meaning supplied by the lifeworld are increasingly shaped by impersonal and objectified social structures. How people think and act is shaped by social structures over which they have very little control and played no part in constructing. Marx (2009 [1852]: 2) claimed that modern society 'weighs like a nightmare on the brains of the living'. This is the view that as modern society develops, human groups create institutions which they eventually lose control of as they grow in power and change in ways that were unintended. Over time, social structures and institutions created by one generation are reproduced through the actions and interactions of subsequent generations, whose minds and actions they dominate and control. Individuals and groups are constrained by human products, in particular social institutions and language.

Social constructions such as the family, gender, corporations, etc. persist over time through individuals acting and interacting in habitualized and patterned ways. Those habitualized interactions have their basis in and are patterned by shared normative ideals and values. The persistence of patterned ways of acting are an essential part of the process by which 'institutionalization' occurs and becomes 'naturalized' (Luckmann, 1984). When a child is born, the process of 'internalization' begins as the institutionally patterned and habitualized ways of thinking and acting are inculcated into their minds (Luckmann, 1978). As the child learns to communicate with other people, those ways of thinking form the basis for acting and interacting in the lifeworld. This is how the 'objectified' status of institutions comes to be affirmed and naturalized in the minds and the actions of the people in the lifeworld. In modern society, the meanings people draw on to construct and make sense of their experience derive not so much from the lifeworld, but ever more powerful and impersonal human constructions and institutions (Berger and Luckmann, 1991 [1966]).

TABLE 3.2 Summary of Berger and Luckmann

Theoretical concepts	
Habitualization	Ways of thinking and acting performed habitually over time; ways of thinking and acting rooted in practical as opposed to discursive consciousness
Objectivation	Occurs when the consequences of human interaction appear to take on an objective existence of their own i.e. independent of individuals
Normalization	A direct function of habitualization and objectivation; occurs when what is socially and culturally arbitrary appears normal and taken-for-granted

What originally consisted of human agents acting and interacting in habitualized and patterned ways starts just to seem natural, inevitable and real. The same is true of language. Language is a form of objectified and institutionally constructed reality. Children are born into a group and acquire language through interacting with others. Over time, the child, along with all the other people in the lifeworld, start to think of the language they use as something real, rather than a human construction. How the world is represented in language appears to them as how the world really is. They think the words they use refer directly to reality. But it is only the way the language specific to that lifeworld constructs a sense of reality. It is not reality in itself.

Basil Bernstein: restricted and elaborate code

While Basil Bernstein (1924–2000) is not strictly a phenomenologist, his work on language provides important insights into the ways language is constrained by the lifeworld and how in turn this shapes consciousness. Like Berger and Luckmann, Bernstein (1971, 1973) regards language as an objectified system of meaning, albeit not one that is the same for all members of society. Instead, Bernstein conceives of language as a form of code, of which there are two main types. By 'code', Bernstein intends the ways of talking specific to the lifeworld of different class-based groups. Restricted code refers to the ways of talking and meanings characteristic of the culture of groups based on strong social ties. Bernstein has in mind here the lifeworlds of working-class groups characterised by low levels of formal education.

Restricted code is language tightly tied to the situations and social roles rooted in the narrow range of habitualized activities found in working-class lifeworlds. Restricted code relies on everyone who uses it possessing large amounts of shared knowledge of the lifeworld in which it is used. Restricted code contains a narrow range of meanings, even if those meanings are highly expressive for those who use and understand them, because the life conditions of the group comprise a similarly narrow range of activities. Moreover, restricted code is like a secret code. Only people who possess shared knowledge of the lifeworld can understand it. For the members of the lifeworld who use restricted code i.e. 'insiders', knowledge of the shared meanings and ways of talking creates a sense of solidarity and belonging. This acts as a barrier to people i.e. 'outsiders' who do not belong to the lifeworld and who do not understand the restricted code used by the people within it.

By contrast, 'elaborate code' refers to the ways of talking and meanings associated with middle-class groups and professionals. As social life becomes more complex and differentiated,

TABLE 3.3 Summary of Bernstein

Theoretical concepts

Restricted code

- rooted in the specific activities and lifestyles of the lifeworld
- requires those who use it to possess large amounts of taken-for-granted and shared knowledge of the lifeworld
- like a secret code: actors in the lifeworld – insiders – know what the code means; those not in the lifeworld – outsiders – do not

Elaborate code

- abstract and impersonal ways of talking and communicating
- used in institutional and professional settings
- not tied to any specific social context

---

so language develops in a number of corresponding ways. Elaborate code involves ways of talking and communicating which are largely impersonal and abstract because they are not tied to any specific social context (lifeworld). An example of elaborate code is the statement 'one cannot help feel nervous at times such as these'. In this statement, neither the person nor the situation referred to is specified in a definitive way. The term *one* includes potentially all people, and the term *times such as these* does not specify a particular time or context. The statement is intended instead to communicate something about how *all* humans feel in *all* situations characterised by nervousness, rather than referring to the feelings of a particular person in a particular situation.

Elaborate code is used in formal institutional settings and professional contexts. Unlike restricted code, which is closed to those outside of the lifeworld of the people who use it, elaborate code is open. The kinds of impersonal and non-specific ways of talking definitive of elaborate code mean that the listener does not necessarily share the same knowledge or social background as the speaker. Bernstein (1971) claims that the people who exist in a lifeworld that operates using restricted code are subject to a kind of double alienation – first, because the lifeworld supplies them with a very narrow range of meanings and ways of talking with which to communicate with others; and second, because it makes it difficult to communicate with people from outside of the lifeworld. As we will see, Bernstein's ideas resonate strongly with Bourdieu's concept of 'linguistic habitus' (Chapter 7) – in particular, the view that socially marked ways of talking are directly implicated in the reproduction of class-based forms of inequality.

Existential phenomenology

Originating in the ideas of Kant, phenomenological ideas and methods developed in a number of different directions throughout the twentieth century within German philosophical thought (Moran, 2000). One of these directions is known as existentialism (Luijpen, 1969). A key figure in taking forward phenomenological methods and ideas within existentialism was the German philosopher Martin Heidegger (1889–1976). Heidegger claimed that since the earliest moments of philosophical speculation, Western thought had privileged abstract theoretical ways of thinking over the lived experiences and practical activities of individuals in the lifeworld. For Heidegger there is no objective point of view from which to understand reality, because any attempt to understand human life always takes place from the point of view of a specific individual, situated in a specific context, at a specific moment in time (lifeworld). As such, any attempt to understand a particular situation or event always involves individuals actively trying to interpret the situation they are in. The true focus of philosophy, according to Heidegger, is human beings' 'being-in the world' – their practical consciousness – and their existence in the world – lifeworld – with other human beings.

A student of Husserl and strongly influenced by the ideas of Heidegger, the French philosopher Maurice Merleau-Ponty (1908–1961) developed a number of existential and phenomenological themes taken from the work of both. Merleau-Ponty's work played a significant part in refocussing social theoretical attention back onto the importance of the body for shaping how individuals perceive and experience the world around them (Crossley, 1995). Merleau-Ponty's ideas about the body strongly inform Pierre Bourdieu's concept of 'habitus' (Chapter 7).

One of the central concerns of Merleau-Ponty's work is the centuries-old analytical distinction within philosophy between mind and body. The term *analytical* is an important one here. It denotes that the distinction drawn between mind and body is one made solely for the purposes of analysis – when we are operating at the level of discursive consciousness (Crossley, 1995). It is not one that exists as part of our lived experience, when we are operating at the level of practical consciousness in the lifeworld. Merleau-Ponty's point was that when we are engaged in thinking, it is not only or necessarily our head we experience as doing the thinking (Matthews, 2006). Instead, it is our whole body we typically experience as doing the thinking e.g. often when I am typing it seems like my fingers have a mind of their own. To talk of 'thinking in our head' is really just a turn of phrase, and not an actual description of our lived experience of the activity that is thinking. Merleau-Ponty regarded the body as fundamental to understanding how we see and experience the world. He claimed that any attempt to explain human experience must take into account the centrality of the body for shaping conscious experience.

Echoing Heidegger, Merleau-Ponty (2013 [1945]) claimed that knowledge of the world can never be objectively understood or known from some disembodied point of view, because subjectivity – consciousness – is always the subjectivity of a particular individual or group. Merleau-Ponty wanted to break down the distinction between mind and body, and the accompanying notion that the two comprise fundamentally separate entities. To do this he developed the term *body-subject*, which is intended to capture the idea that where the mind stops and the body starts cannot be discerned experientially. Rather, who we are, how we feel and what we think are always intimately wrapped up in, and cannot be separated out from, our physical bodies. The mind, or human subjectivity, is constituted by the body, and the body simultaneously constitutes the conscious human subject.

In rejecting the distinction between mind and body, Merleau-Ponty also rejected the view that the individual and the lifeworld are radically separate entities (Schmidt, 1985). To talk of one without the other he regarded as meaningless. Consciousness is always the consciousness of someone in particular, rooted in the body of an individual operating in a specific lifeworld. There is no consciousness in the abstract – only the consciousness of a particular body-subject in a particular lifeworld. The phenomena an individual perceives and experiences at any given moment are determined by the lifeworld in which they are situated. (Merleau-Ponty used the term *visual field* instead of lifeworld.) That which is in our visual field at a particular moment

TABLE 3.4 Summary of Merleau-Ponty

Theoretical concepts	
Body-subject	Intertwining of mind and body of individual
Visual field	Ongoing dialectical relationship between milieu and action

comprises the objects of consciousness, and what we perceive and are conscious of comprises the visual field. Understood in this way, the visual field (lifeworld) is not something that exists outside of the individual any less than the individual can be said to exist outside of the visual field (lifeworld) (Priest, 1998). Rather, as part of the ongoing process of consciousness, we are perceived as objects in the visual field of others, and others become objects of consciousness for us as they enter into our visual field.

Each body-subject is an embodied form of consciousness, and this form of consciousness has a visual field. The body-subject constitutes the field of vision, and the field of vision constitutes the body-subject. This is what Merleau-Ponty (2013 [1945]) refers to as the 'dialectic of milieu and action'. The world is made up of a variety of body-subjects perceiving, constituting and in turn being constituted by the visual fields relative to them. An important point to emphasise here is that the visual field is only intelligible because of the collectively produced categories we use to make sense of what we perceive and experience. That we are able to make sense of situations and interact with others in the lifeworld is because of the primary categories inculcated within practical consciousness. The primary categories supplied to us by the lifeworld and inculcated into practical consciousness through socialization are what make it possible for us to become sense-making body-subjects.

Extending these ideas even further, Merleau-Ponty claims that in actuality individuals *are* embodied forms of practical consciousness. The individual and the lifeworld form an ongoing stream of practical consciousness i.e. they are not separate from one another. We are constituted by and constitute the lifeworld through practical consciousness because, as body-subjects, who we are is utterly wrapped up in and constituted by the lifeworld. To imagine the body-subject as separate from the lifeworld or the lifeworld as separate from the body-subject is to fundamentally misunderstand the ways in which the two simultaneously work to co-produce and reproduce one another all the time, as part of an ongoing and only semi-consciously grasped process.

Applying phenomenological social theory to social work

Entering the lifeworld of the service-user

When a social worker and service-user meet for the first time, it is unlikely they will know very much if anything at all about one another. Even in those cases when a service-user has been referred to social work services for very specific reasons, understanding how the service-user perceives the situation they are in requires to be established. For this to happen, communication must first take place. The social worker needs to try to build up as detailed a picture as they can of how the service-user sees and perceives the situation they are in, and the service-user needs to try to communicate to the social worker what that situation looks like from their particular point of view. Arriving at a shared understanding of an event or situation can be a complex process. The first-order categories of meaning the service-user brings to the social work relationship might be very different from those of the social worker. In this section of the chapter we draw on a number of phenomenological concepts to think more closely about the difficulties that can arise in the communication between social workers and service-users.

Meaning becomes increasingly problematic in modern society. Modern multicultural societies comprise a wide range of different social groups, each of which gives rise to a culturally shaped lifeworld which generates its own sense of reality for the people within it. In the most general sense, culture is made up of and supplies the categories of meaning all the members of a society use to organise and make sense of their experience. Culture contains first-order categories whose meaning are intelligible to all members of society. To speak English, for example, the individual must possess a basic understanding of the most generic meanings captured by a range of first-order categories. For anyone who can legitimately lay claim to speak English, they must possess some understanding of what the first-order category of *school*, for example, means. But beyond the most general meaning the term *school* is intended to convey, what exactly the first-order category of *school* and the related categories of *education* and *learning* mean to a particular individual can vary significantly. More specifically, the meaning depends on the lifeworld to which they belong.

For individuals in a particular lifeworld, the category of *school* contains a number of positively coded typifications. School is a place where children are cared for and made to feel safe. It is where children are encouraged to demonstrate what they know, develop new knowledge and play with their friends. In other lifeworlds, the category of *school* may engender a number of very different and negatively coded typifications: as somewhere bullying takes place; where teachers are to be avoided; and where time is spent learning things which are uninteresting and of little use for getting a job. The point to make here is that different lifeworlds construct reality in different ways for the people within them. The extent to which the categories and meanings supplied by the lifeworld overlap with, share certain aspects in common with or are wholly dissimilar from those of other lifeworlds emphasises the importance of establishing exactly how those categories structure the attitudes and perceptions of those using them.

All lifeworlds arise out of and are shaped by the organisation and structure of society. Certain social-structural factors are more significant than others for shaping how people in the lifeworld perceive and experience the world around them. Class structures, for example, influence strongly how people from socio-economically disadvantaged lifeworlds perceive and experience higher educational institutions, such as colleges and universities (Bufton, 2003; Reay et al., 2009; Francheschelli et al., 2015). Similarly, structures of gender, ethnicity and age are significant for shaping how the world appears in the lifeworld of a particular group. Consider the seemingly mundane activity of taking children to school. As even the most cursory glance will verify, the gender balance in school playgrounds is heavily weighted towards women. The experiences of men who take their children to and from school are typically very different from the experiences of women. School playgrounds are predominantly classified as female social spaces. When men enter what is understood to be a female space, they are more likely to experience their presence in a variety of self-conscious ways. Heightened feelings of self-awareness, suspicion and a sense of being out of place make it more likely that men who enter school playgrounds feel the need to act in ways aimed at demonstrating that their presence is neither out of place or a threat to women and children.

Understanding how the lifeworld depicts reality in socially and culturally specific ways is very important for social workers. When a social worker and a service-user meet for the first time, two lifeworlds come together. For social workers and service-users to communicate successfully, differences in the categories of meaning supplied by their respective lifeworlds need to be identified, and explored. The social worker needs to try to step into and imagine how the lifeworld looks from the particular point of view of the service-user. This involves trying to translate the meanings and typifications embedded in the 'first-order categories' used by the service-user into the 'second-order categories' of the social worker. Exactly how the lifeworld is perceived through the eyes of the service-user can never be fully grasped by the social worker. But it is possible to develop a more refined understanding of the most significant first-order categories the service-user draws on to organise and make sense of their experience. The aim then is to try to unpack the meanings contained within those categories by raising them from a practical to a discursive level.

For a social worker, engaging with service-users from different lifeworlds can be likened to an act of translation. The social worker is trying to identify and translate what certain first-order categories mean from the point of view of the service-user, and the service-user is trying to understand the terms and categories used by the social worker in terms meaningful to them. In some cases, this may mean explicitly asking service-users to try to translate the meaning of the terms they use e.g. 'can you describe to me what kinds of feelings and thoughts you associate with school?' In other cases it may mean quite literally asking the service-user to translate what certain words mean as in the example of young people using slang, or the use of very colloquial terms and dialect – restricted code – by members of a particular community or geographical area.

Phenomenological concepts provide social work with a vocabulary for understanding how a range of cultural and social factors impinge on the categories of meaning different groups use to organise and make sense of their experiences. More specifically still, they draw attention to the interpretative character of all communication by drawing attention to the largely tacitly coded and practical forms of knowledge individuals draw on to communicate with others. Where an absence of shared meanings opens up e.g. when a social worker and service-user belong to very different lifeworlds, phenomenology provides us with a vocabulary for understanding the nature of the issues this gives rise to, as well as providing terms for exploring and developing how best to overcome these.

Making sense of service-users' experiences

In a study of a working-class community in Rotherham, England, sociologist Simon Charlesworth (2000) drew on phenomenological ideas and concepts to try to understand how unemployment impacted on the lives of community members. One of the problems Charlesworth faced when interviewing community members was the difficulty they had articulating their experience of unemployment and how this shaped their interactions with others. The people interviewed by Charlesworth used restricted code to communicate how they felt, specifically a form of dialect used by certain groups in the region. This made it difficult for them to communicate to others exactly how and what they felt. More than this, however, in many cases, it made it difficult for themselves to grasp exactly how and what they were feeling.

Charlesworth's (2000) study is highly instructive for social work in a number of ways. First, it draws attention to the ways the lifeworld shapes the meanings people use to organise and make sense of their experience. Second, it highlights the difficulties that arise when people use restricted code to try to communicate their experiences to people outside of the lifeworld to which they belong. And third, it underscores the view that restricted code works to constrain the capacity of those who use it to interpret, make sense of and communicate the nature of their experiences to others when some aspect of the lifeworld breaks down. These are the socially shaped reasons behind Charlesworth's (2000: 135) remark that often members of the most socially marginalized and 'dispossessed groups are the least able to communicate their experience, or make sense of it'. It is worth examining in more detail why this is the case and the implications this has for considering the power relations animating the social work relationship.

Consider the account of going to the job centre at the beginning of the chapter. How easy was it to understand? Did you have to concentrate hard to make sense of what the service-user was saying? Perhaps you had to read what they said a number of times before you understood? Even then, you may still feel unsure about what certain words mean, or how they were intended to be understood. This is because the experience was communicated in dialect. Dialect is an example of restricted code, because it is restricted to the members of a particular group. Dialect – a form of verbal shorthand – is not part of the official language of wider society. It is a form of communication used by people who belong to a specific lifeworld. Individuals and groups learn to talk in restricted code as part of their socialization. Restricted code enables members of the lifeworld to make sense of and communicate their experiences to other people in the lifeworld. But because restricted code is like a secret code, it can be very difficult to communicate with people who do not belong to the lifeworld.

For service-users who were born into, rarely leave or have never left the lifeworld e.g. young single parents, old people, the long-term unemployed, asylum seekers etc. it can be very difficult to explain how they are feeling when some aspect of the lifeworld breaks down – even to others who share that lifeworld. This is why people who rely on restricted code to communicate with others tend to repeat themselves or restate what they are saying with increasing volume when others fail to understand them. By doing so, they think that the meaning conveyed by the words they are using will become clear to the listener. But the meaning cannot be transmitted in this way, because the meaning does not reside in the words per se – first-order categories. Rather, the meaning of the words is thoroughly wrapped up in and cannot be separated out from the practical activities and lifestyle of the lifeworld to which they belong.

Merleau-Ponty claimed that the lifeworld and practical consciousness are thoroughly co-constituting. This is why the meanings expressed by forms of restricted code such as dialect are almost entirely rooted and only intelligible in the lifeworld. Far more than the case with elaborate code, the meanings conveyed by restricted code are almost entirely contingent on the lifeworld. When some aspect of the lifeworld of the users of restricted code collapses or is radically interrupted e.g. someone is made redundant or a family member dies suddenly and unexpectedly, the meanings contained within restricted code fail to provide typifications adequate for describing how the person is feeling e.g. 'I jist felt mingin''. Without more elaborate forms of code to draw on, service-users constrained to use restricted code can find it very difficult to get outside of the everyday ways of talking they use to objectify and elaborate what and how they are feeling.

Bernstein's concept of 'restricted code' coupled with the concepts of 'practical consciousness' and 'lifeworld' highlights the difficulties that can arise in the interpersonal exchanges between social workers and service-users. The concepts also draw to attention issues of power within the social work relationship. On the one hand, a core tenet of social work practice means encouraging service-users to explain how they see and perceive issues led by them, allowing them to express themselves using terms chosen by and meaningful to themselves. On the other hand, it can be very difficult for service-users to explain how and what they feel because the restricted forms of code they use constrain their capacity to articulate their experiences. This raises the question of how and to what extent social workers should actively seek to assist service-users to communicate their thoughts and feelings? It is important when working with service-users communicating in restricted code or for whom English is not their first language to be mindful of the balance between assisting them to understand and articulate what they are feeling and experiencing (first-order categories), at the same time as trying not to substitute their feelings and experiences with their own socially specific interpretation of them (second-order categories).

Understanding embodiment and experience

At the beginning of the chapter, a number of questions concerning the service-user's account of going to the job centre were raised. One of those questions asked you to consider whether or not you thought the service-user had over-reacted to their experience. Their account of going to the job centre certainly describes a very strong emotional and physiological response. An important point to draw to attention is that from very early on in the account, the service-user makes reference to their body. The body of the service-user was central to shaping how they perceived and experienced the situation unfolding around them.

An emphasis on the body and the embodied nature of human experience is central to Merleau-Ponty's existential-phenomenological account of subjectivity. The concept of 'body-subject' is intended to capture the centrality of embodiment for shaping how people see, perceive and experience situations and events. The body of the service-user was central to the highly emotionally charged and stressful experience of going to the job centre. In this section of the chapter, we use Merleau-Ponty's conceptual ideas to try to arrive at a more insightful and nuanced understanding of why the service-user reacted so strongly and the implications of this for understanding service-users' experiences more generally. On entering the job centre, the service-user quickly became aware of the presence of other body-subjects as they entered their visual field. On perceiving body-subjects from different lifeworlds, the service-user's experience of himself, others and the entire situation rapidly transformed. Central to this transformation in experience was the body of the service-user. Awareness of his own body quickly became heightened as he perceived the woman nearest to him, a woman whose body he described as 'fit, well-dressed an' middle class'. Perceiving the body of the woman in this way immediately transformed the relationship of the service-user to his own body, and the bodies of those around him. His experience of the situation was constituted primarily through and by his awareness of the class-based differences in lifeworlds to which they belonged.

On perceiving the body of the 'middle class' woman, the symbolic dimensions of embodiment came to dominate the service-user's interpretation of the situation. His perception of the role played by his own body as a vehicle for communicating a number of socially coded meanings was heightened. Culture provides the symbolic and normative categories people use to interpret and make sense of the bodies of others. Meaning is actively projected on to and read off of our bodies by others, at the same time as we constitute others through actively projecting onto and reading off meaning from their bodies. In the lifeworld of the service-user, awareness of his body is not something that enters into consciousness very often. The lifeworld of the service-user includes people possessed of similar body types and people he has known long enough such that his body does not shape the nature of their relationship with him – they 'see' past his body. By contrast, his interpretation of the 'fit, well-dressed, middle-class' body of the woman sitting opposite him transformed his relationship to and experience of his own body. Suddenly, he began to experience his own body in a heightened and negative way. Rather than experiencing his body at the level of practical consciousness – as a vehicle for transporting him to and from his home to the job centre – awareness of his body was elevated to the level of discursive consciousness. His body became an object to him, one signifying the differences in the class-based identities of himself and the woman opposite him.

As the service-user's remarks indicate, bound up in his perception of the woman's body as 'fit' and 'middle class' were the character traits of 'confidence' and 'attitude' which he imagined her to possess (in actuality, he did not *know* that the woman felt confident or possessed a confident attitude).

The service-user perceived the woman's body as typifying the very different ways she is shaped by and shapes the lifeworld to which she belongs. The fit body of the woman was perceived by the service-user as communicating the active role she plays in determining her own self-identity and lifestyle. The lifeworld the woman belongs to provides her with the opportunities to develop her self-identity and self-confidence. By contrast, the service-user's relationship to his own physicality – the shape, size and conditioning of his body – heightened his awareness of the constraining nature of the lifeworld to which he belongs, a lifeworld which shapes him in ways he feels unable to control and oppressed by.

The service-user felt estranged from, rather than at one with, his body. In his lifeworld, the lifestyle he is able to lead does not allow him to devote the time, money and care necessary for maintaining his body in the ways he feels reflect his personal identity. His body is negatively constrained by the lifeworld. The body of the woman communicates a relationship to and between the lifeworld and her own self that is enabling, active and self-determined. The lifeworld he belongs to constrains the range and type of activities he is able to undertake and the body and identity he can assume. His relationship to the lifeworld and his own self is constraining, characterised by a lack of control, passive rather than active, and alienating.

In the encounter between the bodies of the service-user and the woman, the service-user's awareness of his body was elevated from the level of practical to discursive consciousness. His body ceased to be experienced as part of, and instead became an object to, him. As awareness of his body became the focus for his full attention, the taken-for-granted flow of practically enacted bodily movements and gestures he normally draws on were interrupted. This had the effect of making him acutely aware of the way he was standing, the look he was wearing on his face, etc. Such acute self-awareness led to a chain of stressful physiological and emotional reactions: he began sweating, felt agitated, shuffled his feet and diverted his gaze.

In a number of very specific ways, the service-user's experience of going to the job centre illustrates the thoroughly co-constituting relationship between the lifeworld and body-subject. For the service-user, going to the job centre did not mean stepping out of the lifeworld he belonged to and leaving behind his socially marginalized identity. Rather, the life conditions of the lifeworld he belongs to came with him – in the most literal sense – ingrained in his physical constitution in ways that when he is in the lifeworld pass largely unnoticed by him of his body. Going to the job centre meant the service-user becoming acutely aware of the ways not only his self-image and identity, but his entire being as an embodied social subject are constrained by the lifeworld.

The service-user's visceral account of going to the job centre demonstrates the valuable insights phenomenological modes of analysis can yield. They allow for the outsider looking in to reconstruct in rich and compelling detail the socially shaped reasons behind the service-user's powerful emotional and physiological reaction to what for others might seem like a rather mundane situation. When understood from the particular point of view of the service-user – what appears like a routine and proactive course of action i.e. going to the job centre – a very different and complex picture begins to emerge. That the service-user wanted to leave the job centre was due to his highly stressful perception and experience of the situation. Another way of thinking about the service-user's desire to leave is that he felt the need to exclude himself from the situation. The notion of 'self-exclusion' is a central one in the work of Bourdieu (Chapter 7). It forms part of his account of the reasons why socially marginalized individuals and groups tend to exclude themselves from mainstream activities and relationships.

Merleau-Ponty's work allows us to see that the socially marginalized position of the service-user constitutes him as much as he constitutes it. The lifeworld is a phenomenon of the flesh and body brought to life through the internalization of socially marked dispositions, sensibilities, feelings and ways of classifying the world. The position of the lifeworld in relation to wider society is one refracted in the body-subject's disposition both away from as well as towards certain types of people, situations, events, etc.

Conclusion

The service-user's account of going to the job centre provides a window onto reflecting on the main concepts and themes covered in this chapter. The service-user's experience of going to the job centre cannot be fully understood without fully grasping how he perceived and experienced the situation. Phenomenologically inspired forms of social theory provide a vocabulary for articulating and reflecting on the ways individuals see, perceive, feel and make sense of themselves, others and the social environment. Operating for the most part at the level of practical consciousness, much of how we perceive and experience the world takes place in taken-for-granted and less than fully conscious ways. Highlighting the socially shaped nature of the natural attitude allows us to unpack and examine the ideas and assumptions rooted in everyday ways of experiencing and seeing the world. Elevating knowledge and processes that for the most part occur at the level of practical consciousness to a discursive level can be highly empowering. It provides us with the opportunity to understand the socially shaped reasons informing our thoughts, feelings and interactions.

Phenomenological concepts occupy a central role in the development of modern social theory. As we have seen, they open up valuable insights across a range of aspects of human experience, including the socially constituted nature of reality, the centrality of the body in shaping human subjectivity and the active part people play, or not, in constructing the lifeworlds to which they belong. Taken on their own, however, phenomenological modes of analysis have been criticized for a number of reasons. One is that phenomenology is unable to progress beyond a merely descriptive level, as opposed to engaging critically with the objects of its analysis. Another is that phenomenologically inspired forms of theorizing fail to deal with issues of power, tending to concentrate instead on how the effects of power are perceived, experienced and understood. In seeking to address these deficiencies, social theorists have sought to combine phenomenological concepts with more critically oriented theories and perspectives. This is particularly true of the work of Pierre Bourdieu, whose work we encounter in Chapter 7.

Further reading

Berger, P. L. and Luckmann, T. (1991 [1966]) *The Social Construction of Reality: A Treatise in the Sociology of Knowledge*. Harmondsworth: Penguin.

Charlesworth, S. A. (2000) *Phenomenology of Working Class Experience*. Cambridge: Cambridge University Press.

Schutz, A. (1970) *On Phenomenology and Social Relations*. London: The University of Chicago Press.

References

Bernstein, B. (1971) *Class, Codes and Control: Volume 1 Theoretical Studies Towards a Sociology of Language*. London: Routledge.

Bernstein, B. (1973) *Class, Codes and Control: Volume 2 Applied Studies Towards a Sociology of Language*. London: Routledge.

Berger, P. L. and Luckmann, T. (1991 [1966]) *The Social Construction of Reality: A Treatise in the Sociology of Knowledge*. Harmondsworth: Penguin.

Black, C. and Enos, R. (1981) 'Using Phenomenology in Clinical Social Work: A Poetic Pilgrimage', *Clinical Social Work Journal*, 9(1): 34–43.

Bufton, S. (2003) '"The Lifeworld" of the University Student: Habitus and Social Class', *Journal of Phenomenological Psychology* 34(2): 207–34.

Charlesworth, S. A. (2000) *Phenomenology of Working Class Experience*. Cambridge: Cambridge University Press.

Crossley, N. (1995) 'Merleau-Ponty, the Elusive Body and Carnal Sociology', *Body and Society*, 1(1): 43–63.

Francheschelli, M., Evans, K. and Schoon, I. (2015) 'A Fish Out of Water? The Therapeutic Narratives of Class Change', *Current Sociology*, 64(3): 353–372.

Heeren, J. (1971) 'Alfred Schutz and the Sociology of Common-Sense Knowledge', in Douglas, J. (ed.) *Understanding Everyday Life: Towards the Reconstruction of Sociological Knowledge*. London: Routledge, pp. 45–56.

Houston, S. (2003) 'A Method from the Lifeworld: Person Centred Planning for Children in Care', *Children and Society*, 17(1): 15–57.

Houston, S. and Mullan-Jensen, C. (2012) 'Towards Depth and Width in Qualitative Social Work: Aligning Interpretative Phenomenological Analysis with the Theory of Social Domains', *Qualitative Social Work*, 11(3): 266–281.

Laing, R. D. (1960) *The Divided Self: An Existential Study in Sanity and Madness*. Harmondsworth: Penguin.

Luckmann, T. (1978) *Phenomenology and Sociology*. Harmondsworth: Penguin.

Luckmann, T. (1984) *Life-World and Social Realities*. Aldershot: Ashgate Publishing Limited.

Luijpen, W. A. (1969) *Existential Phenomenology*. Pittsburgh: Duquesne University Press.

Marx, K. (2009 [1852]) *The Eighteenth Brumaire of Louis Bonaparte*. Gloucester: Dodo Press.

Matthews, E. (2006) *Merleau-Ponty: A Guide for the Perplexed*. London: Continuum.

McCormick, M. L. (2011) 'The Lived Body: The Essential Dimension in Social Work Practice', *Qualitative Social Work*, 10(1): 66–85.

Merleau-Ponty, M. (2013 [1945]) *The Phenomenology of Perception*. London: Routledge.

Moran, D. (2000) *Introduction to Phenomenology*. London: Routledge.

Pascal, J. (2010) 'Phenomenology as a Research Method for Social Work Contexts: Understanding the Lived Experience of Cancer Survival', *Currents: New Scholarship in the Human Services*, 9(2): 1–23.

Pressler, C. and Dasilva, F. (1996) *Sociology and Interpretation: From Weber to Habermas*. New York: SUNY Press.

Priest, S. (1998) *Merleau-Ponty*. London: Routledge.

Reay, D., Crozier, G. and Clayton, J. (2009) 'Strangers in Paradise?: Working-Class Students in Elite Universities', *Sociology*, 43(6): 1103–1121.

Roche, M. (1973) *Phenomenology, Language and the Social Sciences*. London: Routledge and Kegan Paul.

Schmidt, J. (1985) *Maurice Merleau-Ponty: Between Phenomenology and Structuralism*. Basingstoke: Macmillan.

Schutz, A. (1967) *The Phenomenology of the Social World*. Evanston: Northwestern University Press.

Schutz, A. (1970) *On Phenomenology and Social Relations*. London: The University of Chicago Press.

Schutz, A. (1971) *Collected Papers Vol 1: The Problem of Social Reality*. The Hague: Martinus Nijhoff.

Thompson, N. (1992) *Existentialism and Social Work*. London: Routledge.

Thompson, S. (2016) 'Promoting Reciprocity in Old Age: A Social Work Challenge', *Practice: Social Work in Action*, 28(5): 341–355.

Webb, S. (2006) *Social Work in a Risk Society*. London: Sage.

4

SYMBOLIC INTERACTIONISM AND THE SOCIAL SELF

Being in relationships is an integral part of human social life. It is in and through relationships with others that our sense of selfhood and identity emerge and develop. Ask yourself the following question: how well do you know yourself? Take a moment to think about this. As you do, try to be aware of the thoughts and images that come into your mind as you think about your response. Perhaps you imagine yourself through the eyes of family members and friends who know you well. Maybe you imagine scenarios and situations you were once in and how you (re)acted. Maybe you consider how you think and feel when you are alone as the truest gauge of who you really are. Is it the case that you close your eyes and try to look inside of yourself? Is that where the real you resides?

As a social worker, it is important to build up a strong understanding of yourself and personal identity. The self is a key resource for social workers (Urdang, 2010; Dunk-West, 2013). That is why it is so important that you try to develop your self-knowledge and awareness, as well as learning to understand more broadly how selfhood and identity are shaped and develop over time. Just as important is building up an awareness of the ways thinkers working across a range of academic disciplines have sought to understand the self and how it relates to identity. For example, psychoanalytically inspired models of the self have a long tradition within social work. As with more psychologically based models generally, the self, or personality, is conceived of as residing in and intrinsic to the individual. Individuals possess a unique combination of personality traits which develop and are shaped through relatively self-enclosed and autonomous mental conflicts and processes.

The legacy of psychoanalytic ideas and models of selfhood has strongly influenced the notion of personality as something possessed by individuals and that they carry around inside of them (Furedi, 2004). But the concept of personality is exactly that – a concept. Symbolic interactionist (henceforth referred to as SI) conceptions of selfhood instead provide a very different set of perspectives for conceptualizing the self. Rather than the self as residing in mental processes enclosed within the individual, SI thinkers regard the self as developing through and arising out of the interactions and relationships we have with others (Mead, 2011 [1922]: 69). In this view, the self and identity we imagine ourselves to possess is not in spite of social interaction; rather, it is precisely because of the interactions and relationships we have with others that we are able to develop and maintain a coherent sense of self-identity at all.

From an SI perspective, selfhood and identity are fundamentally social entities. The view of the self and identity as developing and changing over time is central to SI thinking. The self cannot be reduced to a series of relatively static attributes or personality traits, but instead comprises an ongoing dynamic process, developing and changing over time through interaction with others across different settings and contexts. The use of SI concepts within social work forms part of a long and established tradition, particularly in North America where SI first emerged (Shaw, 2015). American social reformer, activist and social worker Jane Addams (1860–1935) drew heavily on SI ideas in the running of Hull House, a pioneering settlement home for destitute women and children founded in 1889 (Hewitt, 2006). Jesse Taft (1882–1960), an influential figure in the development of social work education in America, drew on SI thinking to inform her therapeutic work with children and families. Since then, developments in SI accounts of selfhood and identity have continued to provide a highly influential strand in the social work theoretical imagination. This is true of social workers operating across a wide range of practice scenarios and settings including community-based practice, family centred work, criminal justice, group work, and anti-oppressive and discriminatory practice (Forte, 2004a, 2004b; Howe, 1991; Offer, 1999; Dunk-West, 2013).

This chapter identifies and explains the relevance of SI ways of thinking and concepts for social work. We begin by identifying the main intellectual currents underpinning SI concepts, before moving on to discuss the theoretical development of these ideas by the most influential SI thinkers: G. H. Mead, Herbert Blumer and Charles Cooley. Following on from this, we examine the attempts of Goffman, Becker and Cohen to develop and refine SI concepts further, by applying them to a range of empirical phenomena such as small-group settings, stigma, deviance and moral panics. The applied section of the chapter demonstrates the value of SI ideas and concepts by using them to demonstrate the importance of the social work self for empowering service-users, defining the meanings of the situations confronting service-users and working with families and service-users trying to cope with stigma. The chapter concludes by critically reflecting on the strengths and limitations of SI ideas and concepts as applied to social work.

Foundations of symbolic interactionism

The roots of SI thinking draw on two main intellectual currents: early American pragmatist philosophy, and the process sociology of Georg Simmel. Elaborating on the work of pragmatist thinkers such as C. S. Pierce, John Dewey and William James, SI rejects the realist epistemological position known as the Spectator Theory of Knowledge (Mills, 1966). This is the view that social reality is something that pre-exists individuals, already preformed and waiting for them to step into. Instead, pragmatist philosophy emphasises the active role individuals play in shaping their experience and knowledge of reality, as they think and act in purposive ways to achieve specific goals. An emphasis on the active and purposive character of human action was central to the work of William James (1842–1910). Regarded as the founding father of classical pragmatism, James's work was a rich resource in the development of SI thinking (Schubert, 2006). This is especially true with regard to the notion of 'selective attention' and his 'dialogical' conception of the self. Both of these concepts were taken up and developed within SI thinking, most notably in the work of G. H. Mead, whose notions of the 'I' and the 'Me' provided the conceptual foundations on which SI accounts of selfhood subsequently developed (Wiley 2006: 8).

Just as important for shaping the development of SI thinking was the work of the German sociologist Georg Simmel (1858–1918). From Simmel, SI draws and elaborates on the conception of social reality as an ongoing, open-ended process, or event. This is the view that social reality is not pre-given, static and guaranteed once and for all, but instead comprises the sum total of all the actions and interactions – 'forms of sociation' – taking place at any given time (Frisby, 2002). The notion of process is a central one in SI conceptions of selfhood and society as we shall see, and directly informs the view of social agents as actively involved in shaping the relationships and situations of which they form part. Building on the ideas of the early pragmatists and Simmel, the conceptual dimensions of SI were developed across the work of three key thinkers whose most influential ideas we will now address.

Mead, Blumer and Cooley

George Herbert Mead (1863–1931) was a philosopher and social psychologist based at the University of Chicago. Mead's most influential work, *Mind, Self and Society*, was assembled from students' notes and published posthumously in 1967. While first and foremost a social psychological account of human interaction, nonetheless Mead's work is significant for social theory in mainly two ways. First, he regards language as the primary medium through which selfhood emerges and interpersonal communication takes place. And second, he demonstrates the *emergent* properties of the self as realized in, and developing through, interaction with others. The central contentions of Mead's conception of selfhood can be summarized as follows:

- Human agents acquire language as part of their attachment to and interaction within social groups.
- Language is the primary medium through which individual selfhood emerges and develops.
- The concept of selfhood is realized throughout the life course through linguistically mediated forms of social interaction.

Contrary to the kinds of individualistic accounts of selfhood and identity characteristic of philosophic and behaviourist models, Mead regarded the *individual* self as a profoundly *social* entity. The self is a dynamic, processual entity – not an innate set of relatively static attributes – which can develop only in and through 'the act' i.e. through acting and interacting with others (Denizen 1992: 5). This is why, claimed Mead, the self cannot be grasped or known through introspection because it ceases to exist outside of social interaction. Only through language is it possible for a sense of self to develop, a process made possible through the emergence of self-awareness, self-monitoring and self-reflection. This is the view that the self and self-awareness necessarily develop in tandem, for self-consciousness can occur only when 'the individual becomes an object to himself in the presentation of possible lines of contact' (Mead, 1967: 177). The importance of language in the development of selfhood is a recurrent theme throughout Mead's work. As a shared system of symbols and signs, language is enabling for human agents because it allows them to create and signify meanings to one another. Language is what makes culture possible. Language enables the meanings human agents create and designate to things to persist over time and in different contexts. Language allows human beings to talk about or refer to things, people, situations, etc. in ways that are temporally and spatially divorced from the settings in which they first occur. Through language a sense of time and place opens up in the mind of the individual such that it becomes possible to transcend the immediacy of the present.

For Mead, the uniqueness of human communication is made possible and defined by language. A crucial part of this process concerns the importance of dialogue, not just with and between others, but more importantly with oneself (Cook, 1993). Language is the medium through which the self begins to first emerge and form. In making this claim, Mead (1967: 78) draws attention to the fact that language does not simply describe the world; rather, it actively brings things into being, by which is meant that it makes '. . . possible the existence or the appearance of . . . [a] . . . situation or object'. This is a view of language similar to that depicted by Foucault's concept of 'discourse' (Chapter 6). As part of the process by which the self is brought into being and objectified, Mead draws on and develops James's distinction between the 'I' and the 'Me'.

The 'I' refers to the experience of reality we perceive from inside our head and is the stream of consciousness we draw on to formulate possible courses of action. The 'Me' is the name given to the object of self-awareness that is one's own physical body as perceived by others. The 'I' stands for the idiosyncratic and creative aspect of the individual, whereas the 'Me' represents the social component of the self as derived from the internalization of social roles, behavioural patterns, normative values and codes of conduct. In drawing a distinction between the 'I' and the 'Me', Mead (1967) stressed that the latter should not be regarded as merely exerting a constraining influence over the former. On the contrary, the 'I' and the 'Me' are co-constituting such that one could not exist without the other. In this view, the 'Me' is both enabling *and* constraining because it allows for the ongoing self-directed process by which individuals adapt, revise and review their actions in light of the anticipated reactions of others. The notion of others and their relation to the self, specifically self-consciousness, leads us to Mead's concept of the 'generalized other'.

The concept of the generalized other is crucial to Mead's account of self-development, forming the link between the individual and the wider social group. Mead (1967) uses it to refer to the normative attitudes and values contained within wider culture and internalized in the mind of the individual. The concept of generalized other is intended to explain how individuals learn to regulate and monitor their own conduct through assuming the perspective of other members of a group – not any individual in particular, but as the term suggests, an impersonal and generalized other. To explain how this happens, Mead highlights the importance of certain social activities, such as game playing. Through playing games, children learn to assume the generalized perspective of all the other players collectively, as well as the divergent viewpoints of each and any individual player. Learning to empathize with and imagine oneself through the eyes of the generalized other is essential to successful interpersonal communication because the reactions of others intimately shape, and lend form to, the constantly shifting parameters of social situations.

Learning to see oneself from the point of view of the generalized other is an important part in the development of the self. It also forms part of the process by which individuals develop a sense of their own autonomy. As the individual learns to contemplate themselves from the

TABLE 4.1 Summary of Mead

The self

- made up of inter-related parts: the 'I', the 'Me' and the generalized other
- an emergent and socially shaped process; not reducible to fixed or pre-given traits and attributes
- develops primarily through language; realized through action and interactions

point of view of a 'Me' – as an object viewed through the eyes of the generalized other – they develop a sense of their own autonomy and self identity (da Silva, 2007). This allows for a unique perspective of the world to open up to the individual, in turn serving as the basis from which to undertake purposeful and self-considered courses of interaction. In sum, social interaction is possible because of language. Language provides social actors with a shared set of standardized symbols with which to communicate, at the same time enabling them, in various self-consciously directed ways, to reflexively monitor themselves and others during social interaction.

Herbert Blumer

Also based at the University of Chicago, Herbert Blumer's (1900–1987) conceptual ideas overlap with and elaborate significantly on the ideas of Mead. Blumer (1969) wanted to explain the role individuals play in actively constructing and attributing meanings to people and situations. Rejecting the notion that meaning is self-evident and naturally occurring, Blumer argued instead that meaning is actively constructed and socio-culturally specific (Fine, 1993). Blumer (1969) emphasises the importance of 'self-indication' as part of the process by which meaning is made and remade over time. A processual notion, self-indication refers to the notation of people, objects and events as they enter into and flow through consciousness. Actors are actively involved in the meanings they attribute to the objects of consciousness, indicating to themselves which objects to attend to and which to downplay, or ignore altogether. Blumer's point is that individuals become conscious of things only by selecting to direct their attention towards them, by taking note of and indicating them in actively self-directed ways.

The concept of self-indication is a key one for Blumer. First, it captures the notion that individuals actively confer meaning on social situations and other people; and second, it enables potential courses of action to be constructed, modified and/or revised altogether by the individual. This is why Blumer (1969) regarded meaning first and foremost as a social product. By acting and interacting in certain ways and not others, individuals demonstrate their commitment to classifying and defining situations along particular lines. Self-indication enables the individual to impose a sense of structure and coherence onto their experience, even if for the most part the active part they play in doing so is something they lose sight of. By working to define situations in shared and collectively negotiated ways, individuals make social order possible as they come to act and interact in habitualized and predictably patterned ways over time. Social order is an emergent process because human action is premised on and oriented by the shared meanings individuals and groups attribute to the people and events taking place around them.

TABLE 4.2 Summary of Blumer

Meaning and social order

Meaning

- socially produced and not natural or self-evident
- emerges through social actors indicating to themselves – self-indication – which aspects of people, situations and events to attend to
- negotiated and confirmed, or changed and revised, through action and interaction

Social order

- not pre-given, or occurring naturally
- like the self i.e. an emergent phenomenon
- arises through individuals acting and interacting in patterned ways

---

Meaning arises out of actions and interactions between individuals and groups as they seek to achieve specific tasks and goals. While we typically experience a sense of social reality as naturally occurring, in order for it to be maintained requires individuals to constantly check, modify and realign their actions and definition of a situation in line with one another (there are clear parallels here with phenomenological ways of thinking – see Chapter 3). In this view, society and social reality seem real and external to individuals. Yet if individuals deviate from the shared ways of acting and interacting specific to a particular context e.g. people skip the queue while waiting for a bus, then the ordered and predictable nature of social reality quickly falls away, and a sense of disorder and uncertainty arise.

Charles Horton Cooley

The work of Charles Horton Cooley (1864–1929) is an important strand in the formation of SI accounts of selfhood. Cooley's most influential concepts are 'self-idea' and 'looking-glass self' (Cooley, 1907; Jandy, 1969). Like Mead, Cooley (1998 [1908]) holds that language is central to the development of selfhood. Through linguistic forms of communication and interaction, the individual develops a self-idea. The concept of self-idea denotes that the individual self can never be known directly. The idea of one's own self develops and is shaped by the perceptions of others as they are communicated to us verbally and behaviourally through interaction. The self-idea refers to the conceptions of one's own self as arrived at through interacting with others. In the same way that we use a looking-glass to see our own face, we are only able to develop an understanding and sense of our own self – a self-idea – through interpreting the actions and reactions of others towards ourselves (Cooley, 1907). As part of this process, individuals learn to experience 'self-feeling' as they imagine themselves through the eyes and minds of others. Not all interaction is significant for shaping our self-idea and self-feeling. The concept of 'significant others', for example, denotes those individuals whose opinions, and attitudes are significant enough that they are able to influence the type of self-idea and self-feelings we develop.

In addition to the concepts of 'self-idea' and 'self-feeling', Cooley (1998 [1908]) extends SI ideas to develop an account of collective forms of association, such as groups, institutions and society more generally. In essence, Cooley regards collective entities as ongoing, emergent entities structured through lines of individually pursued 'communicative action' (Schubert, 2006: 54).

TABLE 4.3 Summary of Cooley

Self-idea, identity and social institutions

Identity

- rooted in the emergence and development of the self-idea
- can never be known directly but only as understood through the self-idea
- develops through self-consciousness as individuals become aware of how significant others perceive them

Institutions

- abstract term used to refer to aggregates of individuals
- made up of individuals acting in generalized and habitualized ways over time
- require enactment of specific aspects of the 'total self'

The conception of institutions individuals carry around in their minds Cooley regards as being just that – a conception. In actuality, collective phenomena are made up of nothing more than individual actors, in which only specific aspects of their total self are presented (Jandy, 1969). For example, a transnational institution such as the World Bank involves certain individuals acting, reacting and interacting in the patterned ways defined by the roles they play. Were the members of the World Bank to decide not to go to work one day, essentially the World Bank would cease to exist. This example underscores Cooley's view that institutional stability is the product not of external social or internal mental factors, but instead the generalized and habitual patterns of interaction purposively enacted by individuals. More than this, the meanings and values of situations and objects become institutionalized when their practical use or value for lending structure to reality is habitually asserted and reasserted over time. Cooley maintained that while social structures and wider collectives for the most part remain stable, they can always change if individuals consciously elect to define situations in different ways and act and interact along new but mutually shared lines.

The development of symbolic interactionism

Throughout the course of the twentieth century, the theoretical constructs developed by Mead, Blumer and Cooley were taken up and developed by a new generation of thinkers at the University of Chicago. Subsequent SI thinkers were keen to apply and develop these ideas empirically. The work of Erving Goffman (1922–1982) and Howard Becker (1928 – present) was particularly influential in this direction (Drew and Wootton, 1988). Goffman's work focussed on interactions between two or more individuals in small-group settings in and across different social contexts. A key question for Goffman was this: how is social interaction possible in a society characterised by increasingly impersonal and anonymous relations between individuals (Manning, 1992)? Following Durkheim (Chapter 2), Goffman (1983) regarded rules as crucial for lending structure to social life. For the most part, the rules underpinning social interaction are implicit and indeterminate, yet somehow individuals know how and when to use and abide by them. Goffman's work aimed to explain how social actors come to acquire an understanding of these largely tacit rules, as well as knowing how and when to use them.

Goffman's work focussed on the rules of social interaction – in particular, the mechanisms by which agents seek to interpret the actions of others in self-reflexive ways as well as managing their own self-presentation in line with the shifting parameters of social situations. In his early work, Goffman (1959) employed a 'dramaturgical metaphor' to try to understand the dynamics at work during social interaction. This involved likening social life to a theatrical performance, or drama, with individual actors performing roles designed to influence one another. The notion of 'impression management' is an important one here, and draws attention to the knowing importance individuals attribute to ensuring that the impression they give of themselves to others casts them in as favourable a light as possible. To do this, individuals try to enact certain types of 'performance', which in turn requires them to assume certain roles (Goffman, 1959). Over time, other people – the 'audience' – come to know and expect a certain type of performance in a way intended to ensure predictability. Performances can be located anywhere on a sliding scale from successful to unsuccessful. Good actors know how to demonstrate and convince others that their definition of the situation, the particular version of reality they are trying to advance, is the right one. An important aspect of the performances agents enact is the concept of 'role distance'. Sometimes individuals are required to stage performances in the enactment of a particular social role, such as a traffic warden, which means them having to assume a particular 'front' that contradicts their sense of personal identity. The concept of 'role distance' describes the psychological disparity between the roles individuals are required to play and their sense of personal identity.

In the classic studies *Asylums* (1961) and *Stigma* (1964), Goffman shifted his attention to the subject of deviance to cast further light on the construction of selfhood and the ways threats to social order are dealt with and marginalized through processes of exclusion. In *Stigma*, Goffman analyses the behaviour of social actors whose identity is publicly held as soiled or defective in some way. The term stigma refers to 'an attribute that is deeply discrediting' (Goffman, 1964: 13). Stigma threatens our self-identity because it alludes to some aspect of the self that breaches the normative rules underpinning social interaction. Stigma can arise for a range of different reasons, from the possession of certain psychological (mental illness) and physical (disability) traits through to possession of certain forms of ethnic identity (racism) (Goffman, 1964: 15). Each of these attributes can negatively shape the ordinary and predictable patterning of

TABLE 4.4 Summary of Goffman

Dramaturgical model and stigma

Dramaturgical model
- individuals likened to actors
- individual made up of multiple selves used to perform different roles
- performing roles requires actors to know the 'script'
- 'role distance' involves managing the disparity between the actor and the role they are required to perform
- social reality divided into public 'front stage' areas and private 'backstage' areas

Stigma
- occurs when social norms are breached
- emergent property of interactions between individuals and groups
- arises out of disparity between actual and virtual social identity
- attaches to identity of individual

social interactions. This can result in the possessor of the attribute being marginalized and/or excluded. Potentially *any* attribute or act is stigmatizing. Wherever identity norms exist, stigma can occur. A degree of stigmatization is present in all societies because all societies have normative ideas about how people should look, act, interact and so on.

All members of a group or society share common expectations and attitudes regarding what to expect from certain types of individuals and the roles they are expected to perform in a particular context or situation. Mirroring Mead's distinction between the idiosyncratic 'I' and the socially mediated 'Me', Goffman (1964: 2) distinguishes between actual and virtual social identity. The former refers to the self-identity individuals imagine themselves to possess in private, whereas the latter refers to the socially legitimate version of self they are expected to present in public. Stigma arises whenever the disparity between actual and virtual social identity becomes too great and untenable. When this occurs, it can lead to feelings of embarrassment or shame and in some cases interaction breaking down.

Becker on deviance

A contemporary of Goffman, Howard Becker was an influential figure in the second wave of SI thinkers emerging from the Chicago School (Bulmer, 1984). Becker's most influential ideas concern his classic study of deviance entitled *Outsiders* (1963), which was to become a foundational text in the emergence of Labelling Theory. Becker (1963) was critical of attempts to explain deviance in overly psychological terms, on the one hand, and explanations that invoke external social-structural factors such as class background and gender, on the other. Instead, his work focusses on the active part individuals play in learning to think and act in ways considered deviant. To do this, Becker (1953) examined the range of ideas, attitudes and behaviours individuals learn to adopt on the path to becoming marijuana users, and how in turn this process of learning is self-consciously managed and negotiated through interacting with members of the wider group.

Becker (1953) argued that learning to become a marijuana user is a socially learned and collectively negotiated process, one which requires the individual to actively learn and adapt their behaviour in ways consistent with an already established community of marijuana users. Deviance is not a psychological phenomenon, but a social one. As explained by Becker (1963: 9) 'deviance is *not* a quality of the act the person commits, but rather a consequence of the application by others of rules and sanctions to an offender.' In other words, individuals and groups come to be understood both by themselves and others as deviant through the definitions and labels attributed to them through interaction. Moral entrepreneurs was the term Becker (1963) used to refer to individuals and groups involved in maintaining dominant social values and norms. As the moral guardians of society, moral entrepreneurs play a particularly significant part in determining which groups and behaviours are labelled as deviant. Psychiatrists, high-court judges, social workers, teachers and so on are all examples of moral entrepreneurs because they possess the power to influence which individuals, social groups and forms of behaviour come to be labelled as deviant or not.

Moral panics

An emphasis on the socially constructed nature of deviance is at the heart of British sociologist Stanley Cohen's concept of 'moral panics', which he developed in his classic study *Folk Devils and Moral Panics* (1972). Moral panics are purposively instigated by a range of influential social actors and institutions (e.g. moral entrepreneurs). They are liable to occur when a particular individual or group is perceived to act in ways that threaten dominant normative ideals and social values. The word *perceived* is an important one here because it highlights the fact that for certain behaviours and groups to be defined and labelled as deviant, attention first needs to be directed towards them. People and behaviours only become cause for moral panics if they are perceived as presenting a significant threat to dominant social and cultural values. A moral panic takes place over time and involves a number of stages. Each stage forms a necessary part of the overall process by which a moral panic arises. When this happens, dominant social groups and moral entrepreneurs seek to eradicate the perceived threat to order and moral status quo by defining it as morally deviant and cause for action. (Goode and Ben-Yehuda, 1994).

Applying symbolic interactionism to social work

The social work self and service-user empowerment

The organisational environments in which social workers work are subject to increasing 'rationalization' (Chapter 2). This has led to interactions between social workers and service-users becoming more formal, rationally oriented and structured by a range of impersonal and bureaucratically defined criteria. How both social workers and service-users perceive the social work relationship is changing. More than ever, the social work relationship is becoming a mere means to securing a number of narrowly and instrumentally defined ends. This has worked to draw attention away from the importance of the social work relationship in and of itself, as a resource which can be used to empower service-users through interpersonal strategies aimed at self-directed change. The potential for self-development and nurturing embedded in the social work relationship takes on a heightened significance under the increasingly rationalized conditions characteristic of contemporary social work.

The notion that the 'social work self' can be used as a powerful tool for healing and strengthening service-users has a long history (Knott, 1974; Urdang, 2010: 532). Notions of self-work and self-empowerment form the basis for relationship, counselling-based and existential forms of social work (Lieberman and Gottesfeld, 1973; Thompson, 1992). Embedded within these forms of social work relationships is a conception of the self not as a static and fixed entity, a view rejected by SI thinkers, but as capable of developing and changing through interpersonal exchanges and interaction. The interactions between social workers and service-users represent the opening stages of an open-ended and dynamic process. Rather than merely serving as the means for accessing particular services or achieving some predetermined end, the interactions between social workers and service-users provide an interpersonal space in which to explore a number of forms of service-user empowerment (Kuhn, 1962; Kondrat and Teater, 2012).

SI thinkers identify language as essential to the development of selfhood. Language is the primary medium through which the self is realized and objectified. The importance of language, particularly although not exclusively in its verbal form, is emphasised by a range of 'talking therapies' and models (Edwards and Bess, 1998; Dewane, 2006). Talking requires the interlocutor to take up and articulate a particular perspective on the topic they are addressing. When a service-user meets with a social worker for the first time, it may be unclear to the service-user what exactly it is they require assistance with. Encouraging service-users to talk about and explore how they think and feel is an important part of the process by which they come to construct a clearer and more coherent understanding of the issues with which they require assistance. For service-users who are finding it difficult to make sense of their experiences, crucially talking allows them to make the transition from an 'I' to a 'Me'.

Recall that in the work of Mead, the 'I' refers to the self as we experience it from the inside, as it appears to us and is experienced in the mind. The 'I' denotes the stream of perceptions, feelings, impressions and so on as they appear to us in consciousness. For service-users feeling overwhelmed, unclear and confused, objectifying their thoughts and feelings through talking opens up a more distanced and objective perspective from which to view themselves. Talking allows for the service-user to switch from being a subject – an 'I' – to an object – the 'Me' – to themselves. Self-objectification, achieved through talk, can make it easier for service-users to stand back from and de-familiarize their thoughts and feelings, allowing them to view themselves through the eyes of the 'generalized other'. Encouraging service-users to explore and articulate their thoughts and feelings is important. It enables them to construct a clearer and more coherent understanding of the issues facing them.

Constructing an interpersonal space conducive to talking is more likely to occur if the service-user feels that expressing what they think and feel will not be subject to judgement. Being able to talk openly and freely can be a liberating experience for service-users. In the context of their everyday lives, the numerous different roles service-users play e.g. mother, wife, friend, colleague, etc. can all work to constrain their self-image and sense of self-identity. Attached to these social identities are a range of normative expectations and ideals which can inhibit how the service-user thinks and feels, and in turn how they act and interact. Enacting those identities on a daily basis can mean that important aspects of the service-user's self-identity are unexpressed and unrealized. For some service-users, the social work relationship can provide one of the few opportunities to explore and develop aspects of their self-identity that otherwise require to be carefully managed or excluded from interactions with (significant) others.

Regular interaction with a social worker can play an important role in helping service-users to identify how their self-identity is constrained and in some cases negatively affected in and through relationships with others. Contact with a social worker may be the only positive reference point for service-users in abusive relationships characterised by high levels of physical and emotional conflict. Establishing an empathetic and supportive relationship with a social worker can help service-users to identify and separate out more clearly those aspects of their self which only arise in their interactions with certain others, at the same time as providing the space to reflect on how to manage, shut down or terminate conflicted relationships.

Interacting with a social worker can empower service-users who feel negatively constrained by their relationships with others. The social work relationship can also be used to positively affirm the self-image and identity of service-users during periods of personal difficulty and crisis. Interacting with a social worker can provide a fixed and self-affirming resource for service-users trying to negotiate the challenges to selfhood posed by isolation and loneliness, such as when a service-user is faced with the sudden loss of a spouse, partner or child. For service-users experiencing anxiety and stress, or emotions such as grief and despair, interacting with a social worker can provide comfort and self-reassurance. These positive emotions can be used to move through and tackle emotional and psychological difficulties. For elderly service-users, individuals with physical disabilities characterised by limited mobility, ethnic minority groups, lone parents, the long-term unemployed, etc., regular and sustained interaction with a social worker might be one of the few fixed reference points with which to maintain a coherent and stable sense of self-identity.

Constructing a relationship in which the service-user is encouraged to work on and develop a range of self-empowering resources, such as confidence, a positive self-image and a sense of hope, is important. Moreover, once these self-resources have been developed, they can be imported into and used in other areas of the service-user's life (Urdang, 1999). A social work relationship built on the shared values of trust, respect and equality can play a vital part in the process by which service-users come to identify and explore aspects of their self-identity and self-image otherwise denied to them in their everyday lives.

Negotiating meaning in the social work relationship

Communication is a vital part of the social work relationship. Successful communication between social workers and service-users is essential to ensuring that the needs of the service-user are fully met (Prince, 1996). There are a number of socially shaped reasons why communication between social workers and service-users can be problematic (see Chapter 3). A very important aspect of the social work relationship involves service-users communicating to social workers the nature of the difficulties they are experiencing. In the classic social work study by Mayer and Timms (1970), the authors found that the recipients of social work services, particularly service-users from socio-economically disadvantaged backgrounds, often felt that the meanings and definitions social workers attributed to their circumstances differed significantly from their own.

Mayer and Timms's study has attained classic status within social work. This is because it draws attention to a number of general issues to do with the socially shaped nature of meaning and how these can work to impede the social work relationship. How a particular situation or event is understood, and how in turn this shapes the actions and interactions leading out from it, highlights the interpersonal dynamics at play when social workers and service-users try to arrive at shared definitions of a situation. Blumer's (1969) concept of 'self-indication' is an important one here. Self-indication refers to the active role social actors play in directing their attention towards and attributing significance to particular aspects of the social environment, while simultaneously filtering out and playing down the significance of others. Meaning is not something intrinsic to the things we perceive in the world around us, a view first expressed by Kant – see Chapter 3. Meaning does not radiate outwardly from people or things in ways that tell us how we ought to make sense of and understand them. Rather, meaning is negotiated, constructed and realized through the actions and interactions of individuals orienting themselves towards one another in mutually agreed ways. From an SI perspective meaning is a 'relational' entity first and foremost. It arises out of the ways people *relate* to one another and the wider social environment.

Arriving at a shared definition of the issues confronting service-users can be a complicated process, as much for them as the social worker. Service-users actively construct their own definition of situations, even if the extent of the role they play in that process is not necessarily or entirely grasped by them. Often service-users may be unclear of exactly why a particular area of their life has become problematic or difficult to deal with, such as when a parent discovers that their child has been playing truant from school. Service-users may be in a situation that is ongoing, open-ended and difficult to define e.g. their partner continues to leave them only to return some days later. Service-users may feel very strongly about the exact nature of the issues facing them, whereas the social worker may feel differently, or disagree with how the service-user defines the situation e.g. when a social worker suspects that the service-user's understanding of a situation is being influenced strongly by significant others. Electing to frame a situation in certain ways can form part of how the service-user demonstrates their solidarity to significant others such as a partner, family members or close friends. It may be appropriate or helpful to communicate these ideas to the service-user, allowing them to understand that how they have elected to define the situation is just one possible way of defining it. SI accounts of meaning are important not least because they allow us to dispel the notion that there can ever be one 'true' meaning, or 'correct' definition, of a particular situation, person or event.

Developing an awareness of the interpersonal dynamics through which meaning arises and is objectified is very important. It is important to recognise too, however, that many of the problems faced by service-users cannot be dealt with at a symbolic level, by merely redefining the way an issue is being constructed, framed and defined. Not having enough money to pay the electricity bill, for example, is a relatively straight-forward and unambiguous problem. But even in instances such as these, what exactly is meant by 'not having enough money' may be open to interpretation. It may mean that the service-user does not have enough money to pay the electricity bill after certain luxury items have been purchased, or certain problematic behaviours such as gambling, drinking and drug-taking have been accounted for. It is important that the social worker takes the time to explore how the service-user defines their interpretation of the situation.

Developing an awareness of the negotiated character of meaning can also be used to consider the delivery of care packages across multi-agency teams. Operating across a wide range of specialist services and care providers poses a range of challenges. As Forte (2004b: 524) observes, the kinds of issues 'addressed by social workers do not have an independent existence, but are social conditions defined over time by various claims-makers'. Working as part of a multi-agency team can mean social workers trying to bring together and mediate a range of divergent perspectives and frames of meaning in ways that are congruent with those of the service-user. The work of Bywaters (1986), for example, highlights how tensions can arise between medical professionals and social workers due to differing conceptions of health and the factors affecting health and lifestyle. Where multiple 'claim-makers' are involved, social workers can play an important role in mediating discrepancies between various claims, by helping to reconcile them in ways that meet with and best serve the interests of the service-user.

Working with families

The work of Cooley extends SI concepts in order to develop an account of collective forms of association, such as groups and institutions. Social institutions are aggregates of concrete individuals working together to coordinate their actions and interactions on the basis of shared normative ideals and values. This is a very different conception of social institutions from the one contained in the work of structuralist thinkers such as Durkheim (Chapter 2) and Foucault (Chapter 6). Structuralist thinkers adopt a top-down perspective to collective phenomena, which they conceive of as largely independent from and coercing the actions and interactions of individuals. By contrast, SI thinkers adopt a bottom-up perspective, the term *institutions* here merely referring to what in actuality are never more than generalized and habitual patterns of action and interaction.

The account of institutions contained within SI thinking has been developed and applied by social workers working with families characterised by interpersonal tensions and conflict (Forte 2004a, 2004b). As aggregates of purposive individuals, families are made and remade over time through the actions and interactions of individual family members working together to define relationships and situations in line with wider socially shaped roles (La Rossa and Reitzes, 1993). The SI view that human agents interpret situations symbolically is an important one here. The roles of 'mother', 'step-son', 'grandparent', etc. are socially constructed and culturally patterned. Attached to the role of 'step-father', for example, are normative expectations and ideals taken from the wider culture. How exactly these are interpreted, negotiated and realized in the interactions between family members can vary. Where disparities arise between the expectations family members have of one another and the roles they are expected to play, tensions can arise and interaction can break down.

Working on a one-to-one basis with family members and the family as a whole, social workers have used SI ideas to emphasise the active part individuals can play in (re)constructing and (re)negotiating the various roles they play (Forte, 2004b). To this end, SI approaches to family-based work share points of convergence with both cognitive behavioural therapeutic models and Family Systems Theory (Sutton, 2000). Assisting family members to recognise and exercise their autonomy and agency, the possibility opens up for them to reorient how they act and interact with one another in line with the revised definitions and understandings arrived at individually and collectively by the family as a whole.

Stigma and service-users

The final application of SI ideas in this chapter focusses on stigma. It is important that social work professionals understand the interpersonal and social dynamics giving rise to stigma. Understanding how and why stigma occurs forms an important part of trying to fulfil the wider ethical commitment of social work towards challenging prejudice and discrimination in all its forms in society. This is particularly the case for practitioners working in the areas of anti-oppressive and anti-discriminatory practice. From a social theoretical perspective, the social and historical pervasiveness of stigma is significant. It is suggestive of the universal need for human groups to distinguish themselves from one another both socially and symbolically. The relational nature of identity and deviance means that all individuals and groups have the potential to be labelled as deviant and stigmatized. Moreover, to some extent 'all members of society are players in the stigma game' (Burns, 1992: 34). Stigma is the negative flipside of solidarity and cohesion. One of the challenges facing modern multicultural societies is to construct new forms of solidarity and collective identity that do not involve using particular individuals and groups which lay outside of their moral and symbolic boundaries as negative points of reference. Social work plays an important part in trying to construct these new forms of cohesion and collective identity.

Human history abounds with examples of individuals and groups who have been stigmatized. The psychological effects of stigma can be highly distressing, leading to divisions and hostility within communities and society as a whole.

Depending on the circumstances, stigmatization of one individual or group by another can be transient, and while the effects may be unpleasant they may have little consequence on the self-image and self-identity of the individuals concerned. In other cases, the effects of stigma can be psychologically harmful and emotionally distressing. Possession of a stigmatized identity can lead to individuals excluding themselves from particular relationships and situations as they seek to minimize and manage the damage to their self-identity and personhood. Self-preservation through avoidance is a rational response to the effects of stigmatization. In the long term, however, self-exclusion can lead to isolation as those suffering the effects of stigmatization increasingly withdraw from and become cut-off from mainstream society.

Cohen's concept of 'moral panics' can be used to cast light on the collective dynamics whereby certain social groups and behaviours come to be negatively labelled, stigmatized and in some cases criminalized. Moral panics occur when dominant social norms and values are interpreted as being under threat. The emphasis on interpretation in the formation of moral panics is key, highlighting the socially shaped processes by which groups and behaviours come to be identified as threats to the moral order. The concept of moral panics refers to the emotive collective response of society towards a perceived moral threat, one gathering momentum as it passes through a number of mutually reaffirming stages. A range of 'moral entrepreneurs' such as high-ranking professionals and groups, government officials, the tabloid media, psychologists and social workers actively shape the collective response of dominant groups. In recent years, the perceived threat posed to state resources and welfare services by 'benefit cheats' and 'benefit fraudsters' has led to a series of moral panics (Critcher, 2009; Lundstrom, 2011; Pattinson et al., 2016).

Constructing the recipients of social work and social care services as morally ambiguous has long taken place. High-profile government campaigns aimed at targeting individuals who fraudulently claim social welfare services and payments have been influential in framing the claimants in morally charged ways (Department for Work and Pensions and The Rt Hon Lord Freud, 2014). A considerable amount of social resources and activity are devoted to ensuring that the moral identity of the recipients of social welfare services remains morally ambiguous and subject to scrutiny. Assuming the identity of service-user can override other aspects of the individual's identity, connecting them symbolically to wider social and political anxieties about state spending. Assuming the identity of service-user can be damaging to individuals' personal identity often carrying with it a degree of social stigma.

For service-user groups already subject to negative labelling and marginalization, such as ethnic minority groups, asylum seekers, the unemployed, etc., interacting with social work services can compound their already stigmatized identity and status. In other contexts, recourse to social work services is interpreted by members of the wider community, no less the service-user, as signifying a range of moral failings and character blemishes. Framed in this way, service-users are opened up to being negatively classified and defined by others. This includes the view of service-users as lazy and irresponsible; unable to manage themselves and their own lives; failed parents; financially irresponsible; out of control; deviant or criminal; relying on public services for help with private problems; and so on.

Part of being a social worker is likely to involve assisting service-users to try to negotiate and manage the effects of stigma. This requires assisting the service-user to develop strategies for coping with the emotional and psychological pressures this entails. There are a number of ways to support service-users subject to stigmatization. One approach involves working with the service-user on a one-to-one basis to critically question the negative images and labels attributed to them through their interactions and relationships with others. For example, much has been done in the last decade to undermine and challenge the stigma surrounding mental health issues. Mental health problems are far more commonly reported and experienced than in the past. It can be greatly reassuring for a service-user to learn that mental health problems such as depression and anxiety are increasingly commonplace. Recognising that mental health problems are often brought on by situational factors can provide service-users with the comfort of knowing that the difficulties they are experiencing are not intrinsic to themselves. Viewed in this way, mental conditions such as depression and anxiety can plausibly be reinterpreted not as testimony to some personal failing, but as an index of the 'normality' of the service-user e.g. who would *not* feel depressed or anxious in your circumstances? Would it be normal *not* to feel depressed when you experience aspects of your life in the ways you do?

Another approach for combatting stigma involves working with members of service-users' peer group, family or community to challenge the views and attitudes of those enacting stigmatizing practices. This could mean working with individuals on a one-to-one basis or as part of focus groups to challenge negative beliefs and assumptions e.g. does the fact that the service-user is an asylum seeker really represent a threat to the community? If so, why? Is the fact that the service-user experiences mental health problems the defining feature of their identity? Does the mental health problem shape the individual's whole encounter with the service-user? In sum, precisely because stigma and stigmatized forms of identity are socially constructed, they can be deconstructed. Arriving at an understanding of the interactional processes and dynamics giving rise to stigma increases the likelihood that social workers play an active part in eradicating discrimination, stigma and prejudice wherever they encounter it.

Conclusion

For nearly a century, SI models and perspectives have informed the ideas and activities of social workers. Rooted in a conception of human agents as actively involved in the development of selfhood and identity through interaction, SI models lend themselves well to the social work values of self-determination and self-empowerment. The SI conception of the self as open-ended and malleable has been well utilised within social work, providing an analytically robust alternative to more individual-centred and 'psych-' accounts of the self as relatively invariant and static. Founded on the pragmatist view of human agents as self-determining, purposive and capable of enacting self-directed change, SI concepts and perspectives have been taken up and used to inform social work practice across a wide range of scenarios and settings. Like all social theoretical perspectives, however, SI has its critics.

Perhaps most significantly for social work is the charge that SI concepts provide an inadequate conception of power as it is formulated and operates at more macro levels (Alexander, 1987). The refusal to allocate ontological status to social structures other than to regard them as aggregates of individuals acting and interacting in patterned ways has meant that the coercive power of structures such as class and gender, for example, is insufficiently dealt with by SI thinkers. This is true in a general sense but more specifically too, particularly in the failure to account for the only semi-consciously realized ways power works to shape the minds and bodies of individuals (see the work of Foucault, Chapter 6, and Bourdieu, Chapter 7). Similarly, the capacity of SI perspectives to adequately grasp and explain the kinds of long-term historical processes and changes to social relations dealt with in the work of Elias (Chapter 5) has left particular aspects of SI theory vulnerable to critical scrutiny (Maines, 1977; Bourdieu and Wacquant, 1992).

Further reading

Becker, H. (1963) *Outsiders: Studies in the Sociology of Deviance*. New York: MacMillan.
Blumer, H. (1969) *Symbolic Interactionism: Perspective and Method*. California: University of California Press.
Goffman, E. (1968) *Stigma: Notes on the Management of a Spoiled Identity*. Harmondsworth: Penguin.

References

Alexander, J. (1987) *Twenty Lectures*. New York: Columbia University Press.
Becker, H. (1953) 'Becoming a Marihuana User', *The American Journal of Sociology*, 59(3): 235–242.
Becker, H. (1963) *Outsiders: Studies in the Sociology of Deviance*. New York: Free Press.
Blumer, H. (1969) *Symbolic Interactionism: Perspective and Method*. California: University of California Press.
Bourdieu, P. and Wacquant, L. (1992) *An Invitation to Reflexive Sociology*. Chicago: The University of Chicago Press.
Bulmer, M. (1984) *The Chicago School of Sociology: Institutionalization, Diversity, and the Rise of Sociological Research*. Chicago: Chicago University Press.
Burns, T. (1992) *Erving Goffman*. Oxford: Routledge.
Bywaters, P. (1986) 'Social Work and the Medical Profession – Arguments Against Unconditional Collaboration', *The British Journal of Social Work*, 16(6): 661–667.
Cohen, S. (1972) *Folk Devils and Moral Panics*. London: MacGibbon and Kee Ltd.
Cook, G. A. (1993) *George Herbert Mead: The Making of a Social Pragmatist*. Champaign, IL: University of Illinois Press.
Cooley, C. H. (1907) 'Social Consciousness', *American Journal of Sociology*, 12(5): 675–694.
Cooley, C. H. (1998 [1908]) *On Self and Social Organization*. Chicago: University of Chicago Press.
Critcher, C. (2009) 'Widening the Focus: Moral Panics as Moral Regulation', *British Journal of Criminology*, 49(1): 17–34.
da Silva, F. C. (2007) *G.H. Mead: A Critical Introduction*. Cambridge: Polity.
Denizen, N. K. (1992) *Symbolic Interactionism and Cultural Studies: The Politics of Interpretation*. Oxford: Blackwell.
Department for Work and Pensions and The Rt Hon Lord Freud. (2014) *New benefit fraud and error campaign: 'Benefits. Are you doing the right thing?'* [ONLINE] Available at: www.gov.uk/government/news/new-benefit-fraud-and-error-campaign-benefits-are-you-doing-the-right-thing [Accessed 5 February 2017].
Dewane, C. J. (2006) 'Use of Self: A Primer Revisited', *Clinical Social Work Journal*, 34(4): 543–558.
Drew, P. and Wootton, A. (1988) *Erving Goffman: Exploring the Interaction Order*. Cambridge: Polity.
Dunk-West, P. (2013) *How to be a Social Worker: A Critical Guide For Students*. London: Palgrave MacMillan.
Edwards, J. and Bess, J. (1998) 'Developing Effectiveness in the Therapeutic Use of Self', *Clinical Social Work Journal*, 26(01): 89–105.
Fine, G. A. (1993) 'The Sad Demise, Mysterious Disappearance, and Glorious Triumph of Symbolic Interactionism', *Annual Review of Sociology*, 19: 61–87.
Forte, J. A. (2004a) 'Symbolic Interactionism and Social Work: A Forgotten Legacy, Part 1', *Families in Society*, 85(3): 391–400.
Forte, J. A. (2004b) 'Symbolic Interactionism and Social Work: A Forgotten Legacy, Part 2', *Families in Society*, 85(4): 521–530.
Frisby, D. (2002) *Georg Simmel*. London: Routledge.

Furedi, F. (2004) *Therapy Culture: Cultivating Vulnerability in an Uncertain Age*. London: Routledge.

Goffman, E. (1959) *The Presentation of Self in Everyday Life*. Harmondsworth: Penguin.

Goffman, E. (1961) *Asylums*. Harmondsworth: Penguin.

Goffman, E. (1964) *Stigma: Notes on the Management of a Spoiled Identity*. Harmondsworth: Penguin.

Goffman, E. (1983) 'The Interaction Order', *American Sociological Review*, 48(1): 1–17.

Goode, E. and Ben-Yehuda, N. (1994) *Moral Panics: The Social Construction of Deviance*. Oxford: Blackwell.

Hewitt, R. (2006) *Symbolic Interactions: Social Problems and Literary Interventions in the Works of Baillie, Landor and Scott*. Lewisburg: Bucknell University Press.

Howe, D. (1991) 'The Family and the Therapist: Towards a Sociology of Social Work Method', in Davis, M. (ed.) *The Sociology of Social Work*. London: Routledge, pp. 64–81.

Jandy, E. C. (1969) *Charles Horton Cooley: His Life and His Social Theory*. Octagon Books: New York.

Knott, B. H. (1974) 'Social Work as Symbolic Interactionism', *British Journal of Social Work*, 4(1): 5–12.

Kondrat, D. and Teater, B. (2012) 'The Looking-Glass Self: Looking at Relationship as the Mechanism of Change in Case Management of Persons with Severe Mental Illness', *Families in Society: The Journal of Contemporary Social Services*, 93(4): 271–278.

Kuhn, M. (1962) 'The Interview and the Professional Relationship', in Rose, A. (ed.) *Human Behaviour and Social Processes: An Interactionist Approach*. Boston: Houghton Mifflin, pp. 193–206.

La Rossa, R. and Reitzes, D. C. (1993) 'Symbolic Interactionism and Family Studies', in Boss, P., Doherty, W., LaRossa, R., Schumm, W. and Steinmetz, S. (eds.) *Sourcebook of Family Theories and Methods: A Contextual Approach*. New York: Springer US, pp. 135–162.

Lieberman, F. and Gottesfeld, M. (1973) 'The Repulsive Client', *Clinical Social Work Journal*, 1(1): 22–31.

Lundstrom, R. (2011) 'Between the Exceptional and the Ordinary: A Model for the Comparative Analysis of Moral Panics and Moral Regulation', *Crime, Media, Culture: An International Journal*, 7(3): 313–332.

Maines, D. R. (1977) 'Social Organization and Social Structure in Symbolic Interactionist Thought', *Annual Review of Sociology*, 3: 235–259.

Manning, P. (1992) *Erving Goffman and Modern Sociology*. Cambridge: Polity.

Mayer, J. E. and Timms, N. (1970) *The Client Speaks*. London: Routledge and Kegan Paul.

Mead, G. H. (2011 [1922]) 'The Social Self', in da Silva, F. C. (ed.) *G.H. Mead: A Reader*. Abingdon: Routledge, pp. 58–62.

Mead, G. H. (1967) *Mind, Self and Society: From the Standpoint of a Behavioural Social Scientist*, Morris, W. (ed.) Chicago: Chicago University Press.

Mills, C. W. (1966) *Sociology and Pragmatism: The Higher Learning in America*. New York: Oxford University Press.

Offer, J. (1999) *Social Workers, the Community and Social Interactionism: Intervention and the Sociology of Welfare*. London: Jessica Kinglsey Publishers.

Pattinson, R., Crick, A. and Mills, J. (2016) *Benefit dad who whinged house was too small gets plush £425k, 4-bed detached pad*. [ONLINE] Available at: www.thesun.co.uk/news/2081271/fury-as-benefits-dad-of-eight-who-complained-house-was-too-small-handed-keys-to-plush-425000-4-bed-detached-pad-on-posh-street/ [Accessed 5 February 2017].

Prince, K. (1996) *Boring Records? Communication, Speech and Writing in Social Work*. London: Jessica Kingsley Publishers.

Robinson, T. (1978) *In Worlds Apart*. London: Bedford Square Press.

Schubert, (2006) 'The Foundations of Pragmatic Sociology: Charles Horton Cooley and George Herbert Mead', *Journal of Classical Sociology*, 6(1): 51–74.

Shaw, I. (2015) 'Sociological Social Workers: A History of the Present?', *Nordic Social Work Research*, 5(1): 7–24.

Sutton, C. (2000) 'Cognitive-Behavioural Theory: Relevance for Social Work', *Cognitive Behavioural Social Work Review*, 21(1): 6–21.

Thompson, N. (1992) *Existentialism and Social Work*. Oxford: Routledge.

Urdang, E. (1999) 'The Influence of Managed Care on the MSW Social Work Student's Development of the Professional Self', *Smith College Studies in Social Work*, 70(1): 3–25.

Urdang, E. (2010) 'Awareness of Self: A Critical Tool', *Social Work Education*, 29(5): 523–538.

Wiley, N. (2006) 'Pragmatism and the Dialogical Self', *International Journal for Dialogical Science*, 1(1): 5–21.

5

NORBERT ELIAS

Emotions, rationality and self-restraint

Introduction

Part of being a social worker involves dealing with and managing conflict. This might be conflict between family members, between couples who are separating and trying to negotiate childcare or between individuals and groups within communities. Conflict and hostility expressed in a variety of forms might feature directly in your relationship with service-users: in the form of shouting and anger; verbal abuse and intimidating behaviour; or, in the worst case, threats and the actualisation of physical violence (Pahl, 1999). When conflict arises, feelings and emotions become heightened and the capacity to think and act rationally diminishes. This is not to suggest that emotions are necessarily bad, or always lead to conflict. Emotions are an essential part of what it means to be human. Strong feelings and emotional attachments towards friends, family members and loved ones provide the backdrop against which many of the most meaningful and cherished moments of our lives take place.

While all human beings experience powerful feelings and strong emotional urges, not all people are as inclined to act on or react to them. Why are some people's thoughts and actions so emotionally led? How does this shape the ways they perceive people and situations? Why are some individuals better at regulating their emotions than others? How does this relate to their ability to think and act in rational and measured ways? To what extent are differences in emotional temperament and the capacity for self-restraint due to individual differences? And how does this relate to wider group dynamics and social processes? This chapter focusses on the socially shaped nature of human emotions, as well as how changes to the structure and organisation of modern society have influenced the emotional and behavioural dispositions of different individuals and groups.

To do this, we focus on the theoretical ideas of the German Jewish social theorist Norbert Elias (1897–1990). In his most influential work, *The Civilizing Process* (1939), Elias explains how historical transformations to the social relationships characteristic of modern Western society have led to corresponding changes in the emotional and behaviour dispositions of individuals. Elias's central claim is that changes to the type and organisation of social relations in the West have led to rising levels of emotional and behavioural self-restraint and control on the one hand, and an increasing capacity for thinking and acting rationally on the other.

At the heart of Elias's work is the notion of 'process'. Elias regards social reality as an ongoing, dynamic process, constantly developing and changing into new forms and figurations of human relations. Adopting a 'processual' view of social reality allowed Elias to bypass the conceptual pitfalls attached to structuralist forms of social theory on the one hand, and individual-focussed forms of analysis on the other. According to the former, human subjects are seen as being dominated by social structures and institutions, whereas the latter over-emphasises the amount of freedom social agents have. In seeking to go beyond these positions, Elias held that the conceptual carving up of social reality into a series of abstract entities such as individual/society, structure/agency, social stability/social change, etc. fails to grasp the fundamental inter-relatedness of all social phenomena. Instead, Elias developed a conception of social reality as a constant flow of mutating 'networks' and 'figurations' of relations. Human agents, no less than the relationships which bind them to one another, comprise open-ended processes. This is why changes to the types and figurations of social relationships lead to changes in the psychological make-up of individuals and vice versa, such that over time both are transformed in new and largely unintended ways.

Elias used the concepts of 'socio-genesis' and 'psycho-genesis' to highlight how changes to the personality structure of individuals relate to changes to society over time. This is why, he argued, differences in the emotional and psychological make-up of individuals cannot be attributed exclusively to internal factors. At least as important for understanding the psychological and behavioural dispositions of different human groups are changes to the figurations and networks of social relations through which individuals are bound to one another. Viewed in this way, Elias (1970) regarded the separating out of academic life into different disciplines such as psychology, sociology and history as a highly unfortunate albeit largely unintended consequence of wider social change. As we shall see, his work attempts to go beyond the artificiality of this division by demonstrating how changes to the organisation of society (sociology) over time (history) shape the minds of individuals (psychology) (Elias, 1994 [1939]).

Elias's work has been virtually untouched by social work. One notable exception is the work of de Swaan (1988) who adopts Elias's concepts to explain how changes to social relations over time led to shifting attitudes towards the poor and the origins of alms and 'poor relief'. This chapter introduces Elias's most influential conceptual ideas to social work. In doing so it seeks to demonstrate their ability to cast an illuminating light on a range of important issues such as differences in the socialization processes characteristic of marginalized social groups, service-users' experiences of welfare services and the likelihood of coming into contact with and requiring social work assistance. The chapter begins by

TABLE 5.1 Summary of socio-genesis and psycho-genesis

Socio-genesis and psycho-genesis
• refer to inter-relations between social factors and emotional and psychological dispositions
• changes to social organisation of human group shape psychological constitution of individuals, and vice versa
• long-term social change leads to corresponding changes in individual psychology, and vice versa

explaining Elias's organising concept of the 'civilizing process' before moving on to illustrate its value for opening up new ways of thinking with regard to the aforementioned themes.

The civilizing process

Norbert Elias was born in 1897 in Wroclaw, Poland. As a young man, he was forced to quit Germany in 1935 for England as the Nazi Party gained in power prior to the onset of WW2. During the war, Elias's mother perished in the Nazi death camps at Auschwitz. Elias's first-hand experience of the devastating effects of human emotions expressed in such unrestrained and violent ways left a profound mark on him. A concern with the affective dimensions of human life is a central theme throughout Elias's work. Influenced by the work of Weber (Chapter 2), and in particular his claims about the increasingly rational character of culture in the West, Elias wanted to explain how social factors shape the emotional temperament and behavioural dispositions of human groups (Landini, 2013). To do this, Elias's most important work, *The Civilizing Process* (1939), draws on the ideas of a number of influential German thinkers, including the sociologist Georg Simmel (Chapter 4) and Sigmund Freud (Lahire, 2013).

The concept of 'civilizing process' (henceforth referred to as 'CP') refers to a long-term, multi-linear, but ultimately one-directional historical movement, resulting in changes in the nature of social relationships in the West (Elias, 1994 [1939]). These relationships had become ever more rationally organised, a theme developed by Weber. They also involved ever higher levels of emotional, psychological and behavioural self-restraint and regulation. A key point for Elias is that the drive towards greater psychological and corporeal restraint is self-imposed and not the result of greater control forced upon individuals by some external agency. Moreover, the drive towards increasing self-regulation and rising rationality was largely unintended. They are the outcome of changes and developments in social relations that no one could have foreseen or deliberately intended.

Throughout the CP, Elias demonstrates that social relations in Western societies have gradually but steadily changed from the early medieval period onwards. The significance of these changes is the impact they have had for shaping people's capacity to regulate and control the emotional and bodily aspects of their behaviour. To demonstrate this Elias drew on historical data, primarily social etiquette books and manuals. Etiquette books were written and read by aristocratic people from the medieval period onwards. They provided detailed accounts of how to behave, as well as which types of conduct were considered acceptable or not, depending on the situation or context. In comparison with today's standards, people's behaviour in the medieval period was, generally speaking, far less prohibited. Elias demonstrates this by examining and comparing the ways people undertook a range of essential human activities, such as eating, urinating, defecating and conducting sexual relations. On the whole, the emotional temperament characteristic of the medieval period was far more volatile and impulsive than it is today. Human interactions were far less stable, with people's moods and behaviour often vacillating from one extreme to the other, often in very sudden and unpredictable ways. The emotionally charged and volatile nature of the medieval temperament meant incidences of physical violence were far more commonplace. Medieval eating practices were far less constrained too. People used their hands to eat from a communal pot while spitting, belching and farting as and when they felt the urge. People were far more likely to engage in sexual acts in public places too, along with urinating and defecating wherever and whenever they felt the urge. The normative rules that prevent us from acting in these ways in the present day had not yet emerged.

Without the social norms that prevent us from behaving in these ways in the present day, people's behaviour was far less restrained or subject to self-regulation. Compared to the present day, medieval behaviours were characterised by far lower levels of emotional, bodily and psychological restraint. Elias's work shows that from the seventeenth century onwards, an increasing number of human behaviours, particularly those involving bodily functions such as defecating and sexual acts, came to be labelled as 'disgusting', 'repugnant' and 'uncivilized'. As part of this process, those same behaviours were expected to arouse in the individual the socially instilled feelings of shame and embarrassment. Over time, behaviours identified as disgusting and the source of shame and embarrassment steadily disappeared from everyday life. Engaging in sexual acts or urinating and defecating in public places were no longer acceptable. These were now behaviours which when undertaken in front of others were deemed shameful and worthy of embarrassment.

From acts of a sexual nature, to toiletry matters and picking one's nose, these behaviours gradually came to be understood as shameful when performed in public. Correspondingly, such behaviours came to be understood as actions people undertake in private, whether at home in the bedroom, in designated private spaces known as toilets, or anywhere removed from the public gaze. Elias demonstrates the inter-relatedness of the social processes by which these affective and behavioural changes gradually began to occur. In doing so, he is critical of many of the common sense explanations as to why certain behaviours came to be regarded as uncivilized and socially unacceptable. It was not for reasons of hygiene, for example, that people stopped urinating and defecating in public. Changes in behaviour pre-dated knowledge and awareness of hygiene by several centuries. Moreover, it was not for reasons of respect for others that these developments occurred either. People of aristocratic rank continued to behave in ways that were shameful when enacted by people from a lower social position. It was only during the nineteenth century that the stricter codes of bodily conduct and self-regulation came to apply to individuals from *all* social classes and backgrounds.

In accounting for the development of the CP, Elias identifies the emergence of the royal courts of medieval Europe as of central importance. The types of interaction and modes of interpersonal conduct characteristic of the royal courts required individuals to regulate themselves – not just in terms of their interactions with others but in relation to their own emotions and bodies too. As modernity began to develop, the power of the previously ruling class of medieval barons and knights started to decline. Medieval kings and princes assumed power in their place, as greater numbers of people became dependent upon and lived in and around the courts. It was at this time that a new class of courtiers emerged. The emotional and bodily dispositions of the courtiers were very different from those of the unrestrained warlords who preceded them. The courtiers had very different relations to one another in the context of court life as well as to the people below them.

The new types of social relationships characteristic of court society led to changes in interpersonal conduct (Elias, 2006 [1969]). Definitive of these was an emphasis on self-restraint and regulation. Medieval courts were highly controlled, competitive social environments. To secure prestige and favour within the royal courts, courtiers were constantly monitoring the behaviour of one another as they struggled to secure favour and prestige from the royal family. To prove their worth, courtiers sought to demonstrate their refined and gentile nature, which they did by adhering to and enacting very strict and elaborate behavioural codes of conduct and manners. In court life to slip-up with one's manners or to lose one's temper in a way that betrayed a lack of control or self-discipline was read as a flaw in the character of the individual. The need to monitor and regulate one's own behaviour was essential at all times.

For reasons that were largely unintended, Elias demonstrates how wider shifts in the balance of power between the feudal barons and knights in favour of the royal families and princes led to new standardized modes of conduct. As towns and cities grew up around the royal courts, the new, more refined and polite ways of acting and interacting were taken up by wider social groups. A particularly important social group for carrying on the CP was the middle class. The middle classes were keen to identify with and imitate their social superiors as to do so drew prestige from other people. The middle classes embraced and sought to imitate the mannerisms and habits of the social class above them. The role of the middle classes in carrying on the CP was not an example of one group trying directly to copy another. Socially subordinate groups often attempted to resist the imposition and spread of courtly manners and etiquette (Elias, 1994 [1939], 2006 [1969]). Nevertheless, Elias's work demonstrates that for the most part the new norms of conduct and the compulsion towards emotional and bodily self-regulation spread out into wider society. Over the course of the proceeding centuries the emotional and behavioural dispositions found in Western society tended towards increasing levels of self-restraint.

The emergence of court society was a necessary but not sufficient condition for the development of the CP. Just as important was the increasing structural differentiation of society. As society became increasingly complex, the need for shared and uniform behavioural codes grew in equal measure. Without these shared behavioural norms, people from different social spheres such as traders, butchers, clergymen, shopkeepers, etc. would not have been able to interact in patterned and predictable ways. In the rapidly growing towns and cities of early modern Europe, individuals unknown to one another were brought into contact and required to interact with one another. The standardized behavioural codes developing between individuals and groups were passed on and diffused throughout society. These provided the normative and interactional bases for subsequent social interaction.

In addition to these processes, socially shaped emotions such as shame and embarrassment came less to be associated with individuals of a specific rank, and instead became emotions *all* individuals were encouraged to feel if they breached the emotional and behavioural norms governing interpersonal conduct. To avoid experiencing these negative emotions more and more people began to self-regulate their emotions. Shame and embarrassment were feelings anyone could experience if they imagined themselves through the eyes of society. Furthermore, as the CP progressed these emotions stopped being thought about in fully conscious ways, instead receding to a semi-conscious level in the minds of all individuals. The emotions of shame and embarrassment formed part of the normative framework in which all interactions came to be enacted. Rising levels of restraint meant that the sense of self-inhibition to enact certain behaviours became 'part of people's own consciousness and self-steering' (Fletcher, 1997: 17).

By the nineteenth century, the CP had developed to such a point that the reasons for it – changes in social relations – had been lost to view. The conditioning of children to feel shame and embarrassment, for example, is often explained by invoking the notions of hygiene and respect e.g. when a child is chastised for picking his nose at the dinner table. It is precisely the

TABLE 5.2 Summary of the civilizing process

Civilizing process
• origins in medieval court society • long-term multi-linear and one-directional process • historical changes to arrangement and type of social relations • relationships characterised by increasing levels of emotional and behavioural self-control and self-restraint • enables higher levels of foresight, psychologization and rationality • effects distributed unevenly across society

mistaken view of the reasons behind our reactions to these types of behaviours that leads individuals to think of the capacity for self-regulation and the 'senses of embarrassment and shame as something highly personal, something "inward", implanted in them by nature . . .' (Elias, 1994 [1939]: 127–8). The concept of the CP identifies and grasps the social reasons behind changes to the emotional and behavioural dispositions of individuals in the West. A key point to emphasise is that there is nothing natural or inevitable about the type or direction of these changes. Instead, they are the (largely unintended) consequence of changes to the figurations and types of social relations binding individuals.

Social habitus

So far we have explained the concept of the civilizing process from a long-term, historical perspective. In this section, we focus on the ways the CP shapes the emotional and behavioural dispositions of individuals and groups in a number of more specific ways. A key concept for doing this is 'social habitus'. The concept of social habitus allowed Elias to demonstrate how the CP shaped and was shaped by changes to the actions and interactions of concrete individuals. An important point to make here is that the CP does not shape the behaviour of all social groups in uniform and even ways. Instead, the effects of the CP are unevenly distributed across different groups. Characteristic of socially dominant groups is a social habitus characterised by high levels of emotional and corporeal restraint. This is because the individuals who make up dominant groups tend to be integrated into more dense and complex networks of social relations of dependency. By contrast, socially subordinate and marginalized groups tend to be characterised by lower levels of emotional and corporeal restraint. The lifestyles the members of these groups lead tend to exert less pressure on the individual to regulate and restrain their emotions and behaviour.

Elias acknowledged that the pressure to act and interact with self-restraint is exerted over all social groups through a range of external mechanisms of social control. Pressure is exerted both directly and indirectly over individuals through a range of formal institutions, such as schools and universities, the workplace, the police, the army and so on. But if this was all that Elias had said, then the concept of the CP would not take us much farther than what most of us already know. Instead, his most valuable insights lay in his account of the largely hidden and unconscious processes by which the compulsion to act with restraint and foresight are instilled within the individual.

The concept of social habitus draws on and develops the ideas of Sigmund Freud, in partic-ular his later theory of the drives as developed in the classic study *Civilization and Its Discontents* (Cavaletto, 2007; Van Krieken, 1998). Freud (2002 [1930], 2010 [1923]) developed a model of the human mind, or psyche, organised around a tripartite structure. In a natural state such as when babies are born, human beings experience anti-social drives and impulses towards acting violently and, later on in life, sexual gratification. Freud referred to the part of the psyche that produces desires aimed at fulfilling these drives as the 'id'. The need to suppress and control these primal desires is demanded by the part of the mind referred to as the 'superego'. The superego is the socially instilled part of the individual psyche. (The superego plays a similar role to Durkheim's notion of the 'collective conscience' described in Chapter 2.)

The superego develops throughout socialization as the normative ideals and values of the group are internalized in the mind of the individual. The third component of the psyche is the 'ego' – the conscious human mind. In Freud's theory, the id and the superego are forever at war with one another in the ego, a battle enacted daily in the form of daydreams, fantasies and desires, many of which are accompanied by an awareness of the need to suppress such idealiza-tions. The superego must be able to control and restrain the impulses and desires generated by the id. The role of the superego is to regulate and ensure that the individual does not act on these impulses and contravene the normative rules and codes of conduct underpinning social interaction. To do so would pose a threat to social order and the individual too in the form of punishment or, worse still, imprisonment.

Freud's (2002 [1930]) model depicts the human psyche as relatively static and unchanging, uniformly structured in the same way throughout all human groups. Elias was critical of Freud's model, instead viewing the human psyche as an essentially processual entity, more malleable, open-ended and capable of change than Freud had allowed for. The concept of social habitus is intended to capture how the organisation and types of relations binding members of a group directly shapes the component parts of the psyche. How the relations between the different parts of the psyche are arranged and relate to one another is determined 'in accordance with the changing structure of relationships *between* individual human beings' (Elias, 1994 [1939]: 286). As the CP has developed over time, the configuration of relations between the different parts of the psyche has changed in the West. On the whole, the advance of the CP has meant the superego becoming the ever more dominant partner in its relationship to the id. But the ways and extent to which this holds true for different groups within society varies significantly.

In the following section of the chapter we apply the concept of social habitus to illustrate more concretely how the organisation and types of social relations individuals are embedded in shape their capacity for emotional and behavioural self-restraint and the corresponding

TABLE 5.3 Summary of social habitus

Social habitus
• modern society made up of different social habitus • socially shaped emotional, behavioural and psychological characteristics and dispositions of group • enables and constrains individual's capacity for emotional self-restraint and acting with foresight and rationality • shaped by organisation and types of relationships inside and outside of group e.g. 'functional' and 'segmental' solidarity

tendency towards thinking and acting rationally. Social habitus A depicts a lifestyle character-ised by high levels of emotional and behavioural self-restraint and correspondingly high levels of rationality. By contrast, social habitus B depicts a lifestyle characterised by comparatively far lower levels of emotional and behavioural self-restraint and a correspondingly lower capacity for thinking and acting rationally.

Social habitus A

Social habitus A refers to the life conditions of a family comprising two adults, Stephen and Alison, and their two children, Anne and Douglas. The family lives together in a small village not far from a town where Stephen and Alison both work. After leaving university, Stephen and Alison travelled abroad for some time, before returning to the U.K., where they met and got married. Stephen works as a secondary-school teacher, and Alison is a part-time physiotherapist.

The family is positioned within a social habitus comprising multiple, wide-ranging rela-tionships of functional interdependency. In ways that are direct and indirect, conscious and unconscious, partially intended and largely unintended, the social habitus exerts a strong pres-sure over individual family members towards emotional and behavioural self-restraint. This pressure is exerted through and by the relationships between family members, as well as the wider networks and relationships in which they are embedded. For example, Stephen's self-identity is made up of multiple and diverse roles. Stephen is a secondary-school teacher, father, husband, brother, friend, member of the local squash team and so on. These roles position him within multiple intersecting and long chains of relations of functional interdependency. At work and in the classroom, Stephen is responsible for the care of thirty children and is directly and indirectly answerable to all of their parents, his line-manager and the school headmistress. As part of his job he is also involved in running the school football team. This involves liaising with coaches from other schools, as well as parents and children too.

A key point to make here is that other than when things become unusually stressful e.g. when his wife is unwell and unable to help with childcare and domestic tasks, Stephen does not experience the multiple roles he plays as constraining how he thinks, feels and behaves. Instead, he experiences the social habitus he is positioned within as just how life is. In this sense, embedded in Stephen's self-image and self-identity is a conception of 'Stephen-in-relation-to' a wide range of people, groups and institutions (Elias, 1991). These include his children, his wife, his pupils, his colleagues, the school, the squash team, etc. An ongoing and sustained pres-sure is exerted over Stephen, which is both internalized and expressed through the compulsion towards restraining his feelings and emotions and regulating how he acts towards and interacts with others.

In ways that are largely implicit, built into Stephen's subjectivity is a strong compulsion to think through and reflect on how his thoughts, feelings and behaviour could impact on others on whom he depends and who in turn depend upon him. The compulsion towards reflexively monitoring his own feelings and actions is directly bound up with the self-directed pressure Stephen feels to think and act with 'foresight' – thinking through the consequences of certain actions and reactions before enacting them. As part of the disposition to think and act with foresight, Stephen is oriented towards time in future-oriented ways, specifically through the projection of himself into an imagined future and what that means in terms of the demands placed upon him to fulfil certain tasks and commitments. Stephen spends time every week thinking through the days and weeks ahead, making sure to note various commitments in his diary, such as forthcoming school football matches, parents' evenings, his children's extra-curricular activities, matches for the squash team, etc.

Another disposition necessary for meeting the demands placed upon him concerns the capacity for 'psychologization'. This refers to the capacity to see and perceive other people and situations in ways that are based on emotionally detached and 'reality-based observations' (Elias, 1994 [1939]: 400). Instead of disposing individuals to see the world in ways coloured by strong emotional urges and idealizations, a social habitus characterised by high levels of restraint enables an image of the outside world to develop based more on emotionally detached observations and understanding born of experience. An example of psychologization involves being able to perceive people not in poorly differentiated binary ways e.g. friend or foe, good or bad, etc. but instead as being made up of multiple different selves and identities, some of which may directly contradict one another e.g. merely because the police officer who has pulled me over in my car is my wife's cousin does not mean he can turn a blind eye to the fact I have no insurance.

Elias regards the capacity for psychologization as directly related to the increasing structural differentiation of society. As social life becomes increasingly differentiated, the number of selves and identities individuals are required to develop and enact is divided up in corresponding ways. According to Elias (1994 [1939]: 403), the development of psychologization and the capacity to think and act with foresight go hand in hand, both being necessary for thinking and acting in rationally oriented ways. To be able to perform the roles expected of them, individuals have to be able to perceive and interact with others in increasingly emotionally detached and dispassionate ways. That is to say, individuals have to be able to differentiate between those aspects of one another which they do not necessarily like (e.g. the fact my line-manager has strong political views which I disagree with), and those aspects of their identity (e.g. the fact he *is* my line-manager) which enable them to fulfil their professional roles. Being able to relate to and interact with people in a dispassionate and emotionally neutral way is important in a society characterised by high levels of functional differentiation. It enables people whose beliefs and actions might otherwise bring them into conflict with one another to collaborate and get on.

Childhood as emotional and behavioural training

The differentiation of society into an increasingly broad and specialized range of activities forms an important part of the historical changes driving the CP. At a group level, how these changes have filtered through and shaped the personality structure of individuals is directly bound up with changing patterns of childhood socialization. Concurrent with the rising power of the middle class during the nineteenth century, Elias regarded the family as 'coming to play the most important social institution for the instilling of drive controls' (Fletcher, 1997: 22). It is through child socialization that 'adults induce in children the constant restraint and foresight they will need for adult functions' (Elias, 1994 [1939]: 241–4). From an Eliasian per-spective, childhood socialization is first and foremost an exercise in training children to channel and regulate certain anti-social emotional impulses and drives at the same time as encouraging them to develop foresight, psychologization and rationality.

Through the daily round of interactions with one another, the emotional, attitudinal and behavioural dispositions of Stephen and Alison are brought to bear on their children. The habitus-shaped dispositions of Stephen and Alison play a formative role in shaping the emotional, psychological and behavioural socialization of Douglas and Anne. Elias (1994 [1939]: xiii) claimed that in order for children to be inculcated with the dominant standards of behaviour deemed acceptable of the social habitus they belong to, they must be incorporated into the socialization processes of the wider group. An important idea here is that the psychological distance between children and adults varies between different social groups. The greater the number of 'civilizing' institutions parents have had to pass through on their way to becoming adults e.g. school, university, professional institutions, etc. the greater the social distance children have to 'travel' to develop the equivalent levels of emotional and psychological restraint and rationality.

Through childhood socialization and exposure to a wide range of different types of institutions, Stephen and his wife Alison were strongly conditioned to think, feel and act with self-control and restraint at the same time as learning to think and act with foresight and reason. For the most part, the actions, interactions and reactions of Stephen and Alison to and with their children tend towards reproducing within the children the same 'civilizing tendencies' characteristic of their own behaviour. This takes place both in ways that are intentional and consciously directed, and in ways that are unintended and semi-consciously enacted. From the moment the children were born, the high levels of emotional self-regulation and the disposition to act with foresight and rationally were brought to bear on them. Over time and in a steady, stable and concerted way, the children are encouraged to suppress and regulate certain emotions, giving reign to others, and think both with foresight and in psychologically nuanced and rational ways.

At the children's school, they are enrolled in a range of clubs and activities which, in their own small but significant ways, make demands on them, orienting them towards regulating and managing the development of their thoughts, feelings and actions. As the children grow older, their involvement in these activities becomes more demanding and concerted. Douglas receives a team football kit which he is encouraged to take responsibility for, not to be forgotten or left at home or left behind after training. In the gym the family attends, Anne is enrolled in dancing classes. She is responsible for making sure she takes her dancing shoes to and from lessons as well ensuring they are put away and ready for when she needs them next. In sum, from an early age both children develop in a social-relational context characterised by a bourgeoning number and type of relations of interdependency. The experience and (partial) awareness of these social relations and the ways of thinking, feeling and acting they call forth in the children instill within them the compulsion to think and act with self-restraint and foresight.

This steadily widening network of relationships exerts a significant pressure on the children towards emotional, psychological and behavioural self-regulation and self-restraint. Initially, the children experience the demands placed upon them to regulate their thoughts and actions in a self-conscious and often onerous way e.g. through being told to remember their respective sports kits, not to forget to attend training, etc., but over time as they become internalized and normalized, that awareness fades into the background. It strikes them as normal and natural to think and act in self-regulating and future-oriented ways.

Social habitus B

Social habitus B comprises the life conditions of a single parent, Roy, and his son, Jason, who is 9 years old. Social habitus B is characterised by comparatively much lower levels of emotional and behavioural self-restraint and regulation than social habitus A. On the whole, emotional volatility, spontaneity and unpredictability are far less tightly tied to the negative emotions of shame, embarrassment and guilt. In some cases, they are regarded as legitimate ways of responding to people and situations. This has the effect of diminishing the development of the kinds of 'pro-social' dispositions Elias claims are necessary for thinking and acting with foresight, psychologization and rationality. Remember, Elias claims that rational behaviour requires a calculating quality that is only able to develop when emotional and impulsive drives are kept at a distance. The less self-directed pressure individuals feel towards constraining and regulating their emotional and behavioural impulses, the less likely it is they will develop the corresponding dispositions towards thinking and acting rationally.

Roy and Jason live on a council estate not far from the city centre. Roy works full-time as a bus driver, and at the weekend he plays for a local football team. Because Roy's job involves shift work, he often works late and is unable to pick Jason up from school. On these occasions, Jason is collected from school by his grandmother. She lives a few streets away on the same estate. Jason's days are generally less structured than those of the children of social habitus A. Other than playing for the school football team, comparatively fewer demands are placed on Jason in terms of extra-curricular pursuits and the round of activities this involves. The majority of relationships and interactions Jason has with other individuals are informal and personal e.g. family members, neighbours and other children and parents on the housing estate where he lives.

Outside of school, Jason spends most of his time in and around the community where he lives. The lives of Roy, Jason and his grandmother are confined to a relatively small geographical area. Some of the children Jason plays with on the estate are also part of single-parent families, the majority of whom comprise mothers and form part of wider female-centred kin networks. Like many other children on the estate, Jason's experience of gender roles is characterised by clear and rigid distinctions. There is a strong gendered division of parental labour between adults on the estate: women take care of children, and male figures provide the main source of family income. Men feature far less in parental and nurturing duties than women generally.

Jason's life is tightly integrated into a wider group of children and families whose identities and everyday lives intersect and overlap in multiple ways (Hanley, 2007). He has little contact with children or adults outside of the community. When he is at his grandmother's house, Jason plays with the children of friends and neighbours, often at the park or out in the streets in the community. Compared to social habitus A, Jason and his friends are subject to far lower levels of direct parental supervision. The children in the group establish their own relationships and identities which tend to mirror the same highly gendered roles they see at home and in the families around them.

Within Jason's groups of friends, the boys assert their identities through displays of physical strength, toughness and attempts to emulate the male figures in their lives. When disputes break out they tend to be settled with resort to verbal and physical aggression. Parents intervene only occasionally, instead preferring to let the children sort things out among themselves. Jason and his friends regularly come into contact with adolescents and young adults on the estate. Similarly, their identities are based around expressions of machismo, toughness and physical aggression. An identity based on aggressive masculinity is prized among the boys and demonstrated by the tendency to resort to hostility and aggression towards other groups of boys who come to the park from a community nearby.

At the weekend, Roy plays football for a local team and Jason often goes to watch him. While the fathers play football, the women and mothers cheer on their partners and talk among themselves, and the boys play football at the sidelines of the pitch. After the game, sometimes Jason goes with Roy to the local pub. While his father socializes with his friends and members of the team, Jason plays at the park over the road with some of the other children. Other times, Roy and Jason play football together after the match. Roy explains to Jason the need to be tough and to go in strong when tackling other players for the ball. Roy explains to Jason that this is how to win respect from his team mates.

The lives of Roy and Jason form part of a lifestyle characteristic of a social habitus defined by far lower levels of emotional and behavioural self-restraint than that displayed by the members of social habitus A. The social relations binding individuals in the kind of close-knit and marginalized community where Roy and Jason live are characterised not by 'functional', but 'segmental' forms of solidarity (Elias and Dunning, 1986). The concept of segmental solidarity is an attempt to rework Durkheim's notion of 'mechanical solidarity' (Chapter 2): members of the community lead very similar lifestyles; often work and socialize together; and are bound together by shared attitudes, values and beliefs. The main difference between groups bound by segmental (social habitus B) as opposed to mechanical solidarity is that the former are situated in and surrounded by mainstream social groups (such as those of social habitus A) organised around varying degrees of functional dependency.

Communities bound by segmental solidarity are poorly integrated into and detached from mainstream society (Elias and Scotson, 1994 [1965]). They are segments of society excluded from the wider figurations and networks of social relations of interdependency binding members of mainstream society (Elias and Dunning, 1986). Both inside and outside of communities characterised by segmental dependency (social habitus B), the social relations of dependency binding individuals are shorter and less complex. This shapes the type of social habitus characteristic of segmental communities in various ways:

- The pressure towards emotional and physical self-regulation is exerted over individuals far less by the family and wider kinship networks. In certain contexts it is actively discouraged.
- Physical and verbal aggression is much closer to the surface of everyday life.
- The primary sources of emotional and behavioural regulation derive from outside of the family, 'in the form of social agencies such as school, the police, social work' (Elias and Dunning, 1986: 243).
- The mental categories organising and structuring individuals' experiences are cruder and less nuanced. Those categories also tend to be more emotionally charged and rooted in the wider identity of the group.
- The range and types of social roles individuals perform are narrower such that the pressure to think and act with foresight in future-oriented ways is far less keenly felt.

For members of social habitus B, the pressure towards emotional and behavioural self-regulation derives from outside of the community. This pressure is not nearly as strong or powerful as the compulsion to act with restraint directed from within, in the form of internal psychological mechanisms of control. In summary, the lifestyles of social habitus A and B exert very different amounts and types of pressure over the individuals socialized into them. This pressure is directly mediated by the organisation and character of the relations between individuals in the habitus, as well as the relationship of the group to the immediately surrounding networks of social relations and wider society more generally.

Applying Elias to social work

Social habitus and social work services

Elias's concept of social habitus can be applied to think about how the dispositions of marginalized individuals and service-user groups impact negatively on their experience of social work services. It can also be used to consider the experiences of service-users socialized into non-Western contexts characterised by very different nationally shaped habitus dispositions (Elias, 1990). The social habitus of marginalized service-users works to disadvantage them in their encounter with social work services in two main ways. The first concerns accessing the bureaucratic institutions and social relations in which social work services are embedded. The second concerns the increasing bureaucratization of everyday life more generally.

As part of the rationalization of modern society, social work has become heavily bureaucratized. Bureaucratic institutions are founded on the values of rationality, instrumentalism and efficiency (Chapter 2). The organisational basis of contemporary social work is institutional and formal, organised around complex systems of impersonal procedures, regulations and legislation. To access social work services, individuals are required to enter into and navigate these rationally oriented structures and systems of instrumental relations. Bureaucratic relations call forth in individuals certain characteristics and dispositions at the same time as requiring them to regulate and manage others. Bureaucratic relations presuppose individuals who are able to think and act with foresight, as well as relating to others in impersonal and rationally oriented ways. They presuppose individuals possessed of a number of other related dispositions, such as patience, foresight, systematicity, being organised, being capable of thinking logically and interacting formally rather than in overly personal and informal ways.

Dealing with bureaucratic institutions can be an emotionally trying and frustrating experience – particularly when the person we are dealing with face-to-face or on the end of a telephone cannot provide us with the information or assistance we need to achieve a particular goal (Coleman and Harris, 2008). For many service-users, recourse to social work services comes as a last resort and at times of emotional stress and volatility. The capacity to suspend certain feelings and emotional urges can be difficult for anyone feeling this way, but especially for service-users socialized into a habitus characterised by low levels of emotional and behavioural self-restraint (social habitus B). For service-users feeling scared, angry, frustrated and upset, the likelihood of acting and interacting in highly emotionally expressive ways increases. It requires very high levels of emotional and behavioural self-restraint not to react to how we are feeling at such times.

At times of emotional stress, service-users characterised by low levels of self-regulation and restraint are more likely to experience emotional outbursts. This can take a number of forms including the raising of their voice, shouting and use of harsh language. A service-user may behave in overly familiar and personally directed ways, expressing anger, frustration and in some cases making threats of physical violence (Littlechild, 2005; Savaya et al., 2011). Failing to repress and restrain strong emotions and outbursts in bureaucratic contexts can lead to service-users being excluded from the services they need. Their behaviour is deemed unacceptable, unrestrained and uncivilized. This can result in phone calls being terminated, service-users being barred from certain locales and being denied access to certain individuals, relationships and opportunities.

The key point to make here is that the socially shaped dispositions necessary for participating in bureaucratic relations are inextricably bound up with the CP. The CP as we have seen already is unevenly distributed across society. The capacity for acting and interacting in emotionally detached and rational ways depends on the type of social habitus into which individuals are socialized. It is the social habitus, not the individual, which is most influential for shaping the capacity for emotional restraint and acting and interacting rationally. The uneven social distribution of the emotional dispositions called forth by bureaucratic organisations means that often the individuals most likely to require social work assistance are least likely to possess the behavioural dispositions required to access them. On the whole, the social habitus of marginalized groups (social habitus B) makes it far less likely that individuals develop the kinds of emotional and behavioural traits necessary for participating in bureaucratically organised relationships and organisations.

The social habitus of these groups disadvantages the individuals socialized into them in a number of more general ways too. In a culture of rationality, bureaucratic structures extend ever further into the everyday lifeworld. More and more aspects of everyday life are bound up with and draw us into bureaucratic procedures and relations. As part of this process, our personal identities come to be reconstituted in the form of a range of bureaucratically codified reference numbers, online identities, passwords and usernames (Chapter 6). These allow for large amounts of people to be organised and identified. Increasingly, modern society demands that we learn to think and act like bureaucrats.

Learning to think and act bureaucratically involves learning to retain, compile, manage, store and access large amounts of personal information codified in the form of birth certificates, digital identities, passports, drivers licences, bank details and so on. All of these types of information are necessary to access other sources of personal information such as details about our income, medical certification, housing benefits award letters, user identification numbers, etc. For individuals who find it difficult to retain, organise and manage this information it can be very difficult to engage with an increasing number of mainstream institutions and services.

People from a social habitus characterised by ongoing stress, worries and anxieties about money and who are subject to verbal threats and physical violence are denied the social-relational context in which to develop the kinds of rational traits necessary for negotiating bureaucratic structures and systems. A central claim of Elias is that the disposition towards acting with foresight, towards thinking in forward-looking ways, deferring immediate gratification to achieve long-term goals, is not an innate trait or attribute some individuals possess and others do not. Rather this disposition can develop only in a context where strong emotions and feelings are sufficiently bracketed off from consciousness. The social habitus of marginalized groups makes it significantly less likely that the kinds of measured, forward-thinking and systematic approaches to managing one's own life and relationships develop. Taking the time to compile, sort through, follow-up, file and manage personal records and information forms part of a disposition towards everyday life that is far less likely to develop in a social habitus defined by low levels of self-regulation and correspondingly low levels of foresight and rationality.

Viewed from outside of the social habitus, failing to retain, compile and manage personal records, documents and information could be construed as lazy or demonstrative of a lack of care and concern. It may seem as if the service-user does not care to manage their personal affairs. Reconsidered in light of Elias's concept of social habitus, however, such a view appears limited. It involves individualizing what in actuality concerns a range of socially shaped dispositions and an orientation towards everyday life rooted (or not) in the social habitus of the group. To claim that the individual is culpable because they have neglected to think ahead, manage their own affairs, follow procedures, stay within the rules, etc. is to assume that these dispositions and orientations were available to them in the first place, but instead they actively and consciously choose not to enact. But these are not capacities that can be consciously willed or learned overnight – they are socially shaped attributes that form part of and are bound up in a lifestyle far less likely to develop in a social habitus characterised by social conditions hitherto described.

Social habitus, identity and anti-social behaviour

Elias's work pays close attention to the emotional and affective dimensions of human groups. Rejecting the view that differences in emotional temperament are explicable primarily in individualistic and psychological terms, Elias wanted to demonstrate the significance of changes to the type and organization of social relations. The concept of social habitus captures how changes to social relations lead to changes in individual temperament over time, and vice versa. This is true in a general sense, as well as being contingent on and realized across concrete situations and contexts. It is important to take a moment here to discuss the significance of the term 'dispositions'.

Dispositions are not the same as traits. The notion of 'traits' denotes fixed and static attributes that act on the individual in a mechanical cause and effect kind of way e.g. possession of trait A necessarily and always causes behaviour B. By contrast, the term *disposition* alludes to notions of probability, likelihood and/or tendencies e.g. given that individual A is disposed to perceive situations and people in a particular way, they tend to act and react in certain ways and not others. Moreover, whereas traits are presented as being relatively static, *dispositions* are processual.

As opposed to 'traits', dispositions cannot be used to define people in a 'once and for all' kind of way. To say that someone possesses certain traits e.g. a violent, or aggressive temper is to describe a core aspect of their personality. The term *traits* is typically associated with the psychological concept of personality, a notion we have already identified (Chapter 4) as presenting a more static and fixed conception of human agents. Against this view, to say that someone is characterised by certain dispositions involves describing them in a far more open-ended and indefinite way. Dispositions are realized in and through concrete contexts. Dispositions imply a process: the dispositions of the individual are called forth by and shape the situation, and the dispositions shape how the situation unfolds.

Now that we have clarified the difference between traits and dispositions and how they relate to the concept of social habitus, ask yourself the following question: is it more *likely* that an individual from social habitus A or social habitus B will require social work assistance at some point in their life? (Remember, in posing this question we are operating in *general* not *absolute* terms.) The answer is that it is impossible to know for sure. What we can say, however, is that compared to individuals socialized into social habitus A, it is more *likely* that individuals in habitus B will develop certain anti-social dispositions e.g. low levels of emotional and behavioural self-restraint, as well as being less likely to develop certain pro-social dispositions e.g. foresight, psychologization and rationality. On the basis of this reasoning, we can say that it is more likely – not necessary – that an individual from social habitus B will come into contact with social work services.

Why is this more likely to be the case? Members of habitus B are socialized into a habitus that *tends* to validate and legitimize emotional volatility, aggressive forms of masculinity and femininity, and lower levels of behavioural restraint. Individuals in social habitus B are less disposed to enact certain types of practices as part of a lifestyle characterised by sustained emotional and behavioural self-regulation e.g. pursuing certain forms of education and professional training, while being more disposed towards forms of activity and lifestyle characterised by lower levels of emotional and behavioural restraint e.g. when I saw a fight had broken out I went over to see if I could lend a hand. Social habitus B enables certain dispositions to develop, dispositions which allow the individual to participate in the lifestyle characteristic of the group e.g. a capacity to drink heavily; to be a competent fighter; not to back down from conflict and authority figures; to prefer the company of men over women and so on. A lifestyle subject to being negatively classified – as anti-social – outside of the group e.g. he was prone to excessive alcohol consumption; known for using his fists and resorting to violence very quickly; known to be confrontational and aggressive; prone to gang culture, etc.

It is important to clarify here that we are *not* saying that individuals socialized into social habitus B are definitively or necessarily more violent and aggressive, or incapable of thinking and acting with foresight and reason. Rather, the point is that individuals socialized into social habitus B are, generally speaking, more likely to demonstrate some or other of the tendencies that were described. Some individuals will demonstrate very few of those tendencies; others will embody some and not others; and some will demonstrate a great number if not all of those tendencies. Moreover, taken in isolation no one single factor shaping the individuals in social habitus B is necessarily significant in itself. Elias's point was that taken together, these dispositions and tendencies form a 'unity of behaviour' that, while never fully realized in any one individual, can nonetheless be observed to varying degrees in them all (Mennell, 1998).

The extent to which the dispositions of the habitus are realized in any particular individual is contingent on the position they occupy in the wider figuration of relations binding group members. Any attempt to intervene in the behaviour of members of social habitus B would involve viewing the individual 'in relation to' other individuals and the group as a whole – not as the result of purely internal traits or attributes working themselves out through the individual. It would mean applying the concept of social habitus to think about how individual dispositions shape and are shaped by the range of identities and lifestyle practices definitive of the group. It would mean looking at how those individual emotional and behavioural dispositions are informed by as well as forming part of the ways individuals assert their identity within the social habitus to which they belong.

Conclusion

This chapter has introduced the most significant theoretical concepts of Norbert Elias to social work. The aim of developing a conceptually versatile and long-term historical approach to understanding human societies and behaviour is a distinctive feature of Elias's work. His processual conception of human agents and society draws on and elaborates on concepts from a broad range of academic disciplines, including history, psychoanalytic theory, psychology and sociology. The result is a body of work which provides a highly original and innovative treatment of a diverse range of themes and phenomena. Some of those have been covered here, while others, such as old age and dying, insider and outsider groups, and differences in national temperament, comprise a rich source of ideas and insights which to date remain untapped by social work. Given the nature of the themes Elias's work explores in a way that combines theory and empirical research so elegantly, it is surprising that to date his work has not been taken up by social work thinkers and academics. This chapter has sought to address this, by demonstrating the value of Elias's ideas for informing a number of the central social and cultural processes relevant to contemporary social work.

Further reading

Elias, N. (1994 [1939]) *The Civilizing Process: Sociogenetic and Psychogenetic Investigations.* Oxford: Blackwell.
Elias, N. and Scotson, J. L. (1994 [1965]) *The Established and the Outsiders: A Sociological Enquiry into Community Problems.* London: Sage.
Mennell, S. (1998) *Norbert Elias: An Introduction.* Dublin: University College Dublin Press.

References

Cavaletto, G. (2007) *Crossing the Psycho-Social Divide: Freud, Weber, Adorno and Elias.* Aldershot: Ashgate.
Coleman, N. and Harris, J. (2008) 'Calling Social Work', *British Journal of Social Work,* 38(3): 580–599.
Dunning, E. (1994) 'The Social Roots of Football Hooliganism: A Reply to the Critics of the Leicester School', in Giulianotti, R. Bonney, N. and Hepworth, M. (eds.) *Football, Violence and Social Identity.* Routledge: London, pp. 123–153.
Elias, N. (1994 [1939]) *The Civilizing Process: Sociogenetic and Psychogenetic Investigations.* Oxford: Blackwell.
Elias, N. (2006 [1969]) *The Court Society*, Mennell, S. (ed.). Dublin: University College Dublin Press.
Elias, N. (1970) *What Is Sociology?* London: Hutchinson.
Elias, N. (1990) *The Germans: Power Struggles and the Development of Habitus in the Nineteenth and Twentieth Centuries.* Cambridge: Polity.
Elias, N. (1991) *The Society of Individuals.* Oxford: Blackwell.
Elias, N. and Dunning, E. (1986) *Quest for Excitement: Sport and Leisure in the Civilizing Process.* Oxford: Blackwell.
Elias, N. and Scotson, J. L. (1994 [1965]) *The Established and the Outsiders: A Sociological Enquiry into Community Problems.* London: Sage.
Fletcher, J. (1997) *Violence and Civilization.* Cambridge: Polity Press Ltd.
Freud, S. (2010 [1923]) *The Ego and the Id.* Seattle: Pacific Publishing Studio.
Freud, S. (2002 [1930]) *Civilization and Its Discontents.* London: Routledge.
Hanley, L. (2007) *Estates: An Intimate History.* London: Granta Books.
Lahire, B. (2013) 'Elias, Freud and the Human Science', in Depelteau, F. and Landini, T. S. (eds.) *Norbert Elias and Social Theory.* New York: Palgrave, pp. 75–90.

Landini, T. S. (2013) 'Main Principles of Elias' Sociology', in Depelteau, F. and Landini, T. S. (eds.) *Norbert Elias and Social Theory*. New York: Palgrave, pp. 13–30.

Littlechild, B. (2005) 'The Stresses Arising from Violence: Threats and Aggression against Child Protection Social Workers', *Journal of Social Work*, 5(1): 61–82.

Mennell, S. (1998) *Norbert Elias: An Introduction*. Dublin: University College Dublin Press.

Pahl, J. (1999) 'Coping with Physical Violence and Verbal Abuse', in Balloch, S., McLean, J., Pahl, J. and Fisher, M. (eds.) *Social Services: Working under Pressure*. Bristol: Policy Press, pp. 87–106.

Savaya, R., Gardner, F. and Strange, D. (2011) 'Stressful Encounters with Social Work Clients: A Descriptive Account Based on Critical Incidents', *Social Work*, 56(1): 63–71.

Swaan, A. de (1988) *In the Care of the State: Healthcare, Education, and Welfare in Europe and the USA in the Modern Era*. New York: Oxford University Press.

Van Krieken, R. (1998) *Norbert Elias*. London: Routledge.

6

MICHEL FOUCAULT

Social work and professional power

The 'care versus control' debate is a long-standing one within social work (Day, 1979). Is social work primarily about caring for or controlling the recipients of social work services? Or, does social work involve aspects of both? If so, in what ways and to what extent? These are complex and challenging questions, which fall to each generation of social workers to consider and respond. In recent years, the debate about care versus control has resurfaced within social work. A number of high-profile public cases have led to questions being raised about the often contradictory role social workers play as both bound by a duty of care, but also being required to intervene in and take control of the actions of service-users and those involved in their lives.

One approach to considering the debate about care versus control involves looking back in time. Understanding how social work has changed over time allows us to gain a sense of whether or not social work today is more about caring for, as opposed to controlling, service-users. Looking back at how social work was organized and delivered in the past, the image staring back at us seems scarcely recognisable. The overtly religious moral categories social workers used to adjudge individuals as either deserving or undeserving appear crude. The informal knowledge and practice wisdom social workers deferred to was unsystematic and unsophisticated, and the resources and services available to service-users seem limited and inadequate.

Compared to the way it was practiced a century ago, it seems beyond question that social work today is far more about care than control: self-determination and self-empowerment are core social work values in the present day; the knowledge base of social work draws on scientific theories and concepts from the 'psych-' and social scientific disciplines; and the range of opportunities and services available to service-users is broader and more specialized than ever before. Confronted with the image of social work as it was practiced more than a century ago, by comparison social work today seems progressive, emancipatory and person-centred.

But how accurate is this view of social work in the present day? In what ways can social work be said to have positively progressed over time? Are the recipients of social work services subject to less control than they were historically? Are they freer to choose the kind of services provided to them? To what extent can social workers be said to control the knowledge and values informing social work practice? To what extent are social workers subject to control? And how is the care they provide for service-users constrained by the institutional and organisational contexts in which they operate? How aware are social workers of these constraints, and are they able to resist them?

This chapter critically engages with these questions by drawing on the theoretical ideas of French thinker Michel Foucault (1926–1984). Foucault's work has provided a rich set of theoretical resources for social work and healthcare academics (Chambon et al., 1999; Garrity, 2010; Powell, 2012; Powell and Khan, 2012; Hardy, 2015). The concepts of 'discourse' and 'governmentality' in particular have been used to critically interrogate the relations between the state, social workers and service-users. Foucault's work has also been used to raise questions about the rise of surveillance discourse and practice within social work (Garret, 2005; Parrot and Madoc-Jones, 2008; Parton, 2008; Selwyn, 2002). Engaging with these themes, this chapter begins by explicating the concepts of discourse and governmentality and the importance of these for the view that social workers operate now in a 'surveillance society'. We then use these concepts to think about issues of care and control with reference to the social work relationship. Specifically, the categories used to construct the recipients of social work services, the increasing 'digitization' of social work and the rising dominance of individual-centred and 'psych-' discourse within social work education.

Language, discourse and power

Michel Foucault was a French social theorist, historian and philosopher. Foucault's early work was influenced by French structuralist theory, whereas his later work played a formative role in the development of post-structuralism in France. Structuralism employs a depth metaphor for thinking about social reality. In this view, what takes place at the surface level is in actuality determined by social structures operating at a far deeper level of reality. At a surface level, social life appears changeable, characterised by a constant flux of fleeting interactions, situations and events. Structuralists claim that what takes place at a surface level is in fact determined by relatively static and enduring structures operating at a deeper level. Structuralists direct their attention towards the underlying structures that condition what takes place at a surface level.

Structuralism has its origins in the work of Emile Durkheim (Chapter 2) and the French anthropologist Claude Levi-Strauss (1908–2009). From Durkheim, structuralism draws on the conception of culture as akin to a meaning-generating mechanism. Culture provides the collectively shaped symbols and meanings human groups use to construct and classify their experiences in shared and meaningful ways. Language is a primary example of this. From Levi-Strauss, structuralism focusses on the importance of culturally shaped 'myths' (Levi-Strauss, 1978). Cultural myths are the over-arching narratives human groups use to make sense of the world and their place within it in collectively meaningful and coherent ways. The ideas of Durkheim and Levi-Strauss are central to Foucault's earlier work, which combines and elaborates on elements drawn from both. Another highly influential thinker for understanding Foucault's work is the Swiss structural linguist Ferdinand de Saussure (1857–1913).

Saussure's structuralist model of language is central to Foucault's concept of 'discourse'. Saussure wanted to understand the relationship between language and meaning. His central claim is that the meaning of words is not determined by the things they refer to – the common sense view of language – but derives instead from the position words occupy in the wider structure of the language to which they belong (Saussure, 1959 [1906–11]). Saussure developed this claim by distinguishing between two different approaches to the analysis of language. Language can be understood from a *diachronic* perspective. This involves analysing how the meanings conveyed by language develop and change over time. Adopting a *synchronic* perspective involves analysing the internal structure by which language is organised. This remains unchanging and stable over time. Saussure analysed language from a synchronic perspective, focussing on the enduring and fixed structures contained within language as an overall system of meaning (Saussure, 1959 [1906–11]). A key idea here is that the structures hidden within language shape the meaning of words in ways that the users of language do not fully grasp.

Saussure's structuralist account of language forms the basis for Foucault's conception of social reality. Herein, social life is understood as comprising multiple, overlapping and mutually reinforcing systems of meaning. These systems of meaning are made up of different 'languages', which Foucault refers to as 'discourse'. Discourse refers to the ways people think about and communicate ideas and concepts to one another. Sociologists, for example, use sociological discourse to think about and explain ideas about society; psychologists use psychological discourse to explain and talk about the mind. The point to make is that discourse does not reflect or represent the true nature of the things to which it refers e.g. society, the mind. Instead, each discourse creates its own reality, and creates its own objects – the meanings sociologists and psychologists attribute to the concepts of 'society' and the 'mind'. It may *appear* like a discourse is referring to real things, but it is actually merely referring to its own constructions of those things. Discourse works to produce knowledge about the things it refers to, and not, as common sense understandings of language would have us believe, the other way round.

According to Foucault (1977 [1975]), discourse is inextricably bound up with and cannot be separated out from power. Discourse is empowering because it enables people to construct and make sense of their experiences, in turn providing the basis for action and interaction. At the same time, however, discourse exerts power over them by making them think that what they are referring to are real things, when in fact what they are referring to is actually shaped and constructed through discourse. Most of the time people are unaware that their thinking has been shaped by discourse. They think that how they see the world is the way the world is. They do not realize that it is the discourse they use that creates the meanings they attach to things. Discourses exert power over the minds in individuals in ways of which they are largely unaware. This is because generally and without knowing it, we can only ever think and perceive in ways shaped by the discourse (Elden, 2017). The power of discourse is that it constrains the individual to think about the world in certain ways and not others.

Discourse is most powerful when it thoroughly shapes an individual's perceptions at a wholly subconscious level. When this occurs, the ways of thinking and perceiving specific to the discourse appear natural and inevitable. Because they appear natural – just how things are – over time the power exerted by discourse becomes invisible to the people using and shaped by it (Foucault, 1988). In this view, each person is a prisoner of the discourses they draw on and operate within. Foucault aims to bring into consciousness all of these things, by revealing to people the discursive structures which imperceptibly shape how they think and act. More

TABLE 6.1 Summary of discourse

Discourses
• comprise ways of perceiving, thinking, talking
• create the objects to which they refer
• present those objects as real
• become normalized and naturalized over time
• exert power over those who use them and those labelled by them

specifically, his work attempts to 'deconstruct' the dominant forms of discourse structuring the minds of people in modern Western society, by focussing on a number of culturally pervasive and powerful myths about Western science, humanism and Marxism. These include the view of scientific forms of knowledge as objective and impartial; modern society as rational, progressive and 'freer' than in the past; the human psyche as a rational, unified and knowable entity; and power as primarily class-based.

The discourses embedded in these myths work to promote certain ideas, values and beliefs. Rather than seeing the ideals and assumptions embedded in these myths as objective and timeless truths, Foucault regards them instead as forms of discourse like any other. These myths exert power over and constrain the minds of individuals under their sway, primarily by working to conceal the interests and ideals of dominant social groups. A central notion here is that *any* attempt to explain and define reality is a product of discourse. This is true even of scientific forms of knowledge which claim to provide an 'objective' picture of reality as it exists outside of language. In his early work Foucault adopted an 'archaeological' method, whereas his later work employs a 'genealogical' approach to tracing out the operation of power (Foucault, 2001 [1966], 1981). A central notion underpinning both methods is the view that as society has developed throughout history, different types of discourse have emerged, each of which has led to the people within the discourse making sense of and constructing reality in radically different ways. Whether or not these ways of constructing reality can be said to be truer, progressive and rational is not something that can ever be known outside of discourse. It is more accurate instead to note that as the structures of society develop over time, different types of discourse are brought into being and created, which in turn shape how our understanding of reality is constructed (Foucault, 2002 [1969]).

The rise of governmentality

The concept of discourse is central to Foucault's ideas about 'governmentality'. Governmentality refers to the processes by which the state uses powerful forms of discourse to construct, control and coerce the minds and bodies of the population. This is what governmentality means: to 'govern' the 'mentality' of the population. In key texts such as *Discipline and Punish* (1975), Foucault demonstrates a shift in state power away from physical violence and corporeal punishment e.g. public executions and floggings, towards exerting control over the minds of the population. As rising numbers of people throughout the seventeenth and eighteenth centuries began to converge on the growing towns and cities, the threat or actualisation of physical violence became less effective as a way of exercising state power. It often led to violent protests or, worse still, the threat of revolution. Over time, the focus of state authorities began to shift away from the bodies of the citizenry, towards scrutiny and reform of their bodies and minds instead.

A key development informing changes to the organisation and use of state power was the rise of the human sciences (Foucault, 2006 [1961], 1977 [1975]). Unlike the natural sciences which compile information and knowledge about inert matter, the human sciences are used to classify and support rationalizations for practices that take human subjects as their focus. The development of statistical and scientific methods provided governments with important information about population numbers, medical disease, wealth and natural resources. Throughout the seventeenth and eighteenth centuries, the natural and social sciences – natural (e.g. medicine) and social (e.g. criminology) and a fusion of the natural and the social (e.g. psychiatry, psychology and sociology) – developed. These new forms of scientific knowledge were represented as wholly objective, and not as forms of discourse that construct the very things they claim are real.

For example, as a science such as psychology has changed it has moved from being one sort of discourse to another, with the new discourse imagining the human mind in radically new ways from its predecessor. Likewise, as new social sciences were invented, particularly from the eighteenth century onwards, they claimed to investigate particular types of people – 'criminals' in the case of criminology, 'psychiatric patients' in the case of psychiatry – as if such types of people already naturally existed. But it is the discourse that creates the category of 'criminal' and 'psychiatric patient', etc., such that these types of people are invented by the discourses themselves. Far from being objective, the claims of the natural and social sciences actively bring into existence the very things they claim are 'real'. In this sense, each discourse creates its own 'truths', which it then endlessly seeks to confirm and reconfirm.

A discourse creates the very things it takes as its focus. When a discourse such as psychotherapy studies people defined as 'patients', it exerts power over those people. This is why Foucault claims that knowledge and power are thoroughly interpenetrating. Power is exerted on people through discourse because the people who are the focus of the discourse typically take on its labelling of them and its definition of who they are. Discourses such as psychotherapy tell those under its influence what sort of person they are, why this category of person is experiencing certain problems, and, by contrast, what a 'normal' person is. In ways that are often implicit, discourses such as psychotherapy make 'normalizing judgements'. These judgements shape the process by which the people in control of the discourse (e.g. psychotherapists) attempt to remake the person so that they become like the ideal of the 'normal' person depicted by the discourse. The knowledge experts – criminologists, psychiatrists, psychologists – who create and control the discourse collect information about the people who have been labelled. This knowledge is then used to try to turn the individual into the 'normal' person depicted by the discourse.

From the period of the Enlightenment in the eighteenth century, the myths about science as more sophisticated and humane than ways of thinking in the past steadily infiltrated the wider culture. But in actuality, the development of the natural and human sciences has not led, as was claimed they would, to people being freer from the effects of power. Instead, Foucault claimed, the human sciences have led to people being controlled in far less conspicuous, more subtle and efficient ways than was possible in the past. The new 'masters of discourse', such as psychiatric doctors and other forms of social and 'psych-' scientists, while claiming to free those they scrutinized, were able to exert power far more effectively, because the power they yielded was aimed at the minds and souls of the people they examined. At first, these discourses were exercised in newly created institutions, such as mental asylums and certain types of prison. These locales were where the normalizing judgements of the discourse were exercised upon people – institutions which were designed to keep the people contained within them under the constant surveillance of the authorities and those who controlled the discourses.

A particularly striking expression of the shifting focus of power from the body to the mind identified by Foucault (1977 [1975]) was the type of prison designed by the nineteenth century English social reformer Jeremy Bentham. The Panopticon ('all-seeing eye' in Greek) is a ring-shaped building with an all-seeing tower at its centre. The tower is positioned in the middle of the ring such that the windows on the tower enable all of the surrounding cells to be observed. Each cell contains a single individual made visible at all times by the windows positioned at either end. Prisoners are always under scrutiny from the guards in the tower. Their every move can be seen at all times, and the prisoners know this. Because of the way the tower is designed, what the prisoners cannot see is if the guards are actually there. Power resides in the inequality of relations of visibility between the two groups. The prisoners have to assume they are being watched, and the sense of constantly being watched becomes habituated over time. Even when there are no guards in the tower, the prisoners assume the guards are there. The thought that they are being watched exerts power over the minds of the individuals. It is the thought of constantly being watched – and not whether it is necessarily true or not – that compels the prisoners to regulate themselves and how they behave in the ways demanded of them by the prison and its discourse.

A situation where both mind and body are subject to self-regulation is one in which the norms of discourse have become totally normalized. According to Foucault (1977 [1975]: 175), the 'panoptic' principles spread out from prisons in the nineteenth century, infiltrating an ever greater range of institutions, such as hospitals, barracks, orphanages and schools. Each institution is characterised by its own specialist discourse, regimes and techniques of power (e.g. constant visibility, normalizing judgements, use of abstract statistics, etc.). These work upon, shape and coerce the minds and bodies of those within the institution 'with the aim of creating manageable subjects' (Foucault, 1977 [1975]: 107). As modernity has developed, the myth that scientific knowledge will liberate people from traditional forms of power has developed too. But modernity has not led to greater freedom and liberation; it is characterised instead by multiple forms of discourse which produce and exert even more insidious and sophisticated forms of power. Furthermore, these are not operated by a single ruling class, as claimed by Marxists, but develop and are deployed by multiple types of experts and knowledge specialists. Whereas Weber likened modern society to an iron cage of bureaucracy and rationality, Foucault likens modern society to a prison – one made up of different populations, each of which is brought into being and constrained by the multiple forms of discourse exerted over it.

A central claim made by Foucault is that power always creates resistance. Foucault identifies the constraining effects of power, but recognises too how it can work in ways that are productive and in some senses positive too. This is the view that naming and identifying things as in need of being studied and scrutinized – 'criminals' in the case of criminology, 'psychiatric patients' in the case of psychiatry, etc. – plays an important part in bringing those very things into existence. By invoking the concept of 'mental illness', for example, not only are the individuals who are defined as 'mentally ill' monitored and controlled, at the same time their status

TABLE 6.2 Summary of governmentality

Governmentality
<ul><li>state-led process beginning in the sixteenth century</li><li>refers to changes to state power over the population</li><li>characterised by shift in power away from the body to the mind of social subjects</li><li>seeks to reconstitute, classify and evaluate subjectivity of citizenry in line with natural and social scientific forms of discourse</li><li>gives rise to surveillance society</li></ul>

is recognised and legitimized, and certain rights granted to them. In other words, power is not always or exclusively negative and oppressive. It works to reconstitute and reshape things in ways that are positive too. This takes place as power brings into being oppositional categories, dispositions and forces which it identifies as the things over which power is to be exerted.

Governmentality in surveillance society

Foucault invokes the Panopticon as a central metaphor for grasping the nature and dynamics of power in modern society. As the 'panoptic' principles have spread out into wider society, the exercise of power has become increasingly organised around discourses and practices of surveillance (Haggerty, 2006). Significant events such as the terrorist attacks of 9/11, the expansion of the European Union and the global spread of transnational corporations have all led to the intensification of the processes and dynamics of surveillance. This is particularly the case of societies in Western Europe and North America (Lyon, 1994). A degree of surveillance has existed in every society, but modern society is organised around surveillance to such an extent that it has come to be referred to as 'surveillance society' (Lyon, 2001).

Accompanying the rise of surveillance society is what Garland (2001: 195) refers to as a 'culture of control'. Social trust is steadily eroded under the conditions of surveillance society to the extent that surveillance is no longer something undertaken exclusively by government agencies and authorities. Ordinary people in their everyday lives are increasingly concerned with and actively involved in surveillance discourse and practice (Lyon, 1994, 2001). This is so in myriad ways: home security cameras; the use of 'nanny-cams'; cameras on cyclists' helmets and in cars; states encouraging people to identify those who avoid paying tax, engage in illegal activities, fraudulently claim benefit, etc. In Foucault's original model, relations of visibility between the watcher and the watched were uneven and one-directional. In surveillance society, the relationship becomes uni-directional, as all members of society come to assume simultaneously the roles of watcher and watched.

Surveillance involves the systematic and routinized direction of attention on individuals and their personal details (Lyon, 2003, 2007). This is surveillance realized through procedures and legislation, in ways that connect directly with the aims and values of governmentality. As surveillance discourse and practice spread, they become increasingly embedded in and part of the administration of everyday life. Developments in information technologies are integral to this process, particularly in the form of electronic and digital databases. This has led to what Gordon (1990) refers to as the 'electronic panopticon', allied to which is the concept of 'dataveillance'

TABLE 6.3 Summary of surveillance society

Surveillance society
• organised and structured around surveillance discourse and practice • erodes social trust and gives rise to culture of control • transforms subjects into watchers and watched • typically justified using discourses of risk, control and prevention

(Clarke, 1997). Dataveillance refers to the monitoring of people's activities and communications using personal data systems (Clarke, 1997). Dataveillance involves making subjects visible through amassing data about them, in turn creating an inequality of knowledge about subjects. Government organisations and state bureaucracies have always sought to catalogue information about subjects. Traditionally this was very costly, in terms of both time and labour power. Electronic forms of surveillance have proliferated because they provide far more cost efficient ways for states to monitor whole populations (Haggerty and Ericson, 2000).

Changes in surveillance practices are one dimension of surveillance society. Another concerns the processes by which long-held ideals and values come to be undermined and eroded (Lyon, 2007). One of the normative assumptions underpinning surveillance discourse is that there exists something that needs to be watched for, monitored and safe-guarded against. While this is not always or exclusively the case, such as in the case of the surveillance techniques used by powerful corporate agencies such as Amazon to profile consumers' tastes, nevertheless much state-led policy is framed within discourses centring on notions of risk and prevention (Beck, 1992). What exactly constitutes risk, and how prevention of risks is enacted, are contested by different groups. In many cases, this has led to discourses of risk and surveillance practices blurring the boundaries between the private and the public, in turn giving rise to moral ambiguities and the emergence of new ethical questions and debates (Marx, 1988).

Applying Foucault to social work

Social work discourse and the construction of service-users

Foucault's concept of discourse provides a powerful analytical tool for casting light on a number of contemporary developments within social work. This includes the different ways the categories of 'social worker' and 'service-user' have been constructed over time, as well as highlighting the shifting power relations and dynamics embedded in the relations between the two. It also serves as a useful tool for critically considering how the construction of these categories has been shaped by and connects to the wider social and historical processes of governmentality.

What exactly the term *social worker* and the various terms used to refer to those in receipt of social work services mean have changed over time. In line with the restructuring of social work training from the late 1970s, the education of social workers has become an increasingly important site for reconstituting the subjectivity of social work professionals, and by extension, the recipients of social work services (Jones, 1989). This is so in a number of ways but primarily through the formalization and consolidation of an increasingly standardized and professionally regulated curriculum. The education and professional training of social workers vary across different national contexts. In Britain, students are required to undertake a degree in social work approved by the Health and Care Professions Council (HCPC).

From a Foucauldian perspective, the education of social work students is a key moment in the reconstitution of their subjectivity. Over the course of their degree in social work, students are taught and acquire knowledge from a range of academic disciplines including criminology, sociology, developmental psychology, law, etc. By internalizing these forms of discourse, the everyday ways of thinking students import with them into their professional training are reconfigured and reconstituted in the ways demanded by the profession. The subjectivity of social work students is reshaped and reconstituted by the forms of knowledge informing social work discourse. The forms of knowledge – e.g. social work theory, sociology, psychology and so on – construct the category – i.e. 'social worker' – that the people – i.e. 'social work students' – within the discourse come to internalize.

The knowledge social work students acquire during their professional training provides the discursive categories they use to organise their relationship with service-users. The discourse sets the parameters in which the social work relationship is structured. There is nothing natural or inevitable about the meanings contained in the category of 'service-user'. The category of 'service-user' is a discursive construct. The category means different things in different places and has varied over time. The category of 'service-user' derives its meaning from and is constituted by social work discourse. Social work discourse creates the category of 'social worker' at the same time as it brings into being and defines the category of 'service-user'. The category of 'service-user' is determined by the forms of discourse social workers bring to bear on the recipients of social work services. The discourses social workers use to structure their encounters with service-users are not *passive* meanings through which the recipients of social work services are understood. The discourses *actively* reconstitute the recipients of social work services as 'service-users'.

The relationships between social workers and service-users are organised around and by the knowledge social workers acquire during their professional training. Social workers are constituted by and are carriers of discourse. Social workers are shaped by discourse because the knowledge that they internalize during training reconstructs their subjectivity in professionally sanctioned and legitimate ways. They are carriers of discourse because the practices they enact e.g. ways of thinking, acting, interacting, etc. actively reconstruct the recipients of social work services as 'service-users'. Social workers are constituted and shaped by social work discourse, at the same time as the enactment of social work discourse brings into being the category of 'service-user'. The discourse social workers use to construct their encounters with service-users is the product of much wider struggles for power between the state, the social work profession and other professional groups e.g. the legal profession, criminologists, sociologists, psychologists and so on. Irrespective of the personal attitude and ethics of a particular social worker, embedded within the structure of the social work relationship are relations of power. The discursive categories social workers use to construct and organise the social work relationship are shot through with relations of power rooted in the wider historical development of the profession and the wider social struggles in which it is embedded.

A good example of the ways discourse works to reshape and reorganise the subjectivity of service-users comprises children and young people. Historically, children and childhood have been subject to high levels of scrutiny and control. Childhood comprises one of the most intensely governed sectors of human existence (Rose, 1999). As a discursively shaped category, children are understood to embody the future of society (Aries, 1962). How children and young people are discursively framed is closely controlled and highly contested. As counter-intuitive as it may seem, there is no natural or necessary way of understanding the categories of 'children' and 'childhood'. These terms are understood and defined by socially shaped forms of discourse.

Moss and Petrie (2002) use the concepts of 'discourse' and 'governmentality' to critically interrogate how children and childhood are constructed in the present day, and how in turn these discursive categories are used to justify child welfare and policy. They are critical of the ideals and assumptions embedded within developmental psychological forms of discourse which depict early childhood experiences as 'formative' and 'indelible' (Breur, 1999). By drawing on powerful forms of scientific 'psych-' discourse, normative ideas about children being needy, vulnerable, passive and dependent are used by the state to justify a range of behaviours, institutions and policies aimed at regulating the minds and bodies of children (Moss and Petrie, 2002). By constructing a range of abstract and standardized 'developmental stages', the state has framed childhood within a scientific discourse that claims to assert the 'truth' about children and their psychological development. Moss and Petrie are critical of the 'universalizing' claims to truths embedded in scientific discourse. Instead, and like all forms of discourse, those claims are socially shaped, refracting the interests and concerns of the state, other professional groups and a range of expert forms of authority (Moss and Petrie, 2002).

The terms used to categorise the recipients of social work services highlight changes over time in power dynamics within the social work relationship. During the 1970s, the term *client* was widely used within social work discourse, eventually losing currency on the grounds that it depicted individuals as 'passive' (McDonald, 2009). The increasing marketization of social work during the 1980s led to the term *consumer* becoming commonplace. The term *consumer* suggests a balance of power between social workers and consumers, which empowers the latter at the expense of the former. Consumers have expectations. The consumer is always 'king', and the fulfilment of their wishes paramount, irrespective of how realistic those expectations may or may not be (Harris, 1999). More recently, the term *service-user* has become the standard term used to categorise the recipients of social work services (McLaughlin, 2009). The category of 'service-users' is criticized for a number of reasons. First, it creates a semantic link between the term *user* and the users of substances. Second, it fails to differentiate the reason for using welfare services, which runs the risks of depicting service-users as members of one homogenous group. Third, referring to individuals as 'service-users' involves constructing their subjectivity primarily on the basis of the services they use, while foregrounding other aspects of their identity (e.g. mother, worker, wife) at the same time.

The term *expert by experience* emerged as a form of self-conscious resistance on the part of groups in receipt of social work services, particularly those with varying forms of disability (Beresford and Croft, 2001). More broadly, the formation of the 'user-movement' provides an example of how discourse can work to channel power in productive and positive ways. When individuals and service-user groups are classified in certain ways, the identity of those groups is realized and affirmed. Once positioned within and labelled by the discourse, the people in the discourse can renegotiate and redefine the terms and meanings used to classify them. Turning the discourse back on itself by redefining the terms and meanings contained within it results in greater power for the subjects of the discourse.

Social work and surveillance

Referred to as the 'electronic turn', or 'e-turn', the last twenty years have borne witness to the rise of information and communications technology (ICT) in the organisation, distribution and delivery of social work services (Garrett, 2004, 2005). The e-turn represents a key moment in restructuring the activities of social workers, crucially by opening up social workers and service-users to multiple and new forms of electronically mediated surveillance. The term *dataveillance* refers to the monitoring of people's activities and communications using ICT to create personal data systems. Dataveillance involves making human subjects visible through amassing data about them. Under the conditions of surveillance society, social work has becoming oriented towards gathering, sharing and monitoring information about service-users (Parton, 2008).

The rise of ICT within social work has impacted significantly on social work in multiple ways. Many social work academics and professionals regard the rise of ICT as part of the shift towards a government-led culture of managerialism and control within the profession (Rogowski, 2011). As Munro (2004: 1086) notes, 'there is considerable anecdotal evidence' that the digitization of the social work relationship is having a perverse effect on practice, 'with a concern for meeting government targets overriding a concern for the welfare of users'. In a situation of dataveillance, service-users are no longer regarded first and foremost as social subjects. Instead, they come to be reconstituted as objects of a range of powerful discourses. This can be seen in terms of the shifting focus of social work away from the relational and social aspects of the service-user, towards the informational content of the social work relationship instead (Parton, 2008).

In the past, knowledge about service-users was built up over time through person-centred relationships and face-to-face interactions. Knowledge about service-users was stored primarily in the minds of social workers. Personal knowledge formed the basis for constructing shared and meaningful narratives with service-users about the difficulties they were experiencing. Working together on terms negotiated by and meaningful to both parties provided the social work relationship with a sense of coherence and stability. The increasing use of ICT in the relationship between social workers and service-users undermines a narrative-based approach to problem solving (Gilbert and Powell, 2009). Narrative-based methods and models are not conducive to generating and organising the kinds of information that require to be inputted into and stored within centrally managed and shared databases.

Information about service-users is compiled over a number of stages. This involves social workers actively dismantling service-users' thoughts, feelings, actions and experiences and reclassifying and recoding them in line with standardized terminologies and categories (White et al., 2009). Information not relevant to identifying and constructing the most efficient solution to the service-users' issues and problems tends to be filtered out and discarded (Munro, 2004). The terminologies and categories used to classify the service-user belong to one or another type of generic case e.g. housing, healthcare, etc., and are set by the database, not the social worker. The professional discernment of the social worker is bypassed by the instrumental, impersonal and standardized classificatory codes generated by the database (Hudson, 2003). The identity of the service-user is stripped of its unique biography in order to be retranslated into data fragments which can be taken apart, abstracted and reassembled. The living, breathing service-user disappears before reappearing as a reconstituted, disembodied and decontextualized informational category stored in a central database (Parton, 2008).

The abstract categories and codes supplied by electronic databases strip the social work relationship of its unique social, cultural and professional significance. The role played by situational factors, professional wisdom, and emotional insights and intuitions in shaping the social work relationship is diminished (Hasler, 2003). The meanings of the words and modes of expression used by service-users to communicate their thoughts and feelings – meanings often expressed in forms of restricted code rooted in the lifeworld – require to be decoded and standardized to fit with the abstract terms and criteria determined by the database. The opportunity to develop a holistic approach towards working with service-users is diminished. The very real human costs of service-users' problems – the narratives of pain and suffering expressed within and that define the social work relationship – cannot be adequately grasped (Ruch, 2012).

Through the use of ICT and digitized systems, information about social workers and service-users has become increasingly transparent, shared and accessible. As social workers become more reliant on ICT, the social work relationship has become increasingly structured by the normative assumptions contained within the discourse on risk. In a culture of control a concern with managing and controlling people and situations through attempting to anticipate, identify and eliminate risk becomes paramount (Garland, 2001; Beck, 1992). The need to gather information is justified on the grounds that it allows social workers to anticipate and identify potentially high-risk situations. The information is then abstracted from the situations and context in which it first arose, before being taken up and applied to other contexts and cases. Social workers feel under pressure from management to gather information about service-users as the need to anticipate, identify and eliminate risk becomes greater (Community Care, 2017). Supporting clients becomes secondary to a concern with identifying outcomes and risks, and accounting for decisions and practice becomes an end in itself, one that eats into the time available for getting on with the job (Parton, 1996).

Discourses of risk are also used to justify the need for increasing transparency with regard to the decisions and actions taken by social workers. Information enables auditing and the possibility to undertake risk assessment (Parot and Madoc-Jones, 2008). This is particularly true where children and young people are concerned (Garrett, 2004). Operating in a situation of increased transparency – part of which includes increasing awareness of being watched and an object of surveillance – social workers find their professional discretion being steadily eroded. Social workers feel constrained to think and act in ways structured by complex and often contradictory procedures, rather than relying on their experience, sense of professional judgement, situational knowledge and cues to make decisions. Reframed and reconstituted in a discourse of risk, the kinds of creative and collaboratively negotiated responses to service-users' problems are less likely to occur as social workers come to operate in a 'culture of blame and protocolization' (Munro, 2004).

Governmentality and social work

Is social work about caring for or controlling service-users? The concept of governmentality can be used to explore this question in greater depth. It provides an analytical framework with which to critically survey state-led concerns to create and coerce manageable subjects and how in turn these have informed changes to the development of social work education over time. To do this means applying an historical perspective to social work education. In conventional approaches to history, how people thought and acted in the past is represented as being very different from the present. Foucault used the intellectual methods of archaeology and geneal-ogy to reverse this situation. He regarded the role of history and historical change as a way of problematizing and de-familiarizing the ordering of society today. The value of the past is that it provides a range of alternative perspectives for thinking about and seeing the present. It is the present, not the past, which should be viewed as something strange and unfamiliar.

A key point for Foucault is the claim that scientific forms of knowledge and discourse are objective and impartial. Foucault's work focusses on the historical and political processes by which scientific forms of discourse have come to be understood as representing the 'truth' about human subjects, at the same time as dismissing and marginalizing other forms of knowl-edge. The concept of governmentality can be used to think about social work education today and open up new ways of considering the debate about care versus control. Instead of viewing social work education and the curriculum today as the latest point in a much wider histori-cal and progressive trajectory, it requires to be conceived instead as arising out of and marked by struggles for power between the state, social work and the human sciences. Using the past to think critically about how we understand the present allows us to question how and why certain ways of thinking and discursive knowledge shape social work education today. Cast-ing a critical light on the structure and content of social work education in the present day allows us to think about and raise questions about whose interests are served by organising it in this way.

This can be a difficult notion to grasp. The notion that scientific discourse is impartial and progressive, and necessarily brings us closer to a more refined appreciation of reality, is deeply ingrained within modern culture. Discourse makes possible certain ideas and beliefs while closing off and shutting down others. This is exactly what Foucault means when he claims that discourse exerts power over the minds of individuals. When social work students embark on a university degree, the programme of study laid out before them is represented as the culmination of a long period of progress and development. The implicit assumption here is that over time, social work discourse has become normatively more refined and conceptu-ally more sophisticated. In the past, social work was oriented more towards controlling the recipients of social work services; today it is oriented more towards caring for and empower-ing them. Adopting a 'governmentality perspective' involves critically challenging this view, by revealing the structures and relations of power embedded in the structure of social work education today.

Using broad-brush terms this section of the chapter depicts the development of social work education from a governmentality perspective. Key here is a concern to explain how and why social work education in the present day is dominated by individual-centred forms of knowledge and discourse – more specifically still, individual-centred forms of 'psych-', as opposed to sociological and social theoretical, forms of discursive knowledge. How and why these forms of discursive knowledge dominate the social work curriculum in the present day can be explained by drawing on the concept of governmentality.

The institutionalization of social work education in Britain took place in the early moments of the twentieth century. Prior to that, the task of educating and training social workers was loosely overseen by voluntary enterprises organised by the Charity Organisation Society (COS) (Webb, 1996). In 1902, this arrangement changed when the COS founded the School of Sociology at the London School of Economics. A major moral concern behind the founding of the School was to ensure that social workers were provided with the kind of knowledge and training which could shield them from being contaminated by the emotionally distressing situations to which they were exposed (Smith, 1957). The consensus was that social workers exposed to the suffering and distress of the poorest members of society would impact negatively on them: either the social worker would feel discouraged and demoralised by the lives of service-users; or, they would defect from the profession and become radical social critics. In many ways this has remained a central tension within social work through to the present day.

According to Jones (1996: 192), for knowledge to be selected as appropriate for social work education generally it must support the 'primacy of individualisation and endorse the prevailing social order'. For social work to be incorporated into the newly formed welfare state, it had to operate within an intellectual and moral framework that tended towards individualizing the problems of service-users. Otherwise, the state ran the risk of actively training a professional group qualified to identify at close-hand its failure to address a wide range of social problems and inequalities (Lubove, 1966). It is important to note here that social work education developed in a context capable of sustaining two opposing perspectives for understanding the causes of service-users' problems. On the one hand, service-users' problems can be broadly conceived as rooted in the individual and/or the familial context in which they are/were raised. On the other, the causes of those problems derive ultimately from a range of impersonal social-structural factors, such as class-based inequalities, ethnic and gender discrimination. That social work has tended historically towards the former cannot be explained without reference to the wider aims and ideals of the state.

Integration into the bureaucratic and legislative structures of the newly formed welfare state both enabled and constrained the development of social work in Britain. On an ideological level, the overtly religious and moralising discourses brought to bear on service-users were no longer deemed appropriate to the explicitly secular and progressive ideals of a modern secular government. The view of social work as a charitable activity undertaken by members of the educated middle classes was no longer socially acceptable. Social work looked to developments in the human sciences to provide empirically grounded and objective forms of scientific knowledge with which to frame its aims, ideals and activities (Bamford, 2015). To draw on the discursive knowledge produced by these scientific disciplines was beneficial to the profession on two levels. It elevated the professional status of social work vis-à-vis a number of other social service and healthcare services, while providing a legitimate (scientific) discourse with which to frame social workers' activities and the problems confronting the recipients of social work services (Younghusband, 1951).

In the place of the overtly moralising and religiously charged discourse of social work's charitable legacy, the adaptation psychoanalytic discourse and models grew throughout the 1950s and '60s. Psychoanalytic discourse bolstered the professional legitimacy of social work, at the same time identifying the cause of those problems in the mind of the individual and the immediate family unit. While psychoanalytically inspired methods and theories flourished, the critical perspectives contained within sociological and social theoretical discourse were excluded or marginalized (Jones and Novak, 1993). Where sociological discourse continued to feature in the social work curriculum its role tended to be limited to justifying and promoting conservative ideals about the family as a key institution in maintaining social order (Leonard, 1966; Jones, 1996).

Towards the end of the 1960s the influence of psychoanalytic thinking within social work declined. This was due to changes to the internal organisation of social work services and wider shifts in the social and political culture of the period. The unification of personal social services bureaucracies by the 1970s had led to rising numbers of individuals being referred to social work services (Smith, 1965). Individual case work was time-consuming and fundamentally at odds with the bureaucratized and formal settings in which the social work relationship was increasingly situated. Away from social work, the social and political unrest of the late 1960s and '70s provided the conditions for the (re)emergence of more critical forms of social scientific knowledge and theory (Jones and Novak, 1993: 197). These were critical of the individualizing tendencies of psychoanalytic models. During this period the various strands of radical social work began to emerge, such as Marxist and feminist social work as well as emancipatory and anti-discriminatory discourse and practice. Rather than rooting the cause of service-users' problems in the individual psyche, Marxist and feminist social work discourse emphasised the role played by structures of class and patriarchy (see Chapters 2 and 8).

The appointment of Conservative leader Margaret Thatcher as Prime Minister in 1979 signified the beginning of a number of significant changes to the political and intellectual orientation of social work education. The conservative ideologies and policies of the newly elected government meant that sociological forms of discourse were once again regarded as socially and politically subversive because they were openly critical of the state and the unintended consequences of the role played by social work in maintaining a range of inequalities in society. Left in the hands of social workers critical social theory served to confirm many of the government's worst anxieties relating to the view of the social worker as social critic (Jones, 1989). As a response to the perceived dangers that particular forms of knowledge presented to the profession and state respectively, the Central Council for Education and Training in Social Work (CCETSW) was founded in 1971. The purpose of the CCETSW was to modernise social work education by reorganising the curriculum in line with the ideals and aims of the new conservative government.

The CCETSW was highly influential in the transformation of social work education. The composition of the Council was dominated by new managers rather than representatives from higher education institutions (Webb, 1996). From the late '70s until the disbandment of the Council in 2001 and the subsequent formation of the General Social Care Council (known as the Health and Care Professions Council since 2012), social work education has tended towards emphasising the value of practical training. In the reconstruction of social work within a discourse organised around the concept of vocation, the emphasis is on understanding the rules and regulations of the institutions and organisations social workers belong to in order to get the job done.

Since then, a number of critical social work academics have argued that social work education has gradually but steadily been hollowed out of its intellectual and theoretical content (Jones, 1996). Social scientific disciplines such as sociology and social theory where they are included in the curriculum have been steadily marginalized so as to have little impact, and instead the emphasis has shifted towards practice-based learning and evidenced-based forms of practice.

This section of the chapter has outlined, in very broad-brush terms, changes and developments to the social work curriculum in the U.K. Foucault's governmentality perspective means seeing those changes not as taking place in an intellectual vacuum, as the outcome of advances in knowledge about human subjects, but instead as being intimately marked by wider struggles for power between professional groups and the state. In this section of the chapter we have sketched out the ways social work discourse has been forged from and shaped by those struggles – struggles on the one hand rooted in the shift towards the realization of state power through scientific forms of discourse aimed at producing productive and manageable subjects, and on the other, attempts to advance the professional power and status of social work.

Conclusion

Foucault's work has provided a rich theoretical resource for social work. The concept of governmentality has been taken up and used extensively by social work academics and commentators. The appeal of Foucault's work is the relational conception of power contained within it. Foucault's work breaks from Marxist-inspired accounts of power, as something possession-like, and that certain individuals and groups possess more of than others. In place of this view, Foucault develops a far more fluid and dynamic account of power, one made all the more versatile because it enables its productive and positive effects to be brought into view. Foucault's work reminds us that while the effects of power can be negative, working to oppress the minds and bodies of individuals through a range of discursively constituted relations, identities and practices, nevertheless power always creates resistance and resistance can lead to changes in the constitution and ordering of power in new and unforeseen ways.

In this chapter we have drawn on Foucault's concepts to consider the debate within social work about care versus control. This has meant focussing on the ways discourse and power converge upon the recipients of social work services through reconstructing and reconstituting their identities as service-users. Attention was also drawn to the multiple forms of discourse brought to bear on the minds and bodies of social workers, forms of discourse that work to empower them within the social work relationship, while simultaneously making them subject to and objects of state power. Increasingly state power is realized through a range of electronically mediated forms of information technology, surveillance and scrutiny. The result is a situation in which social workers feel increasingly estranged from and disempowered by the professional discourse they bring to bear on service-users and are themselves subject to. Viewed in this way, the debate about care versus control within social work appears now to belong to an earlier stage of modernity. A more pressing question for social work today is how it can resist and reclaim control of the powerful forms of discourse to which it is subject and increasingly controlled.

Further reading

Chambon, A., Irving, A. and Epstein, L. (1999) *Reading Foucault for Social Work*. New York: Columbia University Press.
Foucault, M. (2006 [1961]) *Madness and Civilization*. New York: Vintage Books.
Foucault, M. (1977 [1975]) *Discipline and Punish*. Harmondsworth: Penguin.

References

Aries, P. (1962) *Centuries of Childhood: A Social History of Family Life*. New York: Random House Inc.
Bamford, T. (2015) *A Contemporary History of Social Work: Learning from the Past*. Bristol: Policy Press.
Beck, U. (1992) *Risk Society: Towards a New Modernity*. London: Sage.

Beresford, P. and Croft, S. (2001) 'Service Users' Knowledges and the Social Construction of Social Work', *Journal of Social Work*, 1(3): 295–316.

Breur, J. (1999) *The Myth of the First Three Years: A New Understanding of Early Brain Development*. New York: The Free Press.

Chambon, A., Irving, A. and Epstein, L. (1999) *Reading Foucault for Social Work*. New York: Columbia University Press.

Clarke, R. (1997) *Introduction to dataveillance and information privacy, and definition of terms*. [ONLINE] Available at: www.anu.edu.au/people/Roger.Clarke/DV/Intro.html#DV. [Accessed 5 March 2017].

Community Care. (2017) *Sharing mistakes in social work means you risk being blamed*. [ONLINE] Available at: www.communitycare.co.uk/2017/01/25/sharing-mistakes-in-social-work-means-you-risk-being-blamed-disciplined-and-struck-off/. [Accessed 31 March 2017].

Day, P. R. (1979) 'Care and Control: A Social Work Dilemma', *Social Policy & Administration*, 13(3): 206–209.

Elden, S. (2017) *Foucault: The Birth of Power*. Cambridge: Polity Press.

Foucault, M. (2006 [1961]) *Madness and Civilization*. New York: Vintage Books.

Foucault, M. (2001 [1966]) *The Order of Things: The Archaeology of the Human Sciences*. London: Routledge.

Foucault, M. (2002 [1969]) *Archaeology of Knowledge*. London: Routledge.

Foucault, M. (1977 [1975]) *Discipline and Punish*. Harmondsworth: Penguin.

Foucault, M. (1981) *The History of Sexuality*. Vol. 1. Harmondsworth: Penguin.

Foucault, M. (1988) *Politics, Philosophy, Culture: Interviews and Other Writings, 1977–1984*, Kritzman, L. (ed.). New York: Routledge.

Garland, D. (2001) *The Culture of Control: Crime and Social Order in Contemporary Society*. Oxford: Oxford University Press.

Garrett, P. M. (2004) 'The Electronic Eye: Emerging Surveillance Practices in Social Work with Children and Families', *European Journal of Social Work*, 7(1): 57–71.

Garrett, P. M. (2005) 'Social Work's "Electronic Turn": Notes on the Deployment of Information and Communication Technologies in Social Work with Children and Families', *Critical Social Policy*, 24(4): 529–553.

Garrity, Z. (2010) 'Discourse Analysis, Foucault and Social Work Research: Identifying Some Methodological Complexities', *Journal of Social Work*, 10(2): 193–210.

Gilbert, T. and Powell, J. L. (2009) 'Power and Social Work in the United Kingdom', *Journal of Social Work*, 10(1): 3–22.

Gordon, D. (1990) *The Justice Juggernaut: Fighting Street Crime, Controlling Citizens*. New Brunswick, NJ: Rutgers University Press.

Haggerty, K. D. (2006) 'Tear Down the Walls: On Demolishing the Panopticon', in Lyon, D. (ed.) *Theorizing Surveillance: The Panopticon and Beyond*. Collumpton, Devon: Willan Publishing, pp. 23–46.

Haggerty, K. D. and Ericson, R. V. (2000) 'The Surveillant Assemblage', *British Journal of Sociology*, 51(4): 605–622.

Hardy, M. (2015) *Governing Risk: Care and Control in Contemporary Social Work*. Basingstoke: Palgrave Macmillan.

Harris, J. (1999) 'State Social Work and Social Citizenship in Britain: From Clientelism to Consumerism', *British Journal of Social Work*, 29(6): 915–937.

Hasler, F. (2003) *Users at the Heart: User Participation in the Governance and Operation of Social Regulatory Bodies*. London: SCIE.

Hudson, J. (2003) 'E-Galitarianism? The Information Society and New Labour's Repositioning of Welfare', *Critical Social Policy*, 23(2): 268–290.

Jones, C. (1989) 'End of the Road: Issues in Social Work Education', in Carter, P., Jeffs, T. and Smith, M. (eds.) *Social Work and Social Welfare Yearbook*. Vol. 1. Milton Keynes: Open University Press.

Jones, C. (1996) 'Anti-Intellectualism and the Peculiarities of British Social Work Education', in Parton, N. (ed.) *Social Theory, Social Change and Social Work*. London: Routledge, pp. 190–210.

Jones, C. and Novak, T. (1993) 'Social Work Today', *British Journal of Social Work*, 23(2): 195–212.

Leonard, P. (1966) *Sociology and Social Work*. London: Routledge and Kegan Paul.

Levi-Strauss, C. (1978) *Myth and Meaning*. London: Routledge and Kegan Paul.

Lubove, R. (1966) 'Social Work and the Life of the Poor', *The Nation*, 23(5): 609–611.

Lyon, D. (1994) *The Electronic Eye: The Rise of Surveillance Society: Computers and Social Control in Context*. Oxford: Polity Press.

Lyon, D. (2001) *Surveillance Society: Monitoring Everyday Life*. Buckingham: The Open University Press.

Lyon, D. (2003) *Surveillance as Social Sorting: Privacy, Risk and Digital Discrimination*. Oxford: Routledge.

Lyon, D. (2007) 'The Watched World Today', in Lyon, D. (ed.) *Surveillance Studies: An Overview*. Cambridge: Polity Press, pp. 11–24.

Marx, G. T. (1988) *Undercover: Police Surveillance in America*. Berkeley: University of California Press.

McDonald, C. (2006) *Challenging Social Work: The Context of Practice*. Basingstoke: Palgrave Macmillan.

McLaughlin, H. (2009) 'What's in a Name?: "Client", "Patient", "Customer", "Consumer", "Expert by Experience", "Service-User" – What's Next?', *British Journal of Social Work*, 39(6): 1101–1117.

Moss, P. and Petrie, P. (2002) *From Children's Services to Children's Spaces: Public Policy, Children and Childhood*. London: Routledge.

Munro, J. (2004) 'The Impact of Audit on Social Work Practice', *British Journal of Social Work*, 34(8): 1075–1095.

Parrot, L. and Madoc-Jones, I. (2008) 'Reclaiming Information and Communication Technologies for Empowering Social Work Practice', *Journal of Social Work*, 8(2): 181–197.

Parton, N. (1996) 'Social Work, Risk and "The Blaming System"', in Parton, N. (ed.) *Social Theory, Social Change and Social Work*. London: Routledge, pp. 98–114.

Parton, N. (2008) 'Changes in the Form of Knowledge in Social Work: From the "Social" to the "Informational"?', *British Journal of Social Work*, 38(2): 253–269.

Powell, J. L. (2012) 'Social Work and Elder Abuse: A Foucauldian Analysis', *Social Work & Society*, 10(1): 1–10.

Powell, J. L. and Khan, H. T. A. (2012) 'Foucault, Social Theory and Social Work', *Sociologie Romaneasca*, 10(1): 131–147.

Rogowski, S. (2011) 'Managers, Managerialism and Social Work with Children and Families: The Deformation of a Profession?', *Practice: Social Work in Action*, 23(3): 157–167.

Rose, N. (1999) *Powers of Freedom*. Cambridge: Cambridge University Press.

Ruch, G. (2012) 'Where Have All the Feelings Gone? Developing Reflective and Relationship-Based Management in Child-Care Social Work', *The British Journal of Social Work*, 42(7): 1315–1332.

Saussure, F. (1959 [1906–11]) *Course in General Linguistics*. New York: Philosophical Library.

Selwyn, N. (2002) 'E-Stablishing' an Inclusive Society? Technology, Social Exclusion and UK Government Policy Making', *Journal of Social Policy*, 31(1): 1–20.

Smith, E. D. (1957) 'Education and the Task of Making Social Work Professional', *Social Services Review*, 31(3): 1–10.

Smith, M. (1965) *Professional Education for Social Work in Britain*. London: Allen & Unwin.

Webb, D. (1996) 'Regulation for Radicals: The State, CCETSW and the Academy', in Parton, N. (ed.) *Social Theory, Social Change and Social Work*. Oxford: Routledge, 172–189.

White, S., Hall, C. and Peckover, S. (2009) 'The Descriptive Tyranny of the Common Assessment Framework: Technologies of Categorization and Professional Practice in Child Welfare', *British Journal of Social Work*, 39(7): 1197–1217.

Younghusband, E. (1951) *Report on the Employment and Training of Social Workers*. Edinburgh: T.A. Constable.

7

PIERRE BOURDIEU

Symbolic violence and self-exclusion

Introduction

The value of self-determination is a core one within social work. As long as it brings no harm to others, does not conflict with the interests of society as a whole or lead to the service-user doing harm to themselves, the value of self-determination is one social workers are committed to realizing. Self-determination implies a conception of human agents as morally autonomous individuals, capable of thinking and acting in rational and self-reflexive ways. Implicit in the notion of self-determination is choice. Service-users have the right to determine the course of their own self-development, the lives they lead and the actions they choose to undertake.

A concern with the values of self-determination, autonomy and choice is central to the critical social theory of Pierre Bourdieu (1930–2002). Bourdieu was highly critical of what he regarded as the overly abstract view of individuals as autonomous and free to make choices. Bourdieu wanted to explain how the kinds of social relations organising individuals and groups in modern capitalist society serve to undermine their capacity to think and act in self-determining ways and how in turn this impinges on their capacity to make choices. In Bourdieu's view, the capacity to think and act autonomously is something most people are denied the opportunity to do. For the vast majority of the members of capitalist society the choices they make are for the most part determined for, as opposed to by, them in ways they rarely think to consider or question. While the uneven distribution and wielding of power can be readily discerned in a range of capitalist institutions and organisations, of particular interest to Bourdieu was the notion that power is most effective when it is exerted over people in ways in which they actively take part and collude.

Symbolic violence refers to a situation in which power is exercised over people with their complicity (Bourdieu and Wacquant, 1992: 167). Contained within this idea is the view that members of the most socially oppressed groups think and act in ways that unintentionally serve to reproduce their own domination and oppression. That *inclusion* in certain socialization processes and class-based lifestyles involves the members of socially oppressed groups actively contributing to their marginalization and *exclusion*. According to Bourdieu, this takes place because social actors – from the most privileged individuals to the most oppressed – fail to recognise, they 'misrecognise', the power dynamics constraining them, but that nevertheless constitute the real and enduring causes of their oppression and social suffering (Bourdieu, 1999).

Given Bourdieu's reputation during his lifetime as one of the world's most eminent social theorists his intellectual legacy has been largely overlooked by social work thinkers and practitioners save for a few notable exceptions (Pellion, 1998; Houston, 2002; Emirbayer and Williams, 2005; Garrett, 2007a, 2007b; Huppatz, 2009). This chapter identifies and explicates Bourdieu's main theoretical concepts of habitus, capital and field. It uses these to draw to attention what Bourdieu identified as the main social and cultural processes by which social inequality and symbolic violence are perpetrated. The applied section of the chapter demonstrates the value of Bourdieu's concepts in a range of ways that include identifying how Bourdieu's work can be used as the basis for 'socio-therapy'; highlighting how service-users contribute to their own marginalization through self-exclusion; and demonstrating how the concept of 'field' might be used by social work to try to reclaim the profession's declining status and autonomy.

Bourdieu on habitus and capital

Born in a small rural peasant village in southern France, Pierre Bourdieu (1930–2002) was one of the most influential social theorists of the twentieth century. Bourdieu's most acclaimed theoretical concept is that of 'habitus'. Habitus forms part of Bourdieu's attempt to go beyond the 'structure versus agency' debate, by demonstrating how social structures shape individuals, at the same time as enabling individuals to respond creatively to and shape the social contexts in which they find themselves. Bourdieu regards modern society as made up of opposing social-class groups, each of which gives rise to a specific 'class-based habitus'. Echoing the ideas of Marx (Chapter 2), Bourdieu regarded class as the most significant social structure shaping how individuals think and act. Marx defined class primarily on the basis of material factors. Bourdieu used Weber's ideas (Chapter 2) to expand the notion of class to include the ideal and symbolic dimensions of social life. Habitus (plural: habitus) refers to the ways of thinking, perceiving, feeling, acting, reacting and interacting shared by and characteristic of the members of different class-based groups.

The habitus of a group comprises a combination of material and ideal, subjective and objective, conscious and unconscious, and intended and unintended elements. The material elements are the economic resources of the group, including financial wealth and property. The ideal elements are the shared ideas, normative ideals and values members of the group use to organise and construct their experience. From the moment they are born, individuals are socialized into the habitus of the group. This takes place in ways that are consciously directed and intended, as well as in ways that are only semi-consciously perceived and unintended. Through socialization, the ideal elements of the group habitus are instilled in the mind of the individual. Bourdieu emphasised the ways and extent to which habitus shapes the body too. This is his reworking of Merleau-Ponty's (Chapter 3) ideas about 'milieu and action'. Individuals are socialized into the habitus of the group, and the habitus of the group comes to be *embodied*, in the most literal sense, by the individual. This is true of the ways individuals walk, the postures they adopt, the mannerisms they assume, etc., all of which are shaped by the group habitus. The habitus disposes individuals to think, feel and act in socially distinctive and patterned ways, ways shared by and specific to members of a group.

The dispositions of the habitus generate types of practices. Practices are the ways of thinking, feeling, acting, reacting, etc. individuals enact to make sense of and engage with the world. Practices contain elements that are enabling and creative. Habitus is enabling because it provides socially shaped ways of thinking, feeling and acting. At the same time, however, the practices generated by the habitus are constraining because they always bear the imprint of the wider group. This is true even when the habitus generates practices in improvised and creative ways. In situations that require individuals to improvise how they think and act e.g. when a posh businessman enters a working-class pub, how he responds to the people he encounters are always marked by and refract the habitus of the wider group.

Bourdieu's emphasis on the embodied nature of the habitus is significant in two main ways. First, it highlights that practices are generated at the level of 'practical consciousness' (Chapter 3). Most of the time, we do not have to think about how or why we think and act in the ways we do, because the habitus provides us with the practices we need to take part in situations and interactions. And second, for the most part how we think and act strikes us as natural and inevitable, and not as the result of being socialized into a particular group habitus and not any other. Bourdieu (1977: 80) refers to the taken-for-granted and common sense feel of most social experience as 'doxa'. The 'doxic' ways of thinking, feeling, acting and interacting generated by the habitus form the unexamined basis of the individual's class-based existence in the world.

Closely related to the concept of habitus is the concept of 'capital'. Capitals are socially valuable resources. The concept of capital is an important one because it allows Bourdieu to explain the mechanisms by which individual and social change take place. Habitus is made up of different amounts and types of capital. The habitus is not a fixed and static entity as it is often represented by critics of Bourdieu's work (Jenkins, 1992; King, 2000). Rather, it comprises an ongoing and open-ended process. The habitus *can* and *does* change over time, but crucially and always in ways structured by the amount and types of capital available to the individual.

Bourdieu posits three main types of capital. The first is economic capital, which refers to monetary resources, material possessions and property. The second is cultural capital. Cultural capital refers to socially legitimate forms of practice as well as comprising more embodied forms, such as socially esteemed knowledge and experiences. Attending the theatre and eating in fine restaurants, for example, are cultural practices to which a high social value is attached. By contrast, going to the local cinema to watch a film and eating in fast-food chains are cultural practices that bestow comparatively little prestige on the individual. Cultural capital also refers to the amount and types of knowledge people have e.g. whether they attended a fee-paying or

TABLE 7.1 Summary of habitus

Habitus
• refers to the class-based lifestyles of different groups
• contains material and ideal elements
• provides individual with different amounts and types of capital
• operates for the most part at a practical level e.g. practical consciousness
• embodied in the form of socially shaped dispositions
• realized through socially shaped practices

TABLE 7.2 Summary of types of capital

Capital
• economic capital – material wealth e.g. money, property, etc.
• cultural capital – knowledge of legitimate culture e.g. education, cultural pursuits, linguistic capital
• social capital – social networks and connections

state school, whether they have a university degree, etc. These are embodied forms of cultural capital. Compared to knowledge about football teams and their players, knowledge of French literature and classical music carry a higher social value. The third form of capital is social capital. Social capital refers to the social networks individuals belong to and whether or not the people in those networks have much social power or influence.

A particularly important form of embodied capital is linguistic capital (Bourdieu uses the terms *linguistic capital* and *linguistic habitus* interchangeably). The social-class habitus we possess determines the type of linguistic habitus into which we are socialized. Linguistic habitus refers to the linguistic competencies and ways of talking e.g. turns of phrase, accent, tone, etc. and their relationship to language characteristics of members of a group. The concept of linguistic habitus demonstrates certain affinities with Bernstein's ideas about language as a type of code (Chapter 3). As one of the most conspicuous signifiers of social background, linguistic habitus is directly related to the acquisition and expression of symbolic forms of power such as prestige, authority and status. The linguistic habitus that agents possess communicates – literally and metaphorically – their place in the wider social hierarchy and the amount of social power to which they can lay claim.

All forms of linguistic habitus are subject to classification. Part of the process of being socialized into the linguistic habitus of the group is developing an awareness of its value in the wider 'linguistic market' (Bourdieu, 1991a, 1993). Bourdieu regards linguistic exchanges between people as analogous to transactions between buyers and sellers in a market. Through verbal exchanges with other people, speakers with the most socially valuable linguistic habitus are able to assert their symbolic power e.g. a sense of authority, the right to talk, etc., at the same time as accruing further forms of symbolic power e.g. self-assuredness and self-esteem. Moreover, because the value of one form of linguistic habitus is directly determined through a relationship of difference to all others e.g. a posh accent is perceived as posh only in relation to slang or dialect, the prestige accrued by dominant forms of linguistic habitus comes at the expense of all others.

The ways of talking definitive of the upper-middle-class linguistic habitus are the most socially legitimate. Members of this social group possess high levels of linguistic capital. They talk in ways devoid of slang, of colloquialisms and of regional accents and dialect. The upper-middle-class linguistic habitus is defined by a sense of ease and 'at-oneness', and a mastery of language and linguistic expression (Bourdieu, 1991a). The linguistic habitus of the upper-middle-class is the cultural yardstick against which all other ways of talking are classified and evaluated. The linguistic habitus of working-class groups is the least valuable on the linguistic market. It is defined by a relationship to language that is ill-at-ease and awkward because it lacks proficiency in the use of socially legitimate and formal ways of talking (Bourdieu, 1990b, 1991a, 1993). Bourdieu uses the concept of linguistic habitus to demonstrate how relationships of domination and subordination are enacted in the most mundane ways, as people communicate and interact with one another across a range of settings and contexts.

For Bourdieu, the relationship people from different social groups have to language provides an important site for observing the mundane ways in which power is won and lost during everyday interaction. By talking in certain ways and not others, individuals are complicit in actively reproducing wider structures of social and symbolic power. The words and language we use to express ourselves strike us as one of the most intimate expressions of our identity. We rarely reflect on the socially patterned nature of our relationship to language. For this reason, Bourdieu regards the linguistic habitus as a central mechanism by which our personal identity is opened up and subject to wider social classification, at the same time as being directly involved in the ways we classify others. For members of socially subordinate groups this typically means being subject to negative classification across a much wider range of situations compared to people with a dominant form of linguistic habitus.

Fields, games and distinction

To explain how and why inequalities between social groups persist over time Bourdieu developed the concept of 'field'. Late modern capitalist societies are differentiated into a wide number of interdependent spheres of activity. Bourdieu (1991b) refers to these as fields. The people situated within different fields are involved in playing the kinds of 'games' definitive of that context. In this view, social life is likened to a series of games, in which the individuals involved in those games are 'players'. Irrespective of the field in question e.g. the field of politics, law, commerce, etc. all fields have 'stakes', for which the individuals playing the field-specific games compete with one another. In a capitalist society the games played in fields are 'zero-sum' games. That is to say, the nature of social games is such that there are winners and there are losers, with winning always coming at the expense and to the detriment of the losers.

Bourdieu wanted to understand how the games within fields are played, as well as understanding how the structure of the games shapes what takes place within them. To this end, Bourdieu is less interested in the relatively superficial interactions between the players in games and more interested in the underlying and enduring rules and laws by which the whole game is structured. A key point to make here is that people know how to play games in ways that they typically find difficult to grasp and articulate. They get caught up instead in playing the game in the semi-conscious ways generated by the habitus. For this reason the players in a game rarely think to question why the game is played in the ways it is, how their chances of succeeding are linked to the ways the game is structured, and how in turn this connects to wider inequalities and the uneven distribution of power in society.

A universal property of all fields and the games played within them concerns the notion of 'stakes'. Stakes are the socially valuable resources (forms of capital) for which players in a game compete. Whether or not individuals are disposed to playing a particular game is determined by the relationship between the habitus they possess and the field in which the games take place. Individuals are more likely to play a particular game if they possess the right kind of habitus and capital necessary for playing that game. Before entering a specific field, individuals have to feel that the game is worth playing and that the stakes on offer are of value to them. This feeling is referred to as 'illusio'. The notion of illusio is an important one. It captures the fact that agents tend not to consciously choose the games into which they enter. Instead, it just seems obvious and natural to people to play certain games and not others. This is why when asked for the reasons behind their 'choice' to enter a particular profession, people often need time to think about the reasons why, or are inclined to say things like 'it just seemed like the right thing for me to

TABLE 7.3 Summary of fields

Fields
• structurally differentiated parts making up modern society e.g. legal field, field of social work, etc.
• characterised by struggles between individuals and groups
• social sites in which players compete in field-specific games for prizes on offer e.g. forms of capital
• made up of different positions and position-takings
• characterised by lesser or greater degrees of structural autonomy

do.' This is what Bourdieu means by the notion of 'misrecognition'. Much of how people think and act takes place at a semi-conscious, practical level i.e. the level at which the habitus operates, such that they misrecognise the social reasons shaping the choices they make as individuals.

Irrespective of the games people play, how well they do in those games is determined by the habitus. The habitus of the individual generates the practices necessary for playing the game (Bourdieu, 2000). Game playing takes place in ways that are in part consciously realized and in ways that are (partially) never questioned or come into conscious thought. When an individual enters a field the habitus determines the position they take up as well as the positions they are able to occupy. Particular types of people tend to occupy particular sorts of positions. This is because each position within a field is made up of specific amounts and types of capital (Bourdieu, 2004). To occupy a given position, players need to have the right amounts and types of capital. A high position in a field requires the individual to possess large amounts of capital relevant to the field. Low positions in fields are occupied by individuals with a small amount of capital associated with that field. High positions in a field are occupied by players of the game who are able to dominate other players. Those who occupy low positions and who have low amounts of capital are dominated by other players in the game. It is not just the amount of capital you have within a field that determines the likelihood of you succeeding in the game being played. The types of capital you have are important too. Some types of capital are good in specific fields but in other fields might not necessarily retain their value – they may even have a negative value e.g. when a Polish person's accent (linguistic capital) negatively differentiates them from members of an English community.

Bourdieu regarded the education system as a particularly important field for observing the largely hidden mechanisms by which social inequalities are produced and reproduced. Education and educational achievement are very significant for determining the type of jobs people do, the amount of money they will earn and the kind of (class-based) lifestyle they are likely to lead. According to Bourdieu (1988) the field of education plays a key role in the conservation of the social order as well as consecrating the common sense – doxic – systems of classification contained within the wider culture and that people use to classify themselves e.g. as someone who is clever, lacking in confidence, able to get along with others, etc. As with all social contexts Bourdieu analysed, he uses the metaphor of games to try to understand the field of education. Similarly applicable is the notion that those from socially privileged backgrounds are far more likely to succeed in playing the games within the field of education than those from socially disadvantaged backgrounds (Bourdieu and Passeron, 1990). Bourdieu's analysis led to a set of conclusions that directly challenge the officially held view of modern schooling as based upon meritocratic values – the view that the academic merit of individuals will guarantee their success. Bourdieu claims instead that there is a hidden agenda in the schooling system that works and has effects which operate below the surface level of the conscious intentions of teachers and pupils alike.

Teachers think they are being meritocratic in their approach to children. In actuality, however, they have been socialized into valuing certain types of knowledge and values which are modelled upon and congruent with the knowledge and values held by the upper-middle-class – the socially dominant class. It is these types of class-based knowledge and the values accompanying them that school children are evaluated on and assessed academically. In making this point, Bourdieu (1988, 1990b) highlighted the relationship between the people within the educational system and the wing of the political system dedicated to setting the school curriculum and standards of education, and the upper-middle-class background of those people. In essence, what the education system values and is geared towards is classifying children on the basis of their capacity to demonstrate certain ways of talking and thinking, their attitudes (habitus) and their possession of certain types of knowledge (capital), all of which are consistent with the ways of talking and thinking and the attitudes characteristic of the dominant class.

For children from middle-class backgrounds the type of habitus they embody means they possess many of the types of capital necessary for speaking, thinking and feeling in the ways the education system understands as meritorious. For children with a working-class habitus the capacity to speak, think and feel in the ways the school system demands of them is not as easily attained. This is because the habitus of the groups into which they were socialized does not provide them with the types of capital to play the games specific to the field of education. This has very little to do with intrinsic levels of intelligence. What the education system does is classify and rank people on the basis of the amount and types of capital they possess. These are determined by the habitus. Children who speak in local dialect outside of school or at home are far less likely to be proficient at talking in the 'correct' ways – standard English – used in school because it represents a form of communicating they are far less familiar with compared to middle-class children. By contrast, middle-class parents encourage their children to talk 'properly' because they recognise in ways that are not fully conscious that to do so increases the likelihood the child succeeds at school.

By contrast, talking in dialect or a working-class accent at home, working-class parents actively pass on disadvantage to their children because the types of capital – ways of thinking, talking, feeling – they instil within them are not the right ones for succeeding within education. Children internalize the evaluations and classifications bestowed upon them by teachers in a way that leads them to imagine themselves as more or less intelligent, academically inclined and confident. This leads to a situation where, on the whole, middle-class children tend to experience their relationship to education as something positive and self-affirming, because the values they have and the ways they think and feel are positively recognised and evaluated by teachers. Working-class and lower-middle-class children by contrast tend to have a far less positive, often negative relationship with education, because the types of knowledge, interest and values they are socialized into are subject to far less favourable evaluation.

Distinction games

Bourdieu's analysis of the field of education demonstrates how class structures and relations of power are produced and reproduced over time through culture. Struggles for cultural power form an important part of the processes by which symbolic violence occurs. In his landmark study *Distinction* (2010 [1979]), Bourdieu demonstrated how cultural tastes and preferences correspond with and are shaped by class-based structures and inequalities. To do this, Bourdieu analysed the cultural tastes and preferences of a significant cross-section of French society. His study revealed that the cultural tastes and preferences for a vast range of cultural goods and practices including music, food, fashion, leisure pursuits and so on are highly socially patterned. Bourdieu's study highlights how the cultural tastes and preferences of individuals and groups are strongly shaped by the class-based habitus they possess.

Within the social hierarchy, socially dominant groups tend to possess the highest levels of cultural capital. The members of these groups use their economic capital to acquire the most valorised forms of cultural capital e.g. paying for private education, going to expensive restaurants, attending socially prestigious events, etc. High levels of economic capital lead to the accumulation of similarly high levels of cultural capital, which in turn carry with them high levels of symbolic power e.g. prestige, confidence, a sense of refinement, good taste, etc. Individuals from structurally subordinate groups possess relatively far lower levels of cultural capital. The taste dispositions and preferences associated with dominated social groups e.g. going to the cinema, listening to pop music, watching television, etc. bestow low levels of symbolic power on the individuals who enact these practices. More than this, however, the cultural tastes and preferences of working-class groups typically carry a negative symbolic value. The cultural tastes of these groups serve as a negative point of reference against which all other social groups are classified and evaluated (Bourdieu, 2010 [1979]). The taste dispositions characteristic of these groups are defined as coarse, unsophisticated and vulgar.

Remaining with the metaphor of games, Bourdieu saw everyday life as forming part of the cultural battle ground wherein members of different class-based groups compete with one another in and through various 'distinction games'. People play distinction games all the time in ways that are (partially) knowing as well as in ways that are (partially) unknowing. Distinction games involve individuals classifying as well as being classified by one another. Distinction games take place across a wide range of both formal and mundane settings and activities: talking in elaborate code in a meeting at work, wearing expensive trainers while walking through a shopping centre, choosing which music to listen to at a party, etc. Whether individuals are subject to more or less positive or negative classification by others is determined by the habitus they have and the types of capital they possess. The winners in distinction games tend to be the individuals with the highest amounts of capital. The losers of distinction games tend to possess the lowest levels and types of capital.

How people talk, the ways they dress, the consumer goods they can afford to buy, the lifestyles they lead, the amount of cultural knowledge and education they can lay claim to, all carry a wider social and symbolic value. Within the distinction games enacted out in everyday life, the taste dispositions of socially subordinate social groups are subject to ongoing and negative classification by others. Instead of conferring a personally and socially empowering sense of distinction, prestige and legitimacy, their taste dispositions are classified by others as inferior, vulgar and expressive of a lack of refinement and status. Sometimes in ways that are explicit and personally directed, but more often in ways that are only partially intended and barely perceptible, individuals signify to one another their social position through a range of non-verbal cues, gestures, glances, postures and the attitude they convey (Bourdieu, 2010 [1979]; 1993).

For Bourdieu (2000: 240) the ongoing cumulative effect of defeat in distinction games impacts profoundly on the development of selfhood and personal identity of individuals from

TABLE 7.4 Summary of distinction games

Distinction games
• played within fields and wider culture
• involve (partially) conscious display of amount and types of capital to others
• winners accumulate positive symbolic capital e.g. sense of superiority, social distinction, etc.
• losers accumulate negative symbolic capital e.g. sense of inferiority, shame, etc.

socially subordinate groups. Bourdieu regarded the unequal distribution of symbolic capital as 'one of the most uneven of all distributions, and probably in any case, the most cruel' (Bourdieu, 2000: 240).

For members of social groups to which a low social value is attached, their relationship to the habitus tends to be characterised by a range of negatively constraining and demoralising self-images and perceptions, feelings of inferiority and an overall sense of personal and social estrangement.

Applying Bourdieu

Social work as socio-analysis

Bourdieu's work attempts to examine all aspects of capitalist society and the power relations embedded within them. This led to Bourdieu focussing his attention on the different ways power is produced and operates at a number of levels and across a wide range of fields. The concept of habitus allows us to think about how power is produced and operates at an individual level, specifically by working to constrain the minds and bodies of individuals in a number of mundane and insidious ways. As applied to the level of concrete individuals, Bourdieu regarded his work as a form of 'socio-analysis'. Like the psychotherapist whose job it is to help the patient access what they already (partially) know but find it difficult to put into words and articulate, Bourdieu (1993, 1999) regarded the concepts of habitus, capital and field as supplying the tools for liberating the minds of individuals from the constraining effects of power – primarily, by identifying and bringing into consciousness the *social* causes of their suffering and oppression.

Socio-analysis is Bourdieu's vision of a 'collective counterpart to psychoanalysis' (Bourdieu and Wacquant, 1992: 49). In psychoanalytic discourse, the cause of the patient's difficulties is buried deep inside the psyche, understood as deriving from some inner conflict, or unresolved tension. In contrast to this view, Bourdieu's socio-analytic approach involves trying to seek out and identify the cause of the individual's suffering in the wider social struggles in which they are embedded and oppressed by. Socio-analysis means trying to 'unearth the social unconscious embedded into institutions and lodged deep inside of us' (Bourdieu and Wacquant, 1992: 49). By the phrase 'deep inside of us', Bourdieu is alluding to the habitus, the socially and culturally shaped dispositions the individual develops and comes to embody through socialization.

Habitus works to generate practices. Practices are socially marked ways of seeing, perceiving, thinking, feeling, acting, reacting and interacting with people and situations. As socially shaped categories, self-identity and self-image are constructed by the practices generated by the habitus. For the majority of the time, the types of practices generated by the habitus strike the individual as natural and inevitable. Operating at the level of practical consciousness, people tend not to question or reflect on how the habitus-shaped ways of perceiving, feeling, thinking, etc. shape their experience of reality or themselves. It is only when they come into contact with someone possessed of a very different type of habitus that they are likely to reflect on the socially and culturally shaped nature of their own beliefs and views. Even then, they may try to account for the difference in views by rationalizing to themselves that how and what they think is right. For the most part, habitus generates the practices that enable us to get on in life.

Echoing the ideas of Kant, how things are in actuality can never be directly known. It is the habitus which constructs our experience of social reality – situations, other people and ourselves – and not the things themselves. This is why we tend not to call into question or reflect on the ways of thinking generated by the habitus. We just assume instead that who we think we are, and how others understand us to be, is the person we are. Rather than depicting how reality actually is, the practices generated by the habitus refract the ways of thinking, ideals and values of the class-based group we belong to and the position of that group in the wider social hierarchy. This has very important implications for thinking about the habitus-generated sense of self-identity and self-image individuals develop over time.

The habitus of the group *is* the habitus of the individual. The collective identity and collective self-image of the group habitus are determined by its position in the wider social hierarchy. If the habitus of the group occupies a subordinate position in the social hierarchy e.g. working-class habitus, then the types and range of practices generated by the habitus of the individual will refract their working-class identity and social position. Remember, Bourdieu sees culture in capitalist society as highly ideological. Culture is shot through with relations of power in the form of cultural hierarchies and distinction games in which those with low levels of cultural capital are far less likely to succeed in the struggle for social distinction.

Aside from being highly ideological, modern capitalist culture is highly individualistic. This is why a lack of success tends to be understood and represented as the result of individual failings e.g. lack of effort on the part of the individual, unwillingness to work hard, etc. and not those of wider society (Chapter 1). But how 'successful' people are and how this informs and connects with how they imagine themselves – self-image and self-identity – has very little to do with the person they really are, and everything to do with the amount and types of capital they posses. The amount and types of capital people posses are determined by the habitus of the group. This is exactly what Bourdieu means by the claim that class is the preeminent social fact. It is the social class we are born into, and not any particular attributes we may or may not possess, that determines how successful we will be in the daily struggles and unevenly poised social games of a capitalist society.

A Bourdieu-inspired social work would involve social workers adopting a socio-analytical approach to reframing the self-identity and self-image of service-users. In essence, this would involve assisting service-users to reflect on and explore how their self-identity and self-image are negatively shaped by the habitus they embody and the amount and types of capital available to them. For individuals characterised by very low levels of cultural capital e.g. formal education, talking in restricted code, life experiences, etc., the cultural and symbolic resources available to them for constructing their identity are typically very narrow and constraining. The cultural resources they draw on refract the ideologically marked ideas and values of the wider capitalist culture – individualistic ways of thinking that categorise and classify them in negative ways. (Think about how the types of capital you possess have led to you coming into contact with this book and how in turn the theoretical ideas contained within it provide you with a range of alternative ways of thinking about and understanding your own self and sense of personal identity.)

Drawing on Bourdieu's concepts of habitus and capital, either implicitly or explicitly, social workers can assist service-users to rethink, reassemble and reconstruct an alternative sense of personal identity and self-image redefined on terms that take account of and acknowledge the social-structural reasons feeding into the difficulties and problems they face. The focus of a Bourdieu-inspired socio-analytical, as opposed to psychoanalytical, approach to social work would mean working with service-users to (re)construct a more sociological account of themselves and the issues they face. It would mean working with service-users to recognise and think outside of the limits of the normatively charged attitudes, beliefs and ideals generated by the habitus and that set the parameters in which their self-identity and self-understanding are assembled.

Of course, merely identifying and acknowledging the social-structural forces informing the difficulties and constraints service-users encounter are not the same as removing them. This is a point acknowledged by Bourdieu when he said that 'to subject to scrutiny the mechanisms which render life painful, even untenable, is not to neutralize them; to bring to light contradictions is not to resolve them' (Bourdieu, 1999: 7). But as part of a profession committed to identifying and challenging social inequalities and injustice, social workers can 'within limits' start to 'transform the world by transforming its representation' (Bourdieu and Wacquant, 1992: 14).

Service-users and self-exclusion

Issues of inclusion and exclusion are at the forefront of much of contemporary political policy and debate. The mechanisms by which individuals and entire groups come to be excluded from a range of social activities are complex and assume a wide variety of forms. Exclusion can refer to a lack of or denial of resources, rights, goods and services, for certain communities and groups, as well as individuals being denied the opportunity to participate in mainstream relationships, activities and institutions. Regardless of how it occurs, exclusion from mainstream society impacts negatively on the quality of people's lives as well as affecting the balance and cohesion of society as a whole.

A concern to identify how power works to exclude certain individuals and groups forms a key part of Bourdieu's critical analysis of capitalist society. Of particular interest here are Bourdieu's ideas to do with 'self-exclusion'. Self-exclusion involves individuals actively choosing to exclude themselves from, rather than being excluded by, certain types of social situations, relationships and institutional arrangements. The decision to exclude oneself from certain activities often takes place for legitimate reasons, such as time pressure, lack of interest, etc. But Bourdieu wanted to draw attention to the significance of self-exclusion as both a cause and an effect of symbolic violence. This is the idea that by choosing to exclude themselves from certain social situations, individuals from socially dominated groups actively participate in reproducing their dominated class position.

The notion of 'choice' is an important one here and can be understood as relating directly to Bourdieu's attempt to go beyond the conceptual pitfalls of the 'structure versus agency' debate (Chapter 1). The phrase *it was their choice to act in that way* – or words to that effect – appears frequently in everyday forms of talk and conversation. But take a moment to consider the assumptions contained in the word *choice* as it is used in this way. It assumes a number of things: that the person acting recognised they were making a choice; that the person making the choice had weighed up all the possible consequences of their actions; that the consequences of their actions could be known ahead of making the choice. As it is used in that phrase, the term *choice* carries a number of assumptions, none of which necessarily correspond with or capture how the individual making the choice experienced the situation they were in at the time.

Bourdieu was sceptical of the view that the choices individuals make to act in certain ways are fully consciously grasped. Instead of conceiving of choices as rooted primarily and exclusively in the mind of the individual, Bourdieu saw choices as arising out of the relationship between on the one hand the habitus and capitals embodied by the individual, and the social situation (field) in which the choice was made on the other. Bourdieu likened social life to a series of games. For service-users with a habitus characterised by a very narrow range and low levels of capital, life can seem like a series of games in which they are unable to succeed. This is because they do not have the right amounts or types of capital necessary for playing them. A Syrian service-user, for example, may 'choose' not to attend a local community centre because they are concerned that the linguistic capital they possess e.g. a strong foreign accent, a sense of unease when talking in English, etc. may lead to them being negatively classified by wider members of the community. A single mother may 'choose' not to attend a parent and toddler group because she is anxious that other mothers will make negative judgements about her on account of her single-parent status.

As the previous examples illustrate, the social reasons informing the choices made by individuals to exclude themselves from certain activities cannot be fully grasped by focussing on the individual alone. This is because the choices do not derive from the individuals in isolation, but instead arise out of the relationship, or degree of fit, between the habitus and types of capital they possess and the field in which the choice was made. For service-users with a narrow range and amount of capital, even the most mundane social situations and relationships can dispose them to act in self-excluding ways. It makes sense that people may choose to exclude themselves from situations they imagine will subject them to being classified negatively, in turn giving rise to feelings of embarrassment, shame and inferiority.

Applying the concepts of habitus, capital and field to reconsider the notion of choice allows us to see that much of the time we do not experience the choices we make for what they are – namely, choices. Instead, people experience the practices generated by the habitus, of which choices are merely one example, as something akin to a kind of 'fuzzy logic' (Bourdieu, 1990a [1980]). That is to say, much of what we think and do is only barely and dimly perceived such that were we asked to consciously articulate why we made the choices we did, we would find it very difficult to articulate the reasons. Instead, much of how we think and act can be seen as deriving from a less than fully consciously grasped sense of practical reasoning. Bourdieu was not suggesting that people are incapable of elevating the decisions confronting them to a discursive level and reflecting rationally on the reasoning behind their choices. People do this all the time. But even in such instances, the values on which those choices are based are not chosen by the individual (Bourdieu and Wacquant, 1992). All choices, even those enacted in the most reflexive and rational manner, contain a socially shaped component.

A final point to make concerning Bourdieu's account of self-exclusion concerns the concept of 'misrecognition'. This is the idea that for the most part individuals fail to fully recognise, rather they actively misrecognise, how the choices they make are shaped by the habitus. For individuals characterised by low levels and a narrow range of capital, self-exclusion is far more likely to be rooted in an act of misrecognition, because the individual is unable to grasp how the habitus and types of capital they possess dispose them to think and act in particular ways. Social workers can use Bourdieu's conceptions of self-exclusion and misrecognition to assist service-users to reflect on the choices they make to participate or not in certain forms of activity, relationships and institutions.

By drawing attention to the tacit assumptions and values underlying the choices service-users make, social workers can assist them to identify and challenge the negative and constraining effects of power – in particular as the effects are realized through and exerted over them by the habitus. Social workers accomplish this by demonstrating how the decision not to take part in certain activities may be based on attitudes and beliefs about others and/or themselves which serve to hold them back, or by demonstrating how excluding themselves from certain situations prevents them from accessing additional forms of capital e.g. knowledge that may serve to empower them (cultural capital) and social capital e.g. networks of people who can offer help and support.

This is not the same as saying that social workers should make judgements about the choices service-users make, or try to convince them that they do not know what is best for them. As Bourdieu said, social theory 'can tell us under what conditions moral agency is possible; what it should not try to do is dictate what its course of action ought to be' (Bourdieu and Wacquant, 1992: 57).

The field of social work

Social work often involves dealing with individuals and groups at the sharp end of power in modern society. But the effects of power shape the activities and actions of social workers too. The concept of field can be used to identify and unveil the ways power simultaneously enables and constrains the activities and actions of social workers. It is important that social work students develop an awareness of how power relates to the position of social work within wider society. Doing so forms an important part in trying to counteract the constraining effects of power at the same time as ensuring social work is able to reclaim its professional autonomy.

The concepts of habitus, capital and field provide a theoretical vocabulary for identifying the different forms power can take e.g. economic, cultural and social. Bourdieu adopts a relational approach to social reality. For Bourdieu (Bourdieu and Wacquant, 1992: 97) 'what exists in the social world are relations – objective relations which exist independently of individual consciousness and will . . .' A focus on relations, rather than individuals or social structures, formed part of Bourdieu's attempt to bypass the conceptual antagonisms embedded in the 'structure versus agency' debate. Instead, the trilogy of habitus, capital and field allow for a more versatile and fluid account of the ways social factors simultaneously make possible and enable certain ways of thinking and acting while constraining others at the same time.

The concept of field allows for the mechanisms by which power operates to be revealed and mapped out. A key issue here is that over time, individuals lose sight of the way the fields they are positioned within shape how they think and act. Instead, how they think and act comes to strike them as natural and inevitable. The concept of field allows for power to be conceptualised in a number of different forms, and at different levels, demonstrating how developments and changes at any one of these levels simultaneously shape developments and changes at any and/or all of the other levels. Power resides in: the relations between individuals, institutions and organisations within a field; the relations between people and institutions in and between one field and other fields (wider society); the structure of relations within and between fields over time such that what happens in the present cannot be understood without understanding what came before and how in turn what is happening now shapes what lays ahead.

Bourdieu and Wacquant (1992: 97) define fields as 'networks of objective relations between positions'. When an individual enters the field of social work, the habitus and capitals they posses e.g. formal qualifications, experiences, class-based interests, etc. dispose them towards certain positions and not others e.g. a position in child welfare services as opposed to, say, mental health services. Attached to the positions within a field are various normative attitudes, ideals and behaviours. To assume a particular field position, individuals must possess the necessary amounts and types of capital. It is the combination of habitus, capital and field, and not the individual per se, that disposes them to think and act in certain ways.

The positions in a field are partly defined by the amount and types of capital of which they are made up. But they are also defined by their relation to all the other positions in the field e.g. the position of team manager exists only if there is a team of social workers to manage. The structure of relations through which positions within a field are joined is just as important, if not more so, for shaping how the individuals who occupy those positions act and interact. This is why Bourdieu claims that fields give rise to laws and logics of their own. Fields give rise to ways of acting and interacting that cannot be reduced either to the individuals in the field or to the field itself. Instead, fields give rise to patterned ways of acting and interacting that have a coercive logic, or power, that cannot be reduced to individuals in the field or examined independently of them either; rather it is an emergent, dialectical property arising out of the interactions between the two.

Fields are social sites in which games take place. Games are played for prizes or stakes. The types of capital the players in a field possess shape how and what moves are available to them in the game. The types of capital individuals possess, not the individual themselves, influence how well they will do in the field, the moves they can make and the likelihood they will win prizes e.g. further forms of field-specific capital. Capital exists only in relation to a field. The field of social work is a highly gendered field. The vast majority of social workers are women (Chapter 8). For male social workers, for example, their gender constitutes a form of embodied capital. This can be demonstrated with statistics e.g. statistics show that men are more likely than women to occupy a dominant position within the field of social work. In ways that are (partially) consciously perceived the gender identity of male social workers is a form of embodied capital which disposes them towards positions of power within the field.

The structure of a field directly influences the dynamics and distribution of power within it. These are the relations of power internal to a field. Equally important are the relations of power external to fields. The external relations of power concern the position of the field in relation to the fields around it. Bourdieu uses the notion of autonomy to refer to the way the relations between fields influence and shape what goes on within them. Power and autonomy are inextricably bound up with one another. Moreover, fields are characterised by different levels of autonomy (Bourdieu, Wacquant and Farage, 1994). In fields with high levels of autonomy, individuals are able to define the types and rules of the games they play. The political field, for example, also referred to as the field of power, is a field characterised by very high levels of structural autonomy. The political field exerts power over all other fields of social activity. There is no field of social activity which to varying degrees is not directly influenced by the political field and the events taking place within it.

Within any society, the individuals and institutions that operate in the field of power – the state and state mechanisms of power e.g. administrative organisations, bureaucracies, governing bodies, etc. – have the highest levels of autonomy and social power. In fields with low levels of autonomy, individuals have little influence in determining the roles they play, the rules of the game and the prizes on offer. Instead, these are shaped by the actions and activities of people in the fields surrounding them. The level of autonomy characteristic of the field of social work has changed over time.

At one level, the integration of social work into the newly formed British welfare state was a key moment in the professionalization of social work. The professionalization of social work increased the power and status of social workers vis-à-vis other social and healthcare professions. At the same time, however, it increased the power of the state to intervene directly in the activities of social work. The professional status and autonomy of social work was enhanced through professionalization, at the same time as the influence of social work to define certain values, and practices decreased e.g. social work education is increasingly determined by state policy (Chapter 6) and has led to the increasing marketization and bureaucratization of social welfare services (Chapters 2 and 4); globalization has led to cuts to welfare services due to increasing integration into the world economic system.

The third dimension of the concept of field involves trying to understand changes to the structure of power over time. For Bourdieu the history of a field is akin to the unconscious dimensions of the human mind. He refers to the history of fields as the 'social unconscious'. The term *unconscious* here is intended to convey the forgotten struggles for power both internal and external to fields which shape the structure and distribution of power in the present day. An historical analysis of the field of social work, for example, would involve trying to reconstruct the history of the struggles resulting in the organisation of power-relations structuring the field in the present day. Such an analysis would enable a break with the doxic view that how social work is organised and practised in the present day is natural and inevitable. This is similar to Foucault's emphasis on the contingency of the present. It allows us to understand the present is always the product of past and present struggles within the field but also within fields adjacent to it, as well as being shaped by changes and developments in society more broadly.

Conclusion

At the time of his death in 2002, Bourdieu had established a reputation as one of the world's most influential social theorists (Santoro, 2011). This was an achievement made all the more remarkable, indeed ironic, given the humble social background he was born into, something Bourdieu openly acknowledged throughout his career (Lane, 2000). But it was precisely because of his acute awareness of the limitations of the habitus he was socialized into, and the struggle he faced in trying to overcome the limitations it imposed upon him, that

Bourdieu was so committed to identifying and challenging the material and symbolic mechanisms by which power and inequality are reproduced in modern capitalist society. While politically Bourdieu's commitment to these ideals never wavered and was widely lauded, his theoretical ideas and concepts proved far more divisive.

Bourdieu's most influential conceptual innovation, habitus, has drawn extensive critical commentary. The view that it provides an overly deterministic account of human agents is a recurrent one (King, 2000). Individuals are socialized into the class-based habitus of the group, which operates behind their backs at a practical level, so they are only ever partially able to perceive and change it (Alexander, 1995; Jenkins, 1992; Swartz and Zolberg, 2004). While the concept of field has been used to cast a discerning light on struggles for power across a wide range of social spheres, critics point to the fact that it over-emphasises conflict at the expense of highlighting the collaborative and cohesive dimensions of social life (Becker, 2008; Jenkins, 1992). But leaving these criticisms to one side for a moment, perhaps a more pressing issue from a social work perspective is why to date the work of a social thinker committed to realizing the values of equality and social justice has been largely overlooked within the field of social work. This is an issue to which we will return in greater depth in the final chapter.

Further reading

Bourdieu, P. (1999) *The Weight of the World: Social Suffering in Contemporary Society*. Cambridge: Polity.
Bourdieu, P. and Wacquant, L. (1992) *An Invitation to Reflexive Sociology*. Cambridge: Polity.
Lane, J. (2000) *Pierre Bourdieu: A Critical Introduction*. London: Pluto Press.

References

Alexander, J. (1995) *Fin de Siecle Social Theory: Relativism, Reduction and the Problem of Reason*. London: Verso.
Becker, H. (2008) *Art Worlds*. California: University of California Press.
Bourdieu, P. (1977) *Outline of a Theory of Practice*. Cambridge: Cambridge University Press.
Bourdieu, P. (2010 [1979]) *Distinction: A Social Critique of the Judgement of Taste*. London: Routledge.
Bourdieu, P. (1990a [1980]) *The Logic of Practice*. Cambridge: Polity.
Bourdieu, P. (1988) *Homo Academicus*. Cambridge: Polity.
Bourdieu, P. (1990b) *In Other Words: Essays Towards a Reflexive Sociology*. Cambridge: Polity Press.
Bourdieu, P. (1991a) *Language and Symbolic Power*. Cambridge: Polity.
Bourdieu, P. (1991b) 'Genesis and Structure of the Religious Field', *Comparative Social Research*, 13(1): 1–44.
Bourdieu, P. (1993) *Sociology in Question*. London: Sage.
Bourdieu, P. (1999) *The Weight of the World: Social Suffering in Contemporary Society*. Cambridge: Polity.
Bourdieu, P. (2000) *Pascalian Meditations*. Cambridge: Polity.
Bourdieu, P. (2004) *Science of Science and Reflexivity*. Chicago: University of Chicago Press.
Bourdieu, P., Darbel, A. and Schnapper, D. (1991 [1969]) *The Love of Art: European Art Museums and Their Publics*. Cambridge: Polity.
Bourdieu, P. and Passeron, J. C. (1990) *Reproduction in Education, Society and Culture*. London: Sage.
Bourdieu, P. and Wacquant, L. (1992) *An Invitation to Reflexive Sociology*. Cambridge: Polity.
Bourdieu, P., Wacquant, L. and Farage, S. (1994) 'Rethinking the State: Genesis and Structure of the Bureaucratic Field', *Sociological Theory*, 12(1): 1–18.
Emirbayer, M. and Williams, E. M. (2005) 'Bourdieu and Social Work', *Social Service Review*, 79(4): 689–724.

Garrett, P. M. (2007a) 'Making Social Work More Bourdieusian: Why the Social Professions Should Critically Engage with the Work of Pierre Bourdieu', *European Journal of Social Work*, 10(2): 225–243.

Garrett, P. M. (2007b) 'The Relevance of Bourdieu for Social Work: A Reflection on Obstacles and Omissions', *Journal of Social Work*, 7(3): 355–379.

Houston, S. (2002) 'Reflecting on Habitus, Capital and Field: Towards a Culturally Sensitive Social Work', *Journal of Social Work*, 2(2): 149–167.

Huppatz, K. (2009) 'Reworking Bourdieu's "Capital": Feminine and Female Capitals in the Field of Paid Caring Work', *Sociology*, 43(1): 45–66.

Jenkins, R. (1992) *Pierre Bourdieu*. London: Routledge.

King, A. (2000) 'Thinking with Bourdieu against Bourdieu: A "Practical" Critique of the Habitus', *Sociological Theory*, 18(3): 417–433.

Lane, J. F. (2000) *Pierre Bourdieu: A Critical Reader*. London: Pluto Press.

Pellion, M. (1998) 'Bourdieu's Field and the Sociology of Welfare', *Journal of Social Policy*, 27(2): 213–229.

Santoro, M. (2011) 'From Bourdieu to Cultural Sociology', *Cultural Sociology*, 5(3): 3–23.

Swartz, D. (1997) *Culture and Power: The Sociology of Pierre Bourdieu*. Chicago: University of Chicago Press.

Swartz, D. and Zolberg, V. (2004) *After Bourdieu: Influence, Critique, Elaboration*. Dordrecht: Kluwer Academic Publications.

8

FEMINIST SOCIAL THEORY AND SOCIAL WORK

Introduction

Similar to Marxism, feminism is more than just an intellectual exercise. Feminism is a body of intellectual formulations, political ideas and empirical studies aimed at challenging the subordinate status of women in patriarchal society. To varying degrees these inform the broader activism and political objectives of the feminist movement. The point to emphasise is that feminists, like Marxists, are united by a shared practical aim: to change society, not just understand it.

Patriarchy refers to an oppressive social order organised around, or at least involving in significant ways, gender inequalities and the oppression of women by men. Developing in a number of waves, feminist social work (henceforth referred to as FSW) first emerged in the late 1960s drawing on the momentum of the rising swell of second-wave feminism and work undertaken with female service-users in community settings (Collins, 1986; Dominelli and McLeod, 1989; Stratham, 1978). At the heart of FSW is the goal of improving '. . . women's wellbeing by linking their personal predicaments and often untold private sorrows with their social position and status in society' (Dominelli, 2002: 6). For FSW an important part of realizing this goal means continuing to challenge the conception of women as primarily dependent on and carers of men and children.

From its earliest beginnings, social work was undertaken by and largely for women (Dominelli, 2002; Hicks, 2015). While social work values and ethics transcend gender, the influence of FSW has impacted significantly on the theoretical ideas, policies and practices of mainstream social work. In spite of its strong influence, social work remains a female profession. Women are far more likely than men to become social workers. In England and Scotland, more than 75 per cent of qualified social workers are female (Galley and Parrish, 2016). The vast majority of service-users are women too (Office of the Chief Social Work Adviser, Scottish Government, 2016). Similarly, both in teaching settings and in the provision of frontline practice, men are significantly outnumbered by women. Yet men are disproportionately over-represented in managerial roles at all levels of social work and across social care services more broadly.

Gender bias towards women as both the providers and recipients of social work services remains disproportionately high. Why is this? What does this say about how sex and gender are represented and connect to one another in modern society? How have feminist theorists sought to explain sexual and gender inequalities? What are the main social and cultural mechanisms by which they are produced and reproduced? How do these relate to social work? And how has social work drawn on and applied feminist social theory in practice? All of these questions and many of the wider issues surrounding them are the subject matter for this chapter.

The chapter begins by outlining the development of feminism from its earliest stirrings in the late eighteenth century, through to the present day. This provides the historical backdrop against which to present the ideas of a range of feminist theorists influential for shaping FSW theory and practice. The applied section of the chapter focusses on the ways feminist social workers have drawn on these ideas and perspectives to challenge the (male-centred) knowledge and value bases of social work, as well considering their application across various social work settings and scenarios. In the final section of the chapter, we cast a critically reflexive gaze over the field of social work in the present day by considering how feminist social workers have sought to respond to the prevalence and continuation of gender inequalities therein.

Defining feminism(s): past and present

Intellectually, feminism encompasses a diverse range of ideas, theories and empirical studies. In the present day, it is more accurate to talk of 'feminisms' (plural), as opposed to 'feminism' (singular), the distinction residing in the fact that there are now a broad range of feminist theories and corresponding intellectual and political formulations. Understood in a broad-brush way, feminism is represented as having developed in three main waves.

The rousing of first-wave feminism began in the eighteenth century in the pioneering work of English writers such as Mary Wollstonecraft (1759–1797). Writing her defence of women's rights in the 1790s, Wollstonecraft protested against the unequal and unjust treatment of women by men. Throughout the eighteenth and nineteenth centuries, feminism gathered momentum, culminating in the British suffragette movement and its campaign to secure women with the right to vote. Second-wave feminism emerged during the late 1960s and '70s forming part of the wider social and political unrest of the period and the growing discontent of oppressed and minority groups. It was at this time that feminist ideas and activism began to influence mainstream society and politics. Previously, feminism had comprised a number of loosely organised groups of women campaigning across a range of disparate contexts. The formation of international feminist organisations provided feminists with an institutional basis around which to organise and promote their goals. Promoting slogans such as 'sisterhood' and 'the personal is political', feminist thinkers began to establish themselves within universities and academic settings. This presented a strong challenge to traditionally patriarchal institutions heavily implicated in the production and dissemination of male-centred ways of thinking (Farganis, 1994).

Since the late 1980s, third-wave feminism has led to something of a breakdown in the intellectual identity and unity of second-wave feminism. Third wave-feminism is a fragmented and diverse body of feminist intellectual theories and political formulations. Today, the main forms of feminism include liberal feminism; Marxist/ socialist feminism; radical feminism; and post-modernist feminism. While all feminists share the goal of overturning the subordinate status of women in society, exactly what the category *women* has come to mean has been radically problematized and deconstructed. Women comprise a highly diversified group made up of multiple and in some cases conflicting forms of experience, identity and subjectivity.

The diverse and complex nature of third-wave feminism has impacted on the momentum and direction of feminism more generally. How feminism will proceed in the future is a matter that perhaps will not be clear for generations to come. In spite of this, feminists remain committed to overturning the oppressed status of women, even if what exactly is meant by the term *women*, and what the causes of their oppression are understood to be, continue to divide feminist thinkers and activists.

Liberal feminism

In the continuum of forms of feminist thought, liberal feminism is the least radical. Liberal feminism is premised on the view that sexual inequalities are rooted in a range of socially constructed and culturally pervasive ideas and values centring on the alleged differences between men and women. The ideals and objectives of liberal feminists underpin mainstream social and political approaches to sexual and gender inequalities today. The aim of liberal feminists is to eradicate gender inequalities through reform rather than revolution – reform of existing patriarchal structures and institutions, political policies and cultural forms. These include equality of women's political rights (e.g. securing the right of women to vote); economic equality (the right of women to be financially independent); equality in the workplace (e.g. campaigning for equal pay legislation); and issues of equality within wider society and culture (e.g. legislation such as the Equality Act passed in 2010, and challenging gender stereotypes that impede a culture of mutual respect between men and women in the workplace and wider society).

Since the 1960s and '70s, feminist theories, ideas and values have steadily been taken up and incorporated into mainstream social work (Freeman, 1990; Omre, 1998). FSW has changed the traditional male-dominated knowledge value bases on which the profession was founded. Today, FSW perspectives and values feature in mainstream textbooks and debates, either in their own right or as part of wider discussions to do with 'anti-oppressive practice' (Burke and Harrison, 1998). Mainstream social work discourse and practice adopt the same intellectual and political stance as liberal feminists. This is not to suggest that other forms of feminist-inspired social work do not continue to exert an important influence. Marxist/socialist, post-modern and radical feminist traditions continue to develop and are realized across social work theory and practice. But the extent to which they have influenced mainstream social work has not been as large as the extent of influence of liberal feminism, particularly where this has meant coming into conflict with or openly challenging the state and the profession itself.

Liberal feminists regard inequalities between the sexes as attributable primarily to differences in the social patterning of gender structures. A key thinker in the development of liberal feminism is Anne Oakley (1944 – present). Oakley's work contains elements that are liberal and elements that could be broadly classified as socialist, particularly the view that the labour performed by women in the domestic sphere such as housework and child-rearing is not recognised as labour, but instead regarded as activity women are unquestioningly expected to do (Oakley, 1974, 1976). Oakley's work has been most significant for the conceptual severing of the notions of sex and gender. Simply, 'sex' refers to the biological and physiological differences between males and females, whereas 'gender' refers to the cultural, social and psychological differences between men and women. Oakley's (1974) central claim is that gender is not rooted in the biological differences between men and women. Gender is instead instilled in the minds and bodies of individuals through socialization. On the surface, the variations in physical,

TABLE 8.1 Summary of liberal feminist theory

Liberal feminist theory
• aims and objectives: sexual and gender equality
• focusses analysis on men and women
• conception of social order: liberal democracy; equality can be achieved within existing social structures and culture

emotional and behavioural attributes between men and women appear to be determined by biologically fixed traits and differences in physiology. In actuality, these variations are culturally conditioned and socially patterned.

In *Sex, Gender and Society* (1972) Oakley presents a range of empirical studies to demonstrate the socially shaped nature of gender socialization. Her work identifies four key elements in the socialization process. The first, 'manipulation', refers to the attempts made by parents to manipulate children to behave in ways consistent with what it means to be male or female in a specific cultural context, as well as discouraging those which are not deemed appropriate e.g. boys who want to dress up in clothes for girls. The second, 'canalisation', involves parents directing the behaviour of the child towards certain activities and interests e.g. helping their mother with housework in the case of girls, and being expected to engage more in physical activities like playing outside in the case of boys. The third concerns parents' use of 'verbal appellations' and language more generally. Verbal appellations are used to reinforce appropriate gender identification, such as when a father chastises his son for crying 'like a girl'. The fourth highlights the roles parents actively play in directing their children towards different gender-based activities e.g. encouraging boys to play particular sports such as football and rugby, and girls to pursue dancing or reading.

Oakley's work on gender socialization highlights the active role parents play in 'gendering' their children. In other works, such as *Sex, Gender and Society* (1972) and *The Sociology of Housework* (1974), Oakley elaborates on these ideas to show how gender structures work to constrain the identities, activities and behaviours women are socialized into. The key thing to understand here is that there is nothing natural or inevitable about the roles and identities into which males and females are socialized. They are the product of structures and processes to which a range of patriarchal values, ideals and behaviours are attached. For liberal feminists such as Oakley, these structures and the value systems on which they are based are social constructs. The political objective of liberal feminism is to highlight how and where these structures impinge on and feed directly into inequalities between men and women with the aim of systematically dismantling and eradicating them.

Marxist-socialist feminism

Marxist, or more broadly socialist, feminism has its roots in the later nineteenth century. The origins of Marxist-socialist feminism can be traced back to the early communist and socialist political movement. Marxist-socialist feminists reject the view that gender inequalities can be identified and challenged through changes to existing legal and political structures. Instead, they identify the cause of women's oppression as residing in the highly exploitative and alienating nature of social relations in capitalist society. For Marxist-socialist feminists, only the complete overthrow of capitalism can bring about equality in the relationships between men and women.

A key resource in the development of Marxist-socialist feminism is the work of Friedrich Engels, Marx's close friend, patron and, at times, co-writer. In *The Origin of the Family, Private Property and the State* (1978 [1884]), Engels sets out the intellectual template Marxist-socialist feminists have used to develop much further and comprehensively the implications of Marx and Engels's ideas concerning gender oppression. Engels argues that as a by-product of the wider exploitation of the workforce under capitalism, women are subject to manifold forms of exploitation. Throughout history, the various 'modes of production' – Marx's term for describing social orders based around the exploitation by ruling classes of subordinate ones – have been structured around the control of women. This is true in terms of both the labour they perform and the reproductive capacities they embody. The notion of 'social relations of biological reproduction' is the idea that procreation, childbirth and childcare are structured by the social relations in which family life is rooted. Crucially, this takes place in ways that work to fulfil and serve the wider economic ideals of capitalism.

In capitalist society, the working classes are subject to exploitative and subordinate social positions, women more so than any other social group. Working-class women comprise the most exploited social group of all because in addition to forming part of a socially subordinated class group i.e. the working class, within this class group they occupy a subordinate position in the gender hierarchy i.e. in relation to working-class men. In this view, not only are working-class women exploited by the capitalist system they are born into, but they are also exploited through the social categories of 'wife' and 'mother'. The dual subordination of women as workers and wives is a necessary form of exploitation in a capitalist economy. Working-class men are exploited at, and through, work, but working-class women are subordinated by the capitalist system and their husbands, albeit in ways that are not necessarily intended, or fully consciously grasped by either men or women. Engels's work represents the earliest attempt to use Marxist concepts and ideas to explain the subordinate status of women in capitalist society. Since then, Marxist-socialist feminists have taken up and developed these ideas in a number of different directions.

One such thinker is Canadian sociologist Dorothy Smith (1926 – present). Smith's work draws on ideas from phenomenology (Chapter 3) and Marx's concept of ideology (Chapter 2), in particular the view that knowledge is always marked by and refracts the social context in which it developed. Smith's (1990: 11) central claim is that the modes of consciousness e.g. ways of thinking, feeling, perceiving, understanding, etc. women use to construct their experiences are built on a 'line of fault'. Women's experience of social reality is split between what they intuitively feel, experience and perceive, and the language and concepts at their disposal for articulating those experiences. In a patriarchal society, the ways of thinking and modes of communicating supplied to women through culture do not allow them to capture or articulate the particular nature of their experiences.

In a patriarchal society, the dominant modes of talking and thinking fail to capture and are only marginally shaped by the experiences of women. Instead, they are the linguistic and ideal expressions of men. For Marx, culture in a capitalist society is ideological because the ideas and values of socially dominant groups are imposed on and shape subordinate groups. In patriarchal society, men – the socially dominant sex – oppress women through imposing the cultural ideas and values on women – the socially dominated sex. The concept of 'line-of-fault' is used by Smith to refer to the estrangement women experience when using the linguistic and ideal forms supplied to them by a male-dominated culture. In *The Ideological Practice of Sociology* (1990) Smith extends these ideas to think critically about the status of sociological knowledge. She claims that, similar to everyday ways of thinking and communicating, 'sociology creates a construct of society that is especially discontinuous with the world known, lived, experienced and acted in' by women (Smith, 1990: 2). As the gender composition of the classical theorists demonstrates (Chapter 2), social theory emerged out of the ideas, concerns and values of men. Yet social theory tends to be represented as impartial, objective and value-free. Critical of this view, Smith (1990: 36) argues that only knowledge rooted in 'people's activities and material conditions thereof could be considered non-ideological'. In spite of its claims to objectivity, social theoretical knowledge, and social scientific knowledge more generally, is in fact highly ideological. In its place, Smith (1990) argues for a radical new approach to analysing social life, one which incorporates the view of reality from the standpoint of women. This involves the analyst adopting a standpoint that is situated not 'outside' of knowledge, but 'on the side' of knowledge, and that acknowledges the position of women (Smith, 1987: 15).

The relationship between gender and social position is taken up and explored by British sociologist Beverley Skeggs. Marxist-socialist feminists view gender inequalities as deriving primarily from wider social-class structures. Skeggs's (1997) work takes up and develops these ideas to demonstrate how structures of class and gender interact and shape one another in a number of co-constituting ways. Drawing on Bourdieu's theoretical concepts of 'habitus' and 'capital' (Chapter 7), Skeggs (1997) analyses data taken from ethnographic methods and in-depth interviews with working-class women, highlighting the ways class structures work to undermine gender-based forms of solidarity between women. A specific focus of her work involves the forms of discourse, attitudes and behaviours working-class women use to construct the ideal categories of femininity, sexuality and womanhood. The main conclusion of Skeggs's study was that the attitudes and practices working-class women use to construct those ideal categories were organised around negative interpretations and representations of middle-class women.

Many of the working-class women in Skeggs's study were single parents, whereas others had left school at an early age and had only minimal educational qualifications. This made it much harder, in some cases simply not possible, to construct their identity and lifestyle around education, financial independence and/or a professional career. In ways that were fully consciously grasped and in others that were enacted only semi-consciously, the lack of economic and cultural forms of capital disposed the women to re-appropriate and use their gender as a resource for asserting their agency e.g. through paying close attention to aesthetic appearance and self-presentation, and engaging in recreational pursuits like going to nightclubs with other women.

The conclusions from Skeggs's work are consistent with the view asserted by Bourdieu (1993: 15) that gender tends to be 'one of the last refuges of the dominated classes'. This is the idea that the social-class position of dominated groups, in this case working-class women, systematically denies them the possibility to access legitimate forms of capital with which to construct their identity. Instead, they are compelled to draw on whatever embodied forms of capital they have, in this case their gender, to try to advance their social position. The habitus of the women in Skeggs's study disposed them to construct images and ideals of middle-class women in ways that directly contradicted their own habitus-shaped understandings of how women should aspire to look and behave. Skeggs's work provides a stark demonstration of the ways class and gender combined to compound the oppressed status of working-class women:

TABLE 8.2 Summary of Marxist-socialist feminist theory

Marxist-socialist feminist theory
• aims and objectives: revolutionary action; transformation of existing class and gender hierarchies and relations
• focusses analysis on dominant and dominated classes; subordinate status of women directly related to structure of capitalist class relations
• conception of social order: class-based social structure leads to exploitative gender relations; capitalist society necessarily results in patriarchy

in the first instance, by constructing their self-understanding and identity through sexualised versions of femininity, and in turn conforming to and affirming a number of sexual stereotypes about women; and in the second, by (partially) knowingly trying to undermine constructions of femininity definitive of middle-class forms of habitus.

Radical feminism

Radical feminism first began to develop in the early 1970s. Radical feminists are critical of the view that patriarchy and gender inequalities can be reduced to issues of class relations and the wider capitalist system (Millett, 1977 [1970]; Firestone, 1970). Instead, radical feminists argue that it is patriarchy itself which should be the primary focus for feminist analysis. From a radical feminist perspective, patriarchy is a social order structured wholly and primarily around the interests of men. The central social division is not between ruling and subordinate classes as Marxist-socialist feminists claim, but between all men and all women. In patriarchal society, the systematic subordination of women by men is reflected in all social institutions, ideas and cultural forms. A key assumption for radical feminists is that patriarchy is expressed through both physical and symbolic male violence towards women. In this view, domestic violence and pornography should not be understood as dependent on the dispositions of particular men, but instead are the physical and symbolic expression of a society centred on male control of, and hatred of, women (Brownmiller, 1975).

Radical feminism comprises a number of different positions. These include calls for women to extricate themselves entirely from patriarchal society, and away from all men. Unsurprisingly perhaps, such a radical position has made little impact within social work. Instead, radical feminist theory has tended to inform the view that women should focus their energies on living with and for other women. The ideals captured by this view have informed the formation of organisations run by women for women, such as rape crisis centres, battered women's shelters and incest survivor groups (Dominelli, 2002: 27). For feminists working within a range of perspectives, the claims of radical feminists are overly simplistic and generalizing (hooks, 1984). The main charge is that the category *men* does not comprise a homogenous and unified group as well as it fails to acknowledge the oppression of certain male populations such as homosexuals, male feminists and activists, etc., by men. Critics argue too that radical feminists operate with a colour-blind view towards race and ethnicity and the oppression of working-class women by middle-class women in positions of power (Jaggar, 1983). The radical nature of the claims made by radical feminists has meant its influence within mainstream social work has been limited.

TABLE 8.3 Summary of radical feminist theory

Radical feminist theory

* aims and objectives: analysis and end of patriarchy
* focusses analysis on females and males as fundamentally different; females and males characterised by divergent interests and needs
* conception of social order: organised around and centring on patriarchal relations across all areas of society and culture

Post-modernist feminism

The infusion of post-modernist ideas within feminism began to develop from the 1980s onwards. Post-modernist feminism is also referred to as 'post-structuralist' or 'cultural turn' feminism. This is because post-modernist feminism draws on many of the intellectual resources developed by post-structuralist thinkers such as Foucault (Chapter 6), in particular the view that powerful forms of discourse and the cultural complexities of modern society work to constrain the identities and subjectivity of women. Intellectually, post-modernist feminist thinkers tend to be located more in humanities-based and philosophically inclined disciplines than in the social sciences. Their work tends to be more abstract than concrete, which has shaped the extent to which feminist social workers have been able to apply their ideas. A key idea for post-modernist feminists is that patriarchal discourses oppressively shape the minds and bodies of both men and women. The work of post-modernist feminists seeks to identify and expose the power relations contained within patriarchal forms of discourse.

A hugely influential figure in the development of post-modernist feminism is American thinker Judith Butler (1956 – present). According to Butler, the seemingly straight-forward and natural association between the biological body and the gender scripts of 'male' and 'female' fails to capture the reality that people can feel at odds with, and actively seek to change, the gender script associated with their body (sex). To critically explore the relations between sex and gender, Butler draws on ideas from French post-structuralist thinking and Anglo-Saxon philosophical accounts of language, in particular J. L. Austin's notion of 'speech acts'. Butler (1990) argues that there is no such thing as 'sex' in the sense that there is a biological entity called a 'male' and a biological entity called a 'female'. Instead, the category of 'sex' is just exactly that – a category, a mental construction brought to life by and through language.

During the 1970s, Oakley's distinction between 'sex' and 'gender' was crucial to the development of feminist thought. Butler's work self-consciously seeks to go beyond the widespread assumption that sex is directly determined by biology in ways that mean the division and differences between males and females cannot be changed. Butler (1993, 2004) argues that this division is itself a construction of patriarchal culture and ways of thinking. Her central claim is that gender and sex are not things people have, but instead what people 'do'. Gender is an activity, or form of 'doing', which Butler seeks to capture by the concept of 'performativity'. Gender is not the expression of sex because the categories of sex e.g. 'male' and 'female' do not refer to real things. Rather they are constantly produced and institutionalized through gendered forms of discourse and performativity (Butler, 1990, 1993).

Performativity refers to the effects that gendered ways of thinking and behaving produce on and for the individual. Butler (1990: 140) defines gender performativity as the 'stylized repetition of acts' and forms of 'bodily movement' and comportment. The performative aspects of gender create the impression that human subjects possess a fixed and unalterable sex. Gender performativity is like Austin's speech acts. People bring into existence the very thing they think they are just describing and which already exists – namely, their sex. But gendered performativity is not produced by a fixed-sex subject that exists prior to the act. Gender performativity refers to the processes by which human subjects *become*, not already are, a 'woman' or a 'man'.

Post-modernist feminist thinkers like Butler identify and challenge the discursive categories embedded in and that order the distinction between 'male' and 'female'. The same is true of the work of Raewyn Connell (1944 – present). (Born Robert Connell, Connell is a transsexual who changed her name to Raewyn.) Connell's (1995) most influential work focusses on the concept of 'masculinity', and the performativity involved in the expression of different 'masculinities'. Echoing the ideas of Butler, Connell regards the category of masculinity not as referring to a really existing thing, but instead a mental construct brought into being through performativity. Moreover, there is no such thing as masculinity in the singular. There exist instead multiple discordant and internally contradictory masculinities, organised around oppressively structured practices.

Patriarchal societies are organised around what Connell (1995) refers to as the 'gender order'. The gender order refers to the hierarchy of discourses and practices through which the category of sex is made and remade. At the top of the hierarchy are the patriarchal discourses and practices which construct men as superior to women. Connell refers to these discourses and practices as 'hegemonic masculinity'. This is the dominant form of masculinity in contemporary culture (Connell, 1995: 77). Hegemonic masculinity is constructed through a number of discourses which include the notion that white heterosexual males are more dominant than males from other ethnic groups as well as homosexuals; hegemonic males express certain 'male traits' such as rationality, aggression and the capacity to suppress emotions; hegemonic males realize an ideal physique and body type.

The discourses surrounding hegemonic masculinity shape the minds and bodies of the men who are realized through them. The forms of bodily comportment associated with hegemonic masculinity are integral to the ways men assert their physical and symbolic dominance over women. Not all men are able to realize the discursively shaped performances associated with hegemonic masculinity. This is why hegemonic masculinity is implicated in the subordination of other forms of masculinity. Subordinate forms of masculinity include 'complicit masculinity' e.g. men who aspire and try to imitate the identities and bodily practices associated with hegemonic masculinity; 'subordinate masculinity' e.g. effeminate men and homosexuals; and 'marginalized masculinity' e.g. men who aspire to hegemonic masculinity but are unable to achieve it for reasons of race and disability (Connell, 1995). At the bottom of the gender order are

TABLE 8.4 Summary of post-structuralist and post-modernist feminist theory

Post-structuralist and post-modernist feminist theory

- aims and objectives: identify and deconstruct cultural categories; liberation of human subjects through stimulating difference
- focus analysis on discursive categories used to construct and order human subjectivity
- conception of social order: patriarchal discourses produced and reproduced through culture

'femininities'. Femininity is the negative reference point against which all forms of masculinity are constructed and evaluated. Femininity is differentiated in the following ways: 'emphasised femininity' e.g. females who are compliant with and confer value on the discourses informing hegemonic masculinity; and 'resistant femininity' e.g. women and lesbians who reject appearing and behaving in the ways expected of them.

Applying feminist social theory to social work

Feminist social theory and social work knowledge and values

As a distinct approach to social work, FSW first emerged in Western Europe and America during the 1970s in line with the social and political unrest of the period and the rising tide of second-wave feminism. Since then, FSW has significantly shaped the development of mainstream social work. This is true at a number of levels, including the knowledge and value bases of the profession; social work legislation and policy; and social work discourse and practice. Today, FSW comprises a diverse range of theoretical positions and perspectives, each providing a coherent worldview around which women-centred values, forms of discourse and practice have and continue to take shape.

In terms of the relationship of FSW to mainstream social work, the ideals and objectives of liberal feminism have met with the most success. The ideals and values of liberal feminists have been fully assimilated into every aspect of mainstream social work. Whether they explicitly consider themselves to be feminists or not, the vast majority of social workers root their ideals, attitudes and practices in the moral and political ideals of liberal feminism. The success of liberal feminism to integrate into mainstream social work can in large part be attributed to the view that gender inequalities can be tackled and eradicated from within, as opposed to tearing down and rebuilding anew, the organisational structures in which social work currently exists. Moreover, where they do not overtly challenge or call into conflict mainstream social work values and practice, Marxist-socialist, radical and post-modernist feminist social workers have informed the development of FSW. In this section of the chapter we examine more specifically how the different strands of FSW have impacted on the knowledge and value bases of social work as well as taking a closer look at how this has led to efforts to reorient social work practice along more gender-sensitive lines.

Feminist social theory has provided many of the intellectual resources feminist social workers use to critically interrogate the knowledge and values on which social work was originally founded. Emerging in the nineteenth century, modern social work developed within the social structures and cultural values of Victorian England. Compared to the present day, society then was organised around profound sexual and gender inequalities. Since the late 1960s, feminist social workers have focussed their attention on critically scrutinizing the patriarchal legacy of social work, working hard to identify evidence of its traces in social work thinking, values and practice. Feminist social workers have brought to bear a range of feminist ideas and perspectives on the knowledge base social work draws on and the normative ideals directing practice. It was men, not women, who played the dominant role in establishing many of these ideals.

While the majority of frontline social workers are women, the majority of social work academics and theorists are men (Davis, 1985). Similarly within the 'psych-' disciplines, sociology and social theory, men occupy the majority of dominant field positions. (The vast majority of the theorists featured in this book are men, for example.) Rooted in the ideas of standpoint theorists such as Dorothy Smith, FSW thinkers have challenged the notion that the male-centred forms of knowledge produced by male social work theorists are 'representative and a measure of women's experience' (Dominelli, 2002: 15). FSW scholars have drawn attention to the uneven gendered division of intellectual labour within social work and many of the adjacently positioned disciplines. They claim that the knowledge base of social work is essentially patriarchal because it refracts the interests and normative ideals of men, and men comprise the majority of social work theorists and academics.

From the standpoint of women, a considerable part of the power male-centred knowledge is understood to possess derives from its scientific status (Smith, 1990). Scientific methods and forms of discourse are represented as impartial, objective and value-free. This claim works to obscure how the interests and concerns of men shape the production of this knowledge. The majority of the intellectual constructs structuring the actions and activities of social workers are produced by men, while being taken up and put to work by female social workers working predominantly with female service-users. Under the current intellectual division of labour, female social workers work and interact with other women in ways mediated by constructs and categories produced by men. Smith's work provides a powerful account of the line of fault and sense of estrangement this gives rise to as part of the overall experience of women in a patriarchal society. As the number of women entering academic departments and positions of power has steadily risen since the 1970s, feminist thinkers and FSW have drawn attention to and challenged the dominance of men in positions of intellectual power.

In addition to adopting a critical stance to male-centred knowledge within social work, FSW has drawn on the work of feminist social theorists to interrogate the value base of social work. This has meant critically interrogating the allegedly universal moral principles and normative ideals guiding social work e.g. emancipation, empowerment, self-determination, etc., with a view to explaining how these connect to wider structures of power and the oppressed status of women. Thinking critically about these values is not the same as rejecting them. It means looking closely at how they connect to the lived experiences of women across a range of formal institutional settings and everyday roles and relationships. By bringing these abstract ideals and values back down to the ground, feminist social workers question whether or not the roles and relationships available to women, as mother, wife, worker, carer, etc. provide them with the opportunities to realize those values (Miller, 1991: 40). Feminist social workers are committed to upholding the core social work values of emancipation, empowerment and so on, but not if the realization of these involve women in their everyday lives performing roles which position them as responsible for the '"lesser task" of helping other humans to develop' (Miller, 1991: 40).

A further area feminist social workers have directed their attention towards concerns the essentialist and dualist categories used to order gender relations between men and women. The post-structuralist and post-modernist feminist thought of Butler and Connell respectively has played an important part in challenging the conceptual dualisms e.g. sex/gender, male/female, active/reactive, rational/irrational, etc. implicated in the production and reproduction of antagonistic gender relations and identities. Both seek to deconstruct the notion that the categories of 'male' and 'female' exist outside of the binary forms of discourse through which they are constituted. They claim instead that sexual identity is wholly discursive, and that there are no essential traits and attributes differentiating human subjects. The term *sex* is not rooted in biology, but is an entirely discursive and therefore political construct, one which needs to be abolished altogether. The work of Butler and Connell, for example, has been particularly valuable for social work academics and professionals seeking change to the oppressive classificatory schemes and categories structuring the experiences of non-heterosexual and transgender service-users (McPhail, 2004; Sands, 1996).

Since the 1970s, FSW thinkers have drawn extensively on and put to work many of the ideational constructs developed by feminist social theorists, using them to identify, scrutinize and challenge patriarchal forms of discourse and normative values wherever and whenever they have arisen. Looking to the future, FSW and mainstream social work more broadly need to continue to look to feminist social theory to provide the modes of reasoning and theoretical ideas necessary for deconstructing gender inequalities, patriarchal structures and expressions of power.

Feminist social work practice

Feminist social workers have worked hard to reorganise and enact social work practice along gender-sensitive and feminist lines. Identifying and eradicating 'gender blind' forms of practice is a key objective for FSW. This does not mean, however, that a one-size-fits-all approach to practice can be constructed on the basis of feminist proscribed formulae (Dominelli, 2002; Omre, 1998). For feminist theoretical constructs and conceptual ideas to be of value, they must be able to be translated into the activities and practices of social workers operating across a diverse range of service-user groups and contexts (Foxley, 1979; Payne, 1991). FSW academics and practitioners have made significant process in devising ways to incorporate insights from feminist social theory into social work practice. Testimony to their success can be found in the pages of mainstream journals, specialist feminist journals, social work monographs, and undergraduate and postgraduate textbooks. The body of knowledge concerned with realigning mainstream practice in line with the central tenets of FSW continues to develop in both range and depth.

An important part of FSW practice concerns men. Any serious attempt to tackle the oppressed status of women in society cannot be achieved 'by focussing exclusively on the lives and experiences of women' (Scully, 1990: 3). Part of the challenge of eradicating gender inequality involves social workers working with service-users, particularly men, to understand how and why sexual and gender inequalities are produced and reproduced (Wild, 1999). This means highlighting the ways gender-based roles, identities and behaviours connect to wider structures of power and the inequalities leading out from these. One way feminist social workers have sought to do this has been to work with male service-users and men implicated in the problems of female service-users e.g. women who suffer domestic violence, verbal abuse and family problems. Working with male service-users and men, either on a one-to-one basis or as part of a couple and/or focus group, involves trying to identify, and challenge the ways gender-specific behaviours impact negatively not only on the people around them e.g. partner, spouse, family members, etc., but on men too (Cavanagh and Cree, 1996; Pease, 2001).

Informed by Oakley's (1972, 1974) work on gender and gender socialization, social workers can assist male service-users and men to recognise the active role they play in performing certain gender roles and identities. Rather than something natural or inevitable, the emotional, psychological and behavioural differences between males and females are actively encouraged and developed from a very early age. Whether and to what extent male service-users are aware of it, they actively draw on socially shaped gender identities, relations and practices. Helping men to recognise the agency they exert in electing to identify with and enact certain forms of masculinity and gender practice is an important part of FSW practice. It provides the basis for assisting male service-users and men to explore and develop new forms of gender-based identity and practice.

An important question to consider when working with male service-users and men is why they would choose to relinquish particular ways of 'doing' masculinity which are personally and socially empowering. Working with men to identify the positive gains that might ensue from relinquishing certain forms of gender-based identity and the behaviours attached to them is part of the challenge confronting feminist social workers (Cavanagh and Cree, 1996). As such, Seidler (2006) suggests an approach to working with male service-users that invites them to consider the two-way nature of gender, as a structure which simultaneously enables and constrains how they think, feel and interact. In certain situations and scenarios gender identities and roles can empower men at the same time as disempowering them in other ways. Social workers can work with male service-users and men to identify the advantages and disadvantages attached to different 'masculinities' and the ways these shape their capacity to develop personally fulfilling relationships while undermining them in others.

Following this approach, Pease (2001: 9) claims that men need to be encouraged to 'reflect upon their own socialisation and engage with their own gendered subjectivity'. This could include encouraging male service-users to explore how their own relationships with significant male others e.g. father, uncle, brother, step-father, etc. positively influenced and informed aspects of their own identities. At the same time, drawing attention to the negative impact exposure to certain expressions of masculinity and behaviour had on the service-user is important too, particularly as they relate to their emotional repertoires and capacity to engage in child-rearing and nurturing roles. It may also be the case that some men have not fully considered how the unintended consequences of their actions shape the identity and lives of family members, as well as their own personal identity and development (Dominelli and McLeod, 1989).

Working directly with male service-users and men forms an important strand of FSW practice. Just as important is ensuring that gendered forms of power do not enter into the relationships between service-users and social workers. Skeggs's (1997) work highlights the ways class interacts with and impinges on gender, and how the complex interweaving of the two shapes the experiences and identities of women. As such, Skeggs's work provides a window onto certain assumptions about the social work relationship, in particular the view that women social workers are best suited for assisting female service-users with particular issues and problems (Myers, 2010). The working-class women in Skeggs's study demonstrate that lack of access to economic and cultural forms of capital e.g. money, education and a professional career meant appropriating their gender as a resource for exercising agency.

Class was more significant than gender for shaping the identity of the women in Skeggs's study. This is a valuable point to consider with regard to certain types of social work relationship. It might seem obvious, for example, that a female social worker and mother of two may be better placed to assist a single working-class mother than a male social worker. But a female social worker brings to the relationship with the service-user a range of socially marked dispositions and embodied forms of capital e.g. linguistic capital, bodily gestures and forms of comportment, etc., which are likely to reproduce the same kind of class-based power dynamics found in wider society. In this view, rather than comprising an obstacle to the social work relationship, the gender identity of a male social worker may give rise to a more productive working relationship between the service-user and the social worker. The need to think reflexively about the complex ways gender dynamics interact with other social-structural variables is an important part of incorporating FSW theory into practice.

Connell's work highlights how gender shapes relations of power between men, not just between men and women. Work carried out by Cross and Bagilhole (2002) illustrates how gender impinges on the relationship between male social workers and male service-users. Male social workers may be challenged about their sexuality by male service-users. Men in female-dominated professions are more likely to be subject to 'feminization' and 'stigmatization' (Myers, 2010). A male service-user may have been brought up in an environment where the kinds of traits associated with 'hegemonic masculinity' e.g. athletic physique, toughness and an unwillingness to display emotions are used to assert and gain power (Chapter 5). Male service-users may try to use their masculinity to undermine the personal identity of a male social worker, by trying to gain power in the relationship. The male social worker will have to try to use his professional, as opposed to gender, identity to assert himself in the relationship if an even balance of power is to be maintained.

Up until now we have considered a number of the different ways ideas and insights from feminist social theory have been incorporated into FSW practice. Before moving on to the final section of the chapter it is important to reflect on some of the wider issues concerning the uses and application of FSW theory. The view that human knowledge is necessarily marked by the social conditions from which it arises is a core tenet of standpoint theory (Smith, 1987; Harding, 1991). Human knowledge can never be completely objective or impartial because it always refracts the social and cultural standpoint of the people producing that knowledge. If this is true of all knowledge, then the same principles must be applicable to the ideas and concepts contained within standpoint theory and feminist social theory more generally.

The ideas and values contained within feminist social theory, no less than any other forms of knowledge, are marked by and refract the claims to power of the individuals and groups propounding them, in this case feminist social theorists and feminist social workers. As such, it cannot be assumed that how the categories of 'oppressed' and 'disempowered' are constructed within FSW theory and discourse *necessarily* captures the experiences of the women to whom those categories are applied. At least in part, feminist social theoretical categories, like any other form of social theoretical categories e.g. Marxist, Foucauldian and so on, are shaped by the struggles for power in which the proponents and advocates of those categories are embedded. For example, from the outside looking in, the women in Skeggs's study are presented as subject to a dual form of oppression. Not only are they disempowered by gender, but by the socially subordinate class position they occupy and the nature of the ways the two interpenetrate one another.

To raise this point is not to try to deny the truth claims made in Skeggs's work. It is to highlight that considered from the point of view of the female service-user in the class-based lifeworld she belongs to (Chapter 3), her experience of the roles and identities she assumes might not strike her as either oppressive or disempowering (hooks, 2000). On the contrary, it may seem natural and right that as a woman she assumes, for example, a larger share of the nurturing roles and caring for others because in her lifeworld men are constructed as naturally less proficient than women at caring and nurturing.

Moreover, within the class-based lifeworld of the service-user, her role as a mother may constitute the primary source of her gender-based identity, one she experiences as enabling because it provides a legitimate basis on which to construct a sense of personal and social identity. Not to organise her identity around certain nurturing roles and domestic tasks might impact negatively on her identity, as imagined through her eyes and those of others too. These are important points to consider. They demonstrate the importance of thinking with and applying feminist social theory in a reflexive manner. To do otherwise runs the risk of projecting onto service-users discourses of inequality and oppression because the social worker has failed to consider fully the experiences and perspectives of the individuals and groups in question.

Adopting a rigid and dogmatic approach to gender inequalities implies that the attributes of individuals can be divided out, categorised and controlled for in ways that are very difficult to discern in the messy reality that is human life. As the work of Skeggs demonstrates very clearly, service-users do not live their lives as aggregates of variables; rather, they embody their social class and gender in personally meaningful and often contradictory ways which cannot be prised apart or separated out from their whole identity as a person. How gender interacts with other social variables, such as social class, age and ethnicity, emphasises the need for social workers to adopt a dynamic approach to gender-sensitive practice. Gender is always necessarily mediated by a range of wider social structures, such as class, ethnicity and age. Here we see some of the central tensions at the heart of feminist theory. To return to the point made earlier, FSW cannot be practiced by drawing on a range of ready-made proscriptions or formulae. The challenge for feminist social workers is to remain aware of the complex ways a range of structural factors intersect with and co-constitute one another.

Feminism and social work: dealing with tensions in-house

From its earliest beginnings, social work has been a female-dominated profession. In this final section of the chapter we examine to what extent this remains the case and the ways FSW academics and the profession more generally have sought to explain and address this. Statistics regarding the gender composition of social work across a range of national contexts vary. That women, as opposed to men, are far more likely to become social workers is common to them all. In spite of conscious efforts by the profession to recruit more men into social work, these have met with very limited success (McLean, 2003). Research carried out by the General Social Care Council (GSSC) in 2014 showed that more than 75 per cent of qualified social workers in England are female (Guardian, 2017). In 2015, 84 per cent of all staff working in local authority social work services in Scotland were women (Gov.scot, 2017). Not only are women more likely to become social workers than men, men who embark on undergraduate and postgraduate social work degrees are also more likely than women not to complete their studies (Furness, 2012).

It is neither natural or inevitable that women are more likely to become social workers than men. Powerful and widespread gender stereotypes that depict women as naturally more caring, emotionally driven and sensitive, as well as being more oriented towards nurturing and building relationships, heavily inform the view of social work as a woman's profession (Bruckner, 2002: 269; Christie, 1998; Myers, 2010). The power of these discourses is significant for disposing women towards, at the same time as orienting men away from, social work (Gerstel and Gallacher, 2001; Simpson, 2004). Men who do elect to pursue a career in social work are often viewed as embodying traits and qualities associated with hegemonic forms of masculinity. These include the view of men as emotionally detached, rational and possessing the qualities associated with leadership (Pringle, 2005).

The disproportionately high representation of women within social work raises a number of issues. Feminist social workers have played a leading role in formulating the response to these issues. For liberal feminists, gender equality within social work would mean an even distribution of men and women across social work in all areas and at all levels including management structures and positions of power. From a Marxist-socialist feminist perspective, gender inequalities persist because of more enduring and profound inequalities around which entire social-class groups are organised. The increasing appearance of women in diverse parts of the workforce in more recent times is interpreted by Marxist feminists not as some kind of liberation from the domestic sphere, but rather the result of structural changes in the capitalist economy, as it seeks new sources of cheap labour, such as social care work, to exploit. The radical feminist position regards the under-representation of men within social work in a positive light. Social work should not concern itself with the lack of males within the profession, as to do so means expending what limited resources are available for women to recruit men into one of the few social arenas in which women are dominant (Firestone, 1970).

In sum, the response of feminist social workers towards the gender imbalance within social work is far from unified. Further complicating these issues, and in direct opposition to the views of radical feminists, the general consensus among feminist social workers is that men need to be incorporated more fully into FSW theory. The growing body of research focussing on the experiences and identities of men in social work with regard to time spent in training and in organisational and practice-based settings reflects this consensus (Dominelli, 2002; Cavanagh and Cree, 1996). Research to date suggests that the experiences of men in social work are characterised by a number of ongoing tensions, contradictory roles and relationships (Pringle, 2001; Gerstel and Gallacher, 2001).

The perception of social work as a female profession means that men who enter the profession often face challenges to their masculinity from service-users, the wider public and colleagues too (Pease, 2011). Male social work students and professionals report pressure from friends, relatives and wider cultural stereotypes to assert aspects of their masculinity outside of work e.g. through leisure pursuits and in other areas of their lives. Male social workers are aware of and actively seek to manage the tensions and forms of estrangement they experience. In professional settings male social workers commonly seek to resolve tensions surrounding their identity by actively pursuing more stereotypically masculine roles (Lawler and Hearn, 1997). The propensity of male social workers to pursue managerial positions is in part an unintended consequence of their marginalized status within the profession. This has the effect of further complicating the status of men within social work by increasing their presence within positions of power and authority.

One response to the over-representation of men within managerial positions has been to encourage them to actively assist in the task of dismantling patriarchal structures from inside the profession. Huppatz (2009) has argued that Bourdieu failed to account for the ways gender dispositions and identity can be used as a form of capital within certain occupational contexts (fields). In the field of social work, being male is as a form of field-specific capital which can be used to attain dominant field positions e.g. management roles. For Pringle (2001), male social work professionals need to consider how their gender works to their professional advantage. Echoing these views, Pease (2011) argues that male social workers have an ethical obligation to utilise their awareness to counteract professional advancement on the basis of gender. This seems highly unrealistic, however, and it is far from clear how this would work in practice (Christie, 2006). In many ways, focussing on the experiences and identities of male social workers has tended to complicate, rather than illuminate, the debate about how best to address the gender imbalance within the profession.

Conclusion

This chapter has identified and addressed the main points of intersection and influence of feminist social theory within social work. Emerging in the late 1960s out of the rising tide of second-wave feminism, FSW has continued to develop as a distinct body of knowledge, methods and practice in its own right. As part of the wider intellectual and political fragmentation characteristic of third-wave feminism, FSW similarly began to splinter and diversify, in turn providing the intellectual and political basis for a corresponding series of FSW positions, perspectives and practices. Where these do not call into conflict mainstream liberal social work values and practice, they have contributed to widening the ideational resources inspiring a range of different forms of contemporary FSW practice. In spite of the overall success FSW has achieved in dismantling the remaining patriarchal vestiges of the knowledge and value bases of social work, FSW has made little progress in addressing the highly gendered composition of the profession. Different feminist theoretical perspectives regard this as either more or less problematic. Whether or not and how social work seeks to deal with this in the future as yet remain unclear.

Further reading

Dominelli, L. (2002) *Feminist Social Work Theory and Practice*. Hampshire: Palgrave.
Oakley, A. (1972) *Sex, Gender and Society*. London: Maurice Temple Smith Ltd.
Smith, D. (1987) *The Everyday World as Problematic: A Feminist Sociology*. Toronto: The University of Toronto Press.

References

Bourdieu, P. (1993) *Sociology in Question*. Cambridge: Polity.
Brook, E. and Davis, A. (1985) *Women, the Family, and Social Work*. London: Tavistock.
Brownmiller, S. (1975) *Against Our Will: Men, Women and Rape*. New York: Simon and Schuster.
Bruckner, M. (2002) 'On Social Work and What Gender Has Got to Do with It', *European Journal of Social Work*, 15(3): 269–276.

Burke, B. and Harrison, P. (1998) 'Anti-Oppressive Practice', in Adams, R., Dominelli, L. and Payne, M. (eds.) *Social Work: Themes, Issues and Critical Debates*. Hampshire: Palgrave, pp. 227–236.

Butler, J. (1990) *Gender Trouble: Feminism and the Subversion of Identity*. London: Routledge.

Butler, J. (1993) *Bodies That Matter: On the Discursive Limits of 'Sex'*. London: Routledge.

Butler, J. (2004) *Undoing Gender*. London: Routledge.

Cavanagh, K. and Cree, V. (eds.) (1996) *Working with Men: Feminism and Social Work*. London: Routledge.

Christie, A. (1998) 'Is Social Work a "Non-Traditional" Occupation for Men?', *British Journal of Social Work*, 28(4): 491–510.

Christie, A. (2006) 'Negotiating the Uncomfortable Intersections between Gender and Professional Identities in Social Work', *Critical Social Policy*, 26(2): 390–411.

Collins, B. (1986) 'Defining Feminist Social Work', *Social Work*, 31(3): 214–219.

Connell, R. W. (1995) *Masculinities*. Cambridge: Polity.

Cross, S. and Bagilhole, B. (2002) 'Girls' Jobs for the Boys? Men, Masculinity and Non-Traditional Occupations', *Gender, Work and Organization*, 9(2): 204–226.

Davis, L. V. (1985) 'Female and Male Voices in Social Work', *Social Work*, 30(2): 106–113.

Dominelli, L. (2002) *Feminist Social Work Theory and Practice*. Hampshire: Palgrave.

Dominelli, L. and McLeod, E. (1989) *Feminist Social Work*. London: Palgrave.

Engels, F. (1978 [1884]) *The Origin of the Family, Private Property and the State*. Peking: Foreign Languages Press.

Farganis, S. (1994) *Situating Feminism: From Thought to Action*. London: Sage.

Firestone, S. (1970) *The Dialectic of Sex*. New York: Bantam Books.

Foxley, C. H. (1979). *Non-Sexist Counseling*. Dubuque, IA: Kendall/Hunt.

Freeman, M. (1990) 'Beyond Women's Issues: Feminism and Social Work', *Affilia*, 5(2), 136–151.

Furness, S. (2012) 'Gender at Work: Characteristics of Failing Social Work Students', *British Journal of Social Work*, 42(3): 480–499.

Galley, D. and Parrish, M. (2016) *Why are there so few male social workers?* [ONLINE] Available at: www. theguardian. com/social-care-network/2014/jul/25/why-so-few-male-social-workers. [Accessed 4 March 2017]

Gerstel, N. and Gallacher, S. (2001) 'Men's Caregiving: Gender and the Contingent Character of Care', *Gender and Society*, 15(2): 197–217.

Gov.scot. (2017). *Key statistics – Women and men in Scotland*. [ONLINE] Available at: www.gov.scot/ Topics/People/Equality/18500/StatisticsWomenMenScot#a7 [Accessed 14 March 2017].

Harding, S. (1991) *Whose Science? Whose Knowledge? Thinking from Women's Lives*. Ithaca: Cornell University Press.

Hicks, S. (2015) 'Social Work and Gender: An Argument for Practical Accounts', *Qualitative Social Work*, 14(4): 471–487.

hooks, b. (1984) *Feminist Theory: From Margin to Center*. Boston: South End Press.

hooks, b. (2000) *Where We Stand: Class Matters*. London: Routledge.

Huppatz, K. (2009) 'Reworking Bourdieu's "Capital": Feminine and Female Capitals in the Field of Paid Caring Work', *Sociology*, 43(1): 45–66.

Jaggar, A. (1983) *Feminist Politics and Human Nature*. Totowa, NJ: Rowman and Allanheld.

Lawler, J. and Hearn, J. (1997) 'The Managers of Social Work: The Experiences and Identifications of Third Tier Social Services Managers and the Implications for Future Practice', *British Journal of Social Work*, 27(2): 191–218.

McLean, J. (2003) 'Men as Minority: Men Employed in Statutory Social Work Care', *Journal of Social Work*, 3(1): 45–68.

McPhail, B. (2004) 'Questioning Gender and Sexuality Binaries: What Queer Theorists, Transgendered Individuals, and Sex Researchers Can Teach Social Work', *Journal of Gay and Lesbian Social Services*, 17(1): 3–21.

Miller, J. B. (1991) *Toward a New Psychology of Women*. London: Penguin Books.

Millett, K. (1977 [1970]) *Sexual Politics*. New York: Columbia University Press.

Myers, N. (2010) 'An Exploration of Gender-Related Tensions for Male Social Workers in the Irish Context', *Critical Social Thinking: Policy and Practice*, (2): 38–58.

Oakley, A. (1972) *Sex, Gender and Society*. London: Maurice Temple Smith Ltd.

Oakley, A. (1974) *Housewife*. London: Allen Lane.

Oakley, A. (1974) *The Sociology of Housework*. Oxford: Wiley-Blackwell.

Oakley, A. (1976) *Women's Work: The Housewife, Past and Present*. New York: Random House.

Office of the Chief Social Work Adviser, Scottish Government. (2016) *Social work and social care statistics for Scotland*. [ONLINE] Available at: www.gov.scot/Resource/0049/00493865.pdf. [Accessed 4 March 2017]

Omre, J. (1998) 'Feminist Social Work', in Adams, R., Dominelli, L. and Payne, M. (eds.) *Social Work: Themes, Issues and Critical Debates*. Hampshire: Palgrave, pp. 218–226.

Payne, M. (1991) *Modern Social Work Theory: A Critical Introduction*. London: Palgrave MacMillan.

Pease, R. (2001) 'Developing Pro-Feminist Practice with Men in Social Work', *Critical Social Work*, 2(1).

Pease, R. (2011) 'Men in Social Work: Challenging or Reproducing an Unequal Gender Regime?', *Journal of Women and Social Work*, 26(4): 406–418.

Pringle, K. (2001) 'Men in Social Work: The Double Edge', in Christie, A. (ed.) *Men and Social Work: Theories and Practices*. Houndmills, Basingstoke, England: Palgrave Macmillan, pp. 35–48.

Pringle, K. (2005) *Men, Masculinities and Social Welfare*. London, England: UCL Press.

Sands, R. G. (1996) 'The Elusiveness of Identity in Social Work Practice with Women: A Postmodern Feminist Perspective', *Clinical Social Work Journal*, 24(2): 167–186.

Scully, D. (1990) *Understanding Sexual Violence*. London: HarperCollins.

Seidler, V. J. (2006) *Transforming Masculinities: Men, Cultures, Bodies, Power, Sex and Love*. London: Routledge.

Simpson, R. (2004) 'Masculinity at Work: The Experiences of Men in Female Dominated Occupations', *Work, Employment, Society*, 18(2): 349–368.

Skeggs, B. (1997) *Formations of Class and Gender: Becoming Respectable*. London: Sage.

Smith, D. (1987) *The Everyday World as Problematic: A Feminist Sociology*. Toronto: The University of Toronto Press.

Smith, D. (1990) *The Ideological Practice of Sociology: The Conceptual Practices of Power – A Feminist Sociology of Knowledge*. Toronto: University of Toronto Press.

Stratham, D. (1978) *Radicals in Social Work*. London: Routledge & Kegan Paul.

The Guardian. 2017. *Why are there so few male social workers*. [ONLINE] Available at: https://www.theguardian.com/social-care-network/2014/jul/25/why-so-few-male-social-workers. [Accessed 24 July 2017].

Wild, J. (1999) *Working with Men for Change*. London: University College London Press.

9

GLOBALIZATION AND SOCIAL WORK

Until relatively recently, the term *globalization* was largely confined to academic discussions, books and debates. Globalization was a term used by economists, politicians, scientists and journalists. Today it is hard to think of any sphere of human activity in which concerns and talk about globalization do not feature. The term *globalization* appears as part of the headlines in local and national newspapers, discussions about climate change and conversations about work between couples as they relax at the end of the day. Whether people like it or not, no matter what they understand the term to mean, or even care to know about it at all, globalization and the multiple social processes the term refers to are fundamentally transforming and reshaping the nature of human social life the world over.

Rather than comprising yet another academic buzzword, globalization is highly relevant to social work. At first, it might seem less than clear why this is the case. After all, working with service-users involves dealing with needs and problems that demand local responses oriented towards the here and now. While this is true on one level, in a globalizing world what happens here is increasingly bound up with and shaped by what is happening over there, or a series of over theres, as well as what happens there and now shapes what will happen here in the future, typically in ways that are more immediate and indeterminate than in the past. In a rapidly globalizing world, human social life becomes more uncertain, complex and unpredictable as social relations become increasingly interconnected and stretched such that 'local happenings are shaped by events occurring many miles away and vice versa' (Giddens, 1990: 64).

Globalization and the social processes transforming human life across the planet have profound (unintended) consequences for social work. More than ever, the issues facing social workers and service-users are 'caused as much by global forces as by national forces, and we cannot understand local problems without reference to global economic, political and cultural circumstances' (Ife, 2001: 7). Whether they are aware of it or not, all social workers 'are operating in – or struggling with – conditions affected by globalization' (Lyons, 2006: 378). But globalization does not just present social work with difficulties and problems. It brings new possibilities and opportunities for promoting social justice and wellbeing on a global scale (Payne and Askeland, 2008).

Developing an awareness of the ways globalization is transforming human social life today is steadily becoming part of social work education. It is essential that social workers understand how globalization informs and transforms the nature of what they do and the lives of the people with whom they come into contact. Doing so will ensure that social workers the world over actively harness, rather than being passively subjected to, the effects of globalization. Since the early 1990s, calls within social work to take seriously the changes brought about by globalization have steadily grown (Trevillion, 1997; Pugh and Gould, 2000; Penna et al., 2000; Khan and Dominelli, 2000; Gray and Fook, 2004; Dominelli, 2010). In spite of this, however, the general consensus remains that the 'impact of globalization on social work has yet to be charted in any systematic way' (Khan and Dominelli, 2000: 95). The view of social work as rooted in relatively bounded and self-contained localities, and the overwhelming demands confronting social workers in the here and now (itself a situation intensified by the forces of globalization), continues to hinder the task of promoting globalization to the forefront of the social work theoretical agenda.

This chapter sets out and explains the main debates and theoretical perspectives propounded by theorists of globalization. The chapter begins by highlighting the analytical issues globalization poses for social theory, before explicating the multiple levels at which globalization takes place. The main conceptual terms developed by a broad range of theorists are set out. The applied section of the chapter considers the practical implications of globalization for social work, both in terms of the problems and opportunities to which globalization gives rise. In the final section of the chapter we consider the 'universalization debate' within social work and question whether or not social work would be better placed to realize its aims and values at a transnational level, as opposed to social workers the world over being divided up along particular national and culturally specific lines.

Globalization

From the 1990s onwards, the subject of globalization began to take on increased prominence within the social sciences and humanities. As part of the 'global turn', theorists of globalization began posing questions about the implications of globalization for social theorizing more generally (Urry, 2000a; Albrow, 1996). To remain analytically insightful and conceptually relevant, social theory requires to be fundamentally overhauled and recalibrated, according to theorists of globalization such as Robertson (1992) and Beck (1999, 2000a). Globalization gives rise to multiple, historically unprecedented transnational processes and dynamics which cannot be accommodated by the conceptual ideas first developed by the classical social theorists.

When the classical theorists used the term *society*, they typically intended the patterned social relations of a group of people who exist within a national frame of reference. The same is true of the conception of society contained in much modern social theory. In this view, Canadian society, for example, refers to and is contained within the territorial boundaries constitutive of Canada at any given time. For Beck (1992, 2000b) the notion of society as a relatively self-contained, bounded entity is highly problematic in a globalizing world. It no longer provides an adequate frame of reference for trying to understand the kinds of transnational phenomena and processes characteristic of human life now. Instead, in a globalizing world an ever greater number of social phenomena take place at a level above and beyond the boundaries of nation states. To be able to grasp these global phenomena a new conceptual terminology is required, one which marks the beginning of and operates within a new 'post-societal' paradigm capable of capturing a range of fluid and processual phenomena such as 'global networks and flows' (Urry, 2000a: 186). In the following section of the chapter we look at a number of the most influential attempts to conceptualise the analytically distinct but inter-related levels at which globalization takes place.

Economic dimensions of globalization

Economic developments and processes are fundamental to globalization. A situation of advanced economic globalization is based on a vision of systems of production and consumption which combine to form a transnational capitalist system of trade spanning the entire globe (Friedman, 1999; Klein, 2001; Hardt and Negri, 2000). For advocates of economic globalization such as Thomas Friedman (1999), the global spread of capitalist relations is a positive development. He argues that a capitalist world-order based on free-market capitalism leads to rising levels of material wealth and living standards for everyone.

Theorists of globalization working in a Marxist vein fundamentally disagree with the advocates of economic globalization. The most notable thinker in this direction is the theorist Immanuel Wallerstein. Since the 1970s, Wallerstein (1974) has worked to develop an historically based analysis of the rise of global capitalism, or 'world-system', as he refers to it instead. A world-system is not necessarily worldwide in scope, but refers to a system that creates its own 'world' (Wallerstein, 2004). A world-system is a multi-political and multicultural system which pulls into its sphere of influence different political and cultural formations. A world-system is one in which the actions and interactions between political and cultural units are integrated into and patterned by their position in relation to one another and the wider system. Wallerstein's work focusses on the analysis of world-systems rather than seeing nation states as the primary unit for analysis.

The structure of world-systems is organised around a number of geo-political entities which include a 'core', 'semi-periphery' and 'periphery'. Core states are characterised by large amounts of highly profitable economic activity. Core states are where the forces of industrialization developed first, such as in Western Europe and North America. Peripheral states are states that generate relatively low levels of profit e.g. Africa and parts of Latin America. Within the world-system, the role of semi-peripheral states such as India and Brazil is to serve as mediators. Semi-peripheral states are both subject to domination as well as dominating the peripheral states adjacent to them. By contrast, core states control and regulate the whole system by exploiting the resources of the peripheral states. The role of semi-peripheral states is to ensure that the exploitative relations between core states and periphery states do not become so stark as to disrupt the organisation of the wider system. Like the ruling economic class in capitalist society, core states seek to manipulate the rules of the world-system in ways that serve their own interests. Crucially for Wallerstein (2004), this comes at the cost of the interests of semi-periphery and periphery states.

Wallerstein's concept of the capitalist world-system has been highly influential across a range of academic disciplines including economics, politics and international relations (Robinson, 2011). Wallerstein claims that it is only a matter of time before the spread of global capitalism over-extends its reach and sows the seeds of its own demise. While to date capitalism has indeed been hit by a number of global financial and environmental crises, critics of Wallerstein point to the fact that the world-system has *not* collapsed nor has a new form of social organisation

TABLE 9.1 Summary of Wallerstein

World-systems
• analysis of world-systems • rising dominance of global world-systems of capitalism • division of world into core, semi-periphery and periphery regions and nations • core countries exploit semi-periphery and periphery countries

emerged to take its place. Nonetheless, Wallerstein's ideas continue to inspire economic forms of globalization theory, by prompting further scrutiny of the ways economic factors shape and are shaped by the political, social and cultural dimensions of globalization.

Political dimensions of globalization

The economic and political dimensions of globalization are thoroughly interpenetrating. For commentators and analysts on the political left and right, the spread of capitalism on a global scale has severely undermined the power of national governments in a number of ways. To participate in the various world economic systems, governments must adhere to the international laws and rules governing trade relations such as the General Agreement on Tariffs and Trade (GATT). The rules and laws of international trade ensure that economic interactions between nation states are organised and conducted in predictable and patterned ways. At the same time, submitting to the laws of international trade undermines the autonomy of governments to determine economic policies and activities in their own territories. Increasing economic and political integration has led to rising interdependency between nation states. Negative economic developments in one nation, particularly the economies of core states such as the U.S. and Japan, impact on and have consequences for all other national economies. The collapse of the Greek economy in 2010 threatened to undermine the economic stability of the European Union as a whole. Crisis talks between the heads of member states were held as governments tried to manage and control the effects of the crisis on their own national economies.

Rising levels of economic integration and interdependency undermine the political autonomy of nation states and governments. The global reach of transnational corporations (TNCs) produces a similar effect too. Many economic theorists of globalization regard TNCs as more influential than national governments in shaping the world economy (Ietto-Gillies, 2002; Bonnano and Constance, 2010). The business operations and transactions of TNCs such as Toyota straddle multiple national economies (Dicken, 2015). Toyota has offices and car plants in more than twenty-six countries, spanning the U.K., Australia and South America. In the past, governments were responsible for making decisions about national industry. This was an important part of the overall process by which governments managed and controlled national economic policies. Now, it is more likely to be TNCs, not national governments, which play the decisive role as to where to locate industry.

In terms of both what they do on the global political stage and how they deal with what goes on within their own national domain, the global spread of capitalist relations undermines national governments. What can be said to be inside or outside a particular state has been radically problematized by the economic and political dimensions of globalization (Albrow, 1996). In many parts of Western Europe and North America, governments have sought to respond by actively embracing, rather than trying to resist, the marketization of an ever greater range of social spheres e.g. public health, higher education, social care and so on, spheres of social life that previously were cordoned off from the principles of economic efficiency, productivity and rationality. As we shall see in the applied section of the chapter, this has had a number of negative consequences for the welfare state and social work services.

Social dynamics of globalization

Focusing on the social dimensions of globalization involves trying to understand how globalization reconstitutes the nature and organisation of social life in new and distinctive ways. Giddens (1990: 64) defines globalization as the 'intensification of worldwide social relations which link distant localities in such a way that local happenings are shaped by events occurring many miles away and vice versa'. An important point to make here is that part of the complexity and uncertainty of globalization involves the different ways individuals and groups seek to respond to the *perceived* effects of globalization (Giddens, 2002). Globalization is not just about the world becoming smaller, but also that people's actions and beliefs are affected and change precisely because they believe that is indeed the case. One of the paradoxical effects of globalization is that it creates resistance to itself e.g. forms of social and political activism organised around anti-globalization movements, terrorist groups fighting against the perceived spread of Western values and culture, etc. in ways that tend to accelerate precisely the types of social processes those resisting globalization are seeking to prevent. This is an important point to consider. It frames the ways we are able to think about the forces that shape people's actions and interactions in a globalizing world. What people think and believe globalization to entail shapes how they act and interact at local and national levels, which in turn feed back into and actively shape phenomena occurring at a transnational level.

Ulrich Beck

The increasing perception and proliferation of risk in a globalizing world is the central theme animating the work of German social theorist Ulrich Beck (1944–2015). Beck viewed globalization as an unintended consequence of modernity. Modern society gives rise to powerful social forces that once set in motion take on a life of their own become increasingly hard to anticipate control. Beck distinguishes between 'first' and 'second modernity'. First modernity was characterised by social structures, relations and roles that were relatively fixed and determinate. First modernity was a social order organised around manufacturing industries, class-based identities and politics, the power of the nation state, a belief in social progress and faith in science and expert forms of authority. Second modernity, the current stage of human society referred to by Beck as 'global risk society', developed as an outcome of the unintended consequences of the multiple social processes set in motion during first modernity. Of these the most significant include the declining power of nation states and the rise of the world economy; over-exploitation of the world's natural resources due to the global production of capitalist goods; the rise of problems associated with climate change and global warning; and advances in science such as genetic modification, the outcomes of which are uncertain and raise complex moral and ethical problems.

Beck (1999, 2000a, 2000b) claims that by the latter stages of the twentieth century, global risk society had taken hold. The transition from first to second modernity involves

TABLE 9.2 Summary of Beck

Global risk society
First modernity characterised by:
• relatively fixed roles, identities, and social and political structures
• social life organised around nation state
• cultural values of progress and rationality
• faith in scientific reasoning
Second modernity characterised by:
• loss of faith in scientific progress and forms of reasoning
• loss of trust in governments and expert forms of authority
• proliferation of multiple forms of risk
• growing uncertainty and anxiety about the future

transformations that undermined first modernity in a variety of ways including: increasing public scepticism towards and a lack of trust in scientific forms of knowledge and expert authority due to disagreements between scientists and experts; loss of faith in national governments and politicians to solve social and political problems; and rising levels of anxiety and uncertainty about the future as attempts to resolve problems fail, in turn often giving rise to new and proliferating problems in their place. Global risk society is characterised by ongoing uncertainty, and attempts to control the perceived causes of this uncertainty have the effect of making them worse. Moreover, this predicament shapes developments and changes across all countries because the problems and risks are global in scope. Examples of global risks include economic crises, mass unemployment, wars, the displacement of hundreds of thousands of people, global crime syndicates, environmental crises and the threat of nuclear war.

In global risk society everyday life and social relations are radically transformed: The fact that a worker being in the same job for life has become a thing of the past; communities and community-based forms of solidarity are eroded by economic principles; being mobile and able to travel and relocate becomes increasingly important; and the increasing transfer of labour from core to semi-peripheral areas e.g. the relocation of the textile industries to Asia undermine the relatively stable and fixed forms of identity and outlook characteristic of first modernity. In a world risk society, social relations are radically reconfigured from the ways they were in first modernity. Risk society is one where risk and anxieties about risk become part of everyday life, at the same time as ever more desperate attempts are made to try to control aspects of human life which cannot be controlled.

Giddens and Castells

The work of Anthony Giddens provides one of the most sustained attempts to theorize the ways social relations and the social more generally come to be reconstituted by globalization (1990). Giddens views globalization as a consequence and radicalization of modernity's reconfiguring of the nature of social relations. He argues that modernity has an inherent tendency to spread globally because it creates the kinds of social relations which no longer require people to come into physical contact in a particular location. Developments in modern communications technology mean that individuals can interact with others who are geographically removed from them. The result is that social relations become 'disembedded' from particular local contexts and settings. As modern technology expands across the world, social relations are stretched across space. This means that actions happening in any particular local context could have ramifications for and shape any other place on earth, as long as the necessary telecommunications systems are in place. The ensuing actions and interactions may well transcend the territorial boundaries of nation states.

Giddens' emphasis on the disembedding of social relations due to advances in communication technologies resonates strongly with the work of Spanish social theorist Manuel Castells. Castells regards the changes to social relations characteristic of globalization as part of a wider transformation to the structure and nature of human activity in modern society. Prior to the 1960s and '70s, Western societies were organised around the production of material consumer goods and services. In post-industrial society, human labour activity is directed instead towards the production and dissemination of knowledge, in particular electronic and digital forms of information and data. Driving the shift away from production of material goods towards knowledge and information is the rise of the internet and internet-based forms of technology.

Castells (1996) regards the technological developments behind the rise of the internet as ushering in a new Information Age. Still in its early stages, the Information Age represents a revolutionary phase in the development of human societies. Castells regards networks as the social-structural expression of this new stage in human social development. The social-structural expression of the Information Age *is* the 'network society'. Castells (2000: 5) claims that this mode of social organisation now 'permeates most [nationally based] societies in the world, in various cultural and institutional manifestations'. Network society consists of multiple overlapping networks through which the generation, processing and transmission of information constitute the main forms of human activity and power (Castells, 1996). More and more human activities are undertaken from within a technological paradigm constituted through 'micro-electronics-based information' and 'communication technologies' (Castells, 2000: 5–6).

In the network society, social order is based on and organised around 'informationalism' (Castells, 1998). As internet-based technologies spread across the globe, information is produced and shared through an ever greater number of networks connecting home-based computers, mobile phones and a range of commercial, public and private organisations. A key part of informationalism is the creation and spread of specialist forms of knowledge, such as knowledge about financial markets and information technology no less. Expert forms of knowledge are stored in and managed by electronically based networks. Electronically based networks have replaced bureaucracies as the primary means of organising social relations because they do so more efficiently (Chapter 6). Like the self-perpetuating dynamic propelling the spread of capitalist relations, electronic networks proliferate outwardly, as individuals and groups seek to increase their connectivity through online markets, consumer databases, social media sites and so on. For Castells (1996), a network-based social structure is a highly dynamic, open-ended system of relations, the transformative effects of which tend to permeate all areas of social and economic life.

In earlier stages of modernity, power was organised and exercised through hierarchically arranged structures of relations. In a network society, power and domination are organised around presence and absence in certain networks. Power is tied up with the individual's position within or exclusion from particular networks. Similar to Giddens, Castells (2000) regards networks as radically reshaping people's experience of time and space. Time becomes highly

TABLE 9.3 Summary of Castells

Network society
• organised around informationalism • proliferation of internet-based forms of technology • network as dominant mode of social organisation • increasing number of human interactions take place in the space of flows • the term *space of flows* refers to the online world existing above and beyond national boundaries

compressed as the boundaries between past, present and future become increasingly blurred and harder to distinguish. The distance between the present and the past becomes greater as social life speeds up and changes with increasing rapidity. At the same time, the present becomes ever more 'compressed' as the instantaneousness of electronic communication accelerates the individual's relationship forward in time and into the future (Castells, 2000).

In network society perception of space is reorganised too. Space comes to be organised through the electronically mediated 'space of flows' – the online world. The space of flows is the internet-based online world people can access anytime of the day or night regardless of where they are in the world (providing they have access to the internet). The space of flows refers to the 'non-place' wherein an ever greater number of human actions and interactions take place. This includes the kind of virtual relations and interactions people take part in through social media sites such as Facebook, Twitter, Weibo and dating websites as well as commercial relations and transactions such as e-banking, buying and selling things online, booking aeroplane flights, planning holidays and the like. Crucially, the space of flows exists beyond and above national and territorial boundaries.

While the media people use to access the internet are rooted in particular localities and cultural practices, the space of flows brings together and unties all of these simultaneously. The number of economic and social activities decoupled from the concrete contexts in which they once took place is growing, with an ever greater number taking place instead in the space of flows. This has led to simultaneity in human relations becoming profoundly decoupled from physical co-presence. In his early work, Castells saw the rise of the network society as privileging and working in the interest of elite groups. His later analysis pays more attention to the spread and dissemination of internet technologies to a much broader audience (this requires individuals to possess certain competencies and skills to access the internet) who can use the space of flows to realize their own interests and purposes (Castells and Ince, 2003).

Culture and Globalization

Concomitant with transformations to the economic, political and social dimensions of globalization are the changes taking place at a cultural level. Examining the cultural dimensions of globalization involves looking at how cultural forms and forces shape and are shaped by how people think and feel about the world around them. For the highly influential British theorist of globalization Roland Robertson (1992: 8), globalization refers to the 'compression of the world and the intensification of consciousness of the world as a whole'. Robertson (1992) developed the term *globality* to denote this sense of the compression of the world. Globality refers to a situation in which people across the world are compelled to see and imagine them-selves as merely one part of a far greater global whole, albeit one comprised of a very complex mixture of diverse and differing cultural dispositions and mentalities. Under the conditions of globality the diversity and differences between cultural identities and practices are brought into ever sharper relief. All human groups come to see and imagine those differences as relat-ing to a world where everything is connected to everything else in increasingly complex and changing ways.

Of the many transformations and changes to culture brought about by globalization, the main dispute concerns the view of globalization as a form of cultural imperialism. This is the idea that entities such as Western culture and American consumerism work to produce capitalist and consumerist ideals and values, which they transmit across the world through a range of media e.g. television, film, the internet, etc. in turn undermining and destroying local cultures. Following Wallerstein's terms, the view of a global tidal wave of Western-based media and consumer goods emanating from core Western nations and washing over and destroying the indigenous cultures of the world is a pervasive one (Hannerz, 1989). Closely linked to the notion of cultural imperialism is the cultural homogenization thesis. This is the view that the spread of Western-based cultural forms will have, or indeed is already having, an homogenizing effect on world culture. That is to say, the diversity and differences characteristic of the world's cultures are steadily being over-written by and tending towards centring around an ever diminishing range of mentalities, values, attitudes and ideals, in particular, Western-based cultural forms.

But what exactly is meant by 'Western culture', as well as the often superficial examples and anecdotes used as evidence of its alleged spread across the world, is something that social theorists examine carefully. Western culture is not a homogenous entity. Western cultural forms whether they happen to be ideas, music, films, leisure pursuits, cuisine, values, etc. comprise a mixture of cultural artefacts and forces some of which demonstrate a degree of homogeneity; some contain elements taken from non-Western cultures, and others still are self-consciously anti-Western. The cultural imperialism thesis fails to consider the ways non-Western forms penetrate Western culture, where they are taken up, transformed and in some cases exported back to the contexts from which they originated. Moreover, implicit in this view is that merely being exposed to certain cultural forms is enough to make people adopt them. It presumes that how these cultural forms are interpreted, taken up and incorporated into the lives of the people exposed to them takes place in ways characteristic of the West (Appadurai, 1996).

Rather than being totally over-written by the alleged onslaught of Western culture, many people's experiences today are better imagined as a complex mixture of the (never purely) local and (never purely) global. Robertson (1992) invokes the concept of 'glocalization' to describe this process. Glocalization refers to a situation whereby the more local and more global dimen-sions of culture come into contact and interpenetrate one another in new and transformative ways. When local and global cultural forms and forces interpenetrate, they give rise to new and distinctive combinations of local and global culture. Processes of glocalization feed into cultural hybridization, which occurs when hitherto separate cultural patterns, mentalities, attitudes and values come into contact (Werbner and Modood, 1997; Bhabha, 1994). Specific 'hybrid' prod-ucts emerge in local contexts, while more generic global culture can be seen as a hybridized coming together of what were previously relatively unrelated and distinct cultural traditions. In short, cultural globalization involves far more subtle and complex processes than the notion of the 'rest' being dominated by the 'West' allows for.

TABLE 9.4 Summary of cultural dimensions of globalization

Marxists

- cultural homogenization i.e. homogenization thesis; cultural imperialism

Robertson

- globality – increasing tendency of human groups to see themselves as part of global whole
- glocalization – interpenetration of local and global cultural forms; gives rise to new and distinct cultural entities

---

Applying theories of globalization to social work

Social work and global social problems

The effects of globalization are no longer marginal to the activities and concerns of social workers. Since the 1990s a growing number of social work academics have turned their attention towards trying to understand what exactly globalization means for social work, how it should be theorized and how social workers in particular (local) areas and on a global scale collectively should seek to respond. References to globalization within the social work literature are increasingly commonplace. Yet a number of social work commentators claim that the implications of globalization for social work remain insufficiently grasped. In the view of Hil (2001: 64), the 'changes wrought by globalization necessitate a comprehensive rethinking of the theory and practice of social work.' By continuing to frame social work 'as a locality-specific discipline' concerned primarily with 'practice-based issues', social work professionals remain vulnerable to the global challenges facing them (Dominelli and Hoogvelt, 1996: 95).

At a number of levels and in new and unprecedented ways, globalization is transforming human social life in profound ways. Originating in the earlier stages of modernity, these transformations have fed into and informed the wider backdrop against which social work has developed from the 1970s onwards. Many of the abstract processes the term *globalization* refers to can be discerned in the concrete changes to the organisational and professional contexts social workers are situated. The increasing marketization, bureaucratization and declining autonomy of social work can all be seen as having been intensified, exacerbated and proliferated under the conditions of globalization. The multiple transformative social processes globalization encompasses impact directly on social work as it is organised, delivered and practiced across particular local contexts. Many of the effects of globalization impact on social work in less direct ways, but nonetheless social workers are required to deal with and respond to them. Globalization also gives rise to social problems on a scale and level that present enormous challenges for social work (Fergsuon, Lavalette and Whitmore, 2005).

Differences in the cultural values of ethnic and religious groups lead to conflict and war in many parts of the world. The devastating consequences for entire populations of wars raging in geographically distant and more remote parts of the world are felt across a multitude of local Western contexts. More recently, this has led to the displacement of large numbers of people from their homelands to many parts of Europe and other parts of the world too. The economic, social and political impact this has for national governments is profound. National governments are forced to respond in ways that seek to balance their own particular local interests and circumstances with those of the wider international community. Tensions arise between nation states as disagreements about how to respond and react to the problems posed by ethnic tensions, racial discrimination and social unrest spill out into and threaten to disrupt everyday life and the wider international community.

At the same time as heightening the need for social work services and assistance, the capacity for social work to adequately respond is increasingly hampered and constrained. International migration means that problems caused by poverty, ethnic and religious discrimination, political oppression and lack of civil rights in a range of countries have consequences felt in others. The illegal trafficking of women and children in particular for sexual exploitation calls into action law enforcement agencies and criminal justice systems from a range of disparate locations. Low wages, inhumane working conditions, and the use and exploitation of child-labour in one part of the world raise questions over the employment policies of TNCs and the moral choices of consumers in another.

Economic markets and transactions are ever more global in scale. The pursuit and maximization of economic efficiency and profit have penetrated an ever greater number of spheres of human life. National governments experience increasing pressure to ensure national economies are as productive and streamlined as possible. Economic policies organised around austerity and rationalization have led to extensive cuts to the welfare state, national health services and social benefit systems (Khan and Dominelli, 2000; Caragata and Sanchez, 2002). At the same time as reducing expenditure on public sector spending and social services, governments seek to generate economic revenue through privatizing welfare services and opening up the public sector to non-statutory and commercial enterprises. This is particularly the case regarding the provision of care for old people as well as proposals to privatize children's welfare services (Dominelli and Hoogvelt, 1996).

Increasingly, national governments on the left and right make reference to 'globalization' as both the cause and justification for economic reforms to state welfare policy and spending. The pressure on national governments to be at the forefront of economic globalization encourages cheaper alternatives to 'costly social services and works to privatise social problems through a rhetoric of self-determining individuals, responsible for managing their own lives and use of life chances' (Trevillion, 1997: 5). Political decisions made in one state are increasingly shaped by political and economic forces deriving from outside of that state's national boundaries.

National governments that seek to resist the marketization of welfare services are under increasing financial pressure from the economic world-systems into which they are pulled. Countries such as Sweden, for example, a nation that has a long tradition of adopting a statist welfare model, have witnessed the rise of the phenomenon referred to as 'shunting' (Gould, 1993; Trevillion, 1997). As they are discharged from the hospital, individuals – along with the costs of caring for them – are shunted to social service departments, such as social work, in an effort to defray the costs incurred by the health service. Where the marketization of social welfare is opened up to commercial and non-statutory organisations, certain service-user groups come to be regarded as financially more lucrative than others. The care of old people in particular has become highly marketized. By contrast the organisation and provision of services relating to young families, service-users with disabilities and ethnic groups yield comparatively far smaller profit margins with the result that the range and quality of services available to these groups are diminished (Gould, 1993).

As the social processes characteristic of globalization accelerate and intensify, frequent technological, economic and political changes compel vast alterations to the ways people think, feel and act. Insecurity, uncertainty and risk (Beck, 1992, 1999; Bauman, 1998, 2007) characterise not only the material aspects of people's lives, such as job security and standards of living, but how they individuals feel about their place in the world, as their experience of everyday situations and relationships comes to be characterised by disruption, agitation and anxiety (Giddens, 1991; Beck, 1999). A culture of insecurity, uncertainty and anxiety about the future is becoming part of the everyday lives and experiences of people all over the world today.

Globalizing the social work consciousness

In place of the overly narrow conception of social work as primarily a locality-based profession, advocates of a global social work perspective argue that social work needs to reconceptualise its identity, aims and values in ways that allow for connections between the local and the global to develop (Hong, 2010). To do this, social workers the world over need to adopt a more proactive stance towards thinking both locally and globally if they are to have any chance of meeting the challenges facing them and those working in the social professions more generally (Midgley, 1996, 2001; Otto and Lorenz, 1998). Just as theorists such as Beck (1992, 2000a) and Robertson (1992) have claimed that the changes wrought by globalization require social theorists to critically re-evaluate and where necessary jettison certain foundational assumptions and concepts, so social work needs to reconceive its knowledge base, values and practices, along globally oriented lines (Ahmadi, 2003; Dominelli, 2009, 2010; Dominelli and Hackett, 2005; Midgley, 2001).

Echoing Robertson's (1992) concept of 'globality', Ahmadi (2003: 14) argues for the development and careful reconstruction of social work consciousness along more globally oriented lines. For many social work practitioners, the call to redirect their attention towards globalization and thinking and acting globally is unrealistic. Like the notion of climate change – a predicament exacerbated by globalization – globalization is something most people are aware of but are unclear as to how to respond. Globalization intensifies and accelerates a range of social processes which directly shape the concerns and activities of social workers, at the same time as making it harder for social workers to know how to address, manage and respond to those processes. It is important to acknowledge this tension. It is one of the core tensions to which globalization gives rise. Globalization sets in motion and accelerates social processes that radically transform human life on a global scale, at the same time as how people across the world imagine and respond to those transformations feeds back into and adds momentum to those processes in new and unforeseen ways. Faced with the complexity and enormity of the challenges globalization poses, the debate as to whether social work should universalize its aims and objectives by elevating them to a transnational scale has gathered increasing momentum in recent years.

Many of the transformations to human societies in a globalizing world are giving rise to social problems on an unprecedented scale. This is particularly the case for individuals and groups already situated on the margins of society. That said, it is important to acknowledge that globalization is not an inherently or entirely good or bad phenomenon – a way of thinking that the majority of social theorists tend to challenge and go beyond. Globalization brings in its wake transformations and changes on multiple levels. Really, it is far more accurate to say that globalization poses new problems and challenges many of which have consequences that bring those affected by them into the sphere of social work services, as well as giving rise to unprecedented possibilities and potential for positive change.

Understanding how globalization impacts negatively on the values and objectives of social work is important. Just as important is that social work finds ways to identify the possibilities and potential of the transformations to social life opened up by globalization. Commentators such as Ahmadi (2003: 18) emphasise the potential globalization engenders for positive social change, such as 'the promotion of greater solidarity, democracy and a greater possibility to prevent conflicts'. Social theory can play an important part in tapping these changes, providing social workers with the conceptual constructs and ways of seeing necessary for reshaping them in positive and enabling ways. Globalization can no longer be regarded as an abstract or marginal concern of social work. In a rapidly globalizing world, 'all social workers require at least minimum exposure to ideas about the local-global dialectic, comparative welfare policies and inter-cultural relations' (Lyons, 2006: 371). By fostering a global consciousness, social workers across the world will develop fuller awareness that individually and collectively they can actively shape the welfare and wellbeing of the people whose lives they come into contact with.

Towards a universal social work?

Globalization accelerates and intensifies a number of the fundamental tensions and contradictions at the heart of human social life. Globalization is characterised by rising standards of living and wealth for a very small minority at the same time as poverty is exacerbated and more widespread for an ever growing majority. Globalization has resulted in the proliferation and spread of universal cultural forms and practices at the same time as the identities and cultural mentalities of particular local traditions are becoming more distinct. Globalization leads to ever greater levels of interconnectivity, dependency and integration between disparate human groups at the same time as heightening divisions and hostility between different peoples, and cultures.

Arising out of these contradictory processes and tensions, the debate about whether or not social work would be best placed to meet the challenges presented by globalization has gathered momentum. Discussion and debate about the desirability of universalizing social work have grown up in the pages of social work journals, monographs and textbooks in the last thirty years or so. The term *universal social work* is used to refer to a 'form of social work that would transcend national boundaries and which gives social work a global face such that there are commonalities in theory and practice across widely divergent contexts' (Gray and Fook, 2004: 628). Presently, the International Federation of Social Workers (IFSW), a body the origins of which date back to 1928, facilitates international social work collaborations as well as providing 'a global voice for the profession' (Ifsw.org, 2017). While founded on the universal values of social justice, human rights and social development, as well as issuing a universal definition of social work, to date the IFSW has not sought to construct a universal approach to social work (Hare, 2004).

What would a universal social work look like? How would it be organised? Would a universal social work serve the interests of some, or all, social workers? Around what values would a universal social work be organised? What obstacles and difficulties would have to be overcome for the vision of a universal social work to be realized? The debate about the universalization of social work provides a clear window onto surveying and exploring a number of the tensions engendered by globalization and which social work is under pressure to respond. In this next section of the chapter we examine those tensions and how various social theoretical concepts can be used to illuminate and cast light on them.

Starting with the political dimensions of the universalization debate, one view is that increasingly social work in Western Europe and North America is overly constrained by its relationship to the state. Professional social work is a Western convention, originating in modern Western capitalist society during the latter stages of the nineteenth century. Taking place at different times across different national contexts, the professionalization of social work was closely bound up with the aims of gaining greater collective status and autonomy for social workers. This was achieved through integrating into the institutional, legal and bureaucratic structures of the modern welfare state (Chapter 6). For a number of social work academics and commentators, however, the (unintended) consequences of professionalization have weakened and continue to undermine the activities of social workers.

The main argument in favour of universalization advanced by Western social work commentators is that a transnational social work would be able to bypass its relationship with the state. A transnational social work operating above and beyond the boundaries of any particular national government would enable social work to extricate itself from the local and national constraints currently imposed upon it. In a scenario whereby all national governments would contribute financially to the maintenance of a transnational social work, it would become possible for social work to define the nature of its value and knowledge bases in self-determined ways as well as being able to operate outside of the ideological agenda of any particular national government.

As a free-floating transnational entity, a global social work would provide a collective platform for social workers to organise and direct their resources towards regulating and, where necessary, intervening in the socially destructive actions and activities of powerful corporations, TNCs and national governments. The construction and consolidation of universal standards and criteria for social work delivery and practice could be used at national and local levels as benchmarks against which to measure the provision and delivery of social work and welfare services. The same centrally organised criteria could also be used to bypass government policies and epistemological biases e.g. the primacy attributed to Western scientific knowledge and forms of reasoning that form part of wider state-led forms of control and political governance (de Sousa Santos, 2014).

From a Western perspective, the vision of a global social work capable of bypassing the economic and political constraints of the state is a highly appealing one. Viewed from a non-Western perspective, however, such a vision seems far less attractive. Given the perceived failure of Western social work ideology and practice to acknowledge and address the structural dimensions of service-users' problems make it difficult to see what the appeal of such models and practice would be for those in a non-Western context (Nagpaul, 1993; Nimmagadda and Cowger, 1999). In South Africa, for example, indigenous forms of social work have a strong radical focus, emphasising the importance of social work in helping to bring about structural changes to society. The emphasis here is on action models to tackle a range of social problems such as poverty, inequality, unemployment and health problems such as limiting the spread of HIV/AIDS (Patel and Hochfeld, 2012).

At the level of culture, globalization involves the interpenetration and coming together of divergent values, ideals, beliefs and practices. These are realized and expressed through individuals, groups and artefacts from different cultural contexts coming into contact and interacting with one another. The benefits of being exposed to the values and practices of social workers working within different (local) contexts has a long and established tradition within social work (Otis, 1986; Irvine and Payne, 2005). The value of knowledge exchange forms the basis of the international and comparative traditions within social work as well as providing the impetus behind the many exchange and work placement schemes promoted through internationalization initiatives such as the Erasmus programme and the World Universities Network (WUN). Awareness of what social work means and how it is practiced across different contexts highlights the arbitrary ways in which social work is organised and enacted in one's own local (or global when viewed from afar) context. Powerful forms of professional discourse coerce and reconfigure the subjectivity of social workers in ways that work to foreclose the development of alternative ways of seeing (Chapter 6). This is the constraining power of discourse. The international exchange of experiences and knowledge provides an important opportunity for social workers to import and build on forms of discourse and practice that have proven successful in other parts of the world.

While cultural diversity tends to be constructed within Western liberal democracies as both achievable and desirable, fears that a universal social work would lead to a form of cultural imperialism centring on Western social work models and values have been voiced by a wide range of social work scholars and commentators (Midgley, 1981; Prager, 1985; Ife, 1998). Critics of the universalization debate argue that to date, the internationalization of social work has been heavily biased towards Western social work models which are typically and uncritically represented 'as having global applicability' (Gray and Fook, 2004: 632). Advocates of indigenous social work models are critical of the top-down approach implicit in Western depictions of a universal social work (Midgley, 1981; Ife, 1998; Tsang and Yan, 2001). This is the view that Western social work models contain a range of culturally specific assumptions and ideals which serve as the hidden basis on which claims regarding best practice are premised. These views echo the claims made by Marxist-inspired critics of globalization who argue that global culture is really just a Western European and North American culture imposed upon and overwriting the indigenous ideals and practices of those found in particular local contexts.

Fears that the universalization of social work would necessarily entail the spread of Western social work values and knowledge are valid and need to be taken seriously. But they also require to be considered carefully and critically too. Implicit in those fears is a conception of Western social work as comprising a single 'homogenous, monolithic entity' (Ife, 2001: 15). What exactly is meant by the notion of 'Western social work' needs to be critically unpacked and clarified. Furthermore, a growing body of social work literature suggests that rather than displacing indigenous values and forms of practice, social work models imported from outside of a particular culture tend to be 'glocalized', with social workers working to actively appropriate and adapt what they have learned to suit the particular conditions and needs of practitioners (Harris and Chou, 2001; Cheung and Liu, 2004; Gray, 2005; Hong, 2010).

In addition to culture, social relations are also reconfigured and organized by the transformative effects of globalization. A universalized social work would allow social work to organise and manage its response to the growing precariousness and risk characteristic of human social life in a 'world risk society' (Beck, 1999). The work of Castells offers a number of possibilities for thinking about how a universal social work operating at a transnational level might be better equipped to deal with the difficulties and forms of suffering concomitant with the proliferation of risk. Castells (1996) regards networks as the social-structural expression of the Information Age. Making use of the expanding scope of internet-based forms of technology, a universalized social work could organise itself through the online space of flows. This is the vision of a universal social work as comprising multiple interconnecting networks of social work professionals situated across a range of local, national and transnational settings connected through internet-based forms of technology. To some extent, the increasing interconnectivity of social workers around the world is already becoming a reality, with transnational networks being established through various formal and informal channels. Whether or not the social structure of non-Western industrialized nations is equally as conducive to the reordering of social work through associations of networks is questionable, however.

The social-structural development of society directly determines how its members conceive of and imagine themselves and others. As Durkheim's account of social solidarity demonstrates (Chapter 2), the ideology of individualism – the propensity to conceive of ourselves as individuals first and foremost – is a phenomenon specific to industrialized and for this reason largely Western and North American societies characterised by highly complex divisions of labour. Social work values and models from the industrial West have developed out of cultural conditions characterised by organic forms of social solidarity and correspondingly high levels of individualism. The organisational forms and social practices arising out of Western social work are shot through with individualistic conceptions and ideals of human agents as morally autonomous and self-determining.

This raises the question as to how and which moral values and normative ideals would inform the value base of a universal social work. The normative assumption that social work is committed to assisting service-users to realize their self-potential in ways determined by the service-user is a good case in point. Ideas and discourses about the self and selfhood contained within Western social work refract the wider ideology of individualism characteristic of organic forms of social solidarity. For service-users in non-industrialized, non-Western societies, such as China and India, the values of self-realization and self-determination are actively shunned unless they are tied to the values and goals of wider collectives such as the family and community (Bose, 1992). Similarly, the emphasis on equality of relations between social workers and service-users is not necessarily compatible with the hierarchical ordering of social relations and selfhood characteristic of non-Western societies. As Hokenstad and Midgley (1997: 4) observe, service-users in India, for example, actively look to social workers for guidance and instruction as part of the assistance offered to them, the problem being that this involves inheriting 'unquestioned assumptions about who has expertise, the superiority of a professional model, what is "development" . . . and so on'. Western social work models and values are marked by the social relations of power attached to them and in which they grew up, making it problematic for them to be extrapolated from the societies in which they developed.

In the context of the U.K. and North America, the structure and organisation of social life in line with a highly differentiated division of labour have led to a highly individualistic culture (Chapters 1 and 2). Awareness of how social work is undertaken to assist individuals through more collective-based forms of social work could serve as a basis on which to try to counteract and correct the individualizing tendencies of Western and North American social work. This would involve Western social work borrowing from more collectivist models in order to promote social cohesion and solidarity. Social workers could play an important part in trying to counteract the pathological individualism characteristic of Western societies, and would form part of social work's contribution to the 'organisation of individuals and groups into broader collectivities in order to oppose many of the excesses of global capitalism' (Hil, 2001: 57).

Conclusion

Far from being of marginal concern, globalization has profound implications for social work and those working in the welfare and social care professions more broadly. Globalization gives rise to social processes and transformations of a kind and on a scale never seen before. The attempts of social theorists to make sense of and grasp the nature of those processes are of central importance to social work. Developing an awareness of the ways globalization is transforming human social life is something social workers need to embrace wholeheartedly if they are to respond and actively shape how those processes develop now and in the future. Globalization is transforming the world in ways which have negative human consequences, many of which fall to the lot of social workers across the planet to deal with, respond to and try to manage. At the same time, globalization entails the possibility for new forms of solidarity, association and collective identity. If social workers are to harness these, it is vital that they cultivate a more globally oriented mindset towards the local organisational settings and practice scenarios in which they are embedded. Doing so will allow for connections to be made and shaped between happenings in the here and now, and events taking place elsewhere in the world.

Further reading

Beck, U. (1999) *World Risk Society*. Cambridge: Polity.
Giddens, A. (2002) *Runaway World: How Globalization is Reshaping Our Lives*. 2nd ed. London: Profile.
Robertson, R. (1992) *Globalization: Social Theory and Global Culture*. London: Sage.

References

Ahmadi, N. (2003) 'Globalisation of Consciousness and New Challenges for International Social Work', *International Journal of Social Welfare*, 12: 14–23.
Albrow, M. (1996) *The Global Age*. Cambridge: Polity.
Appadurai, A. (1996) *Modernity at Large: Cultural Dimensions of Globalization*. Minneapolis: University of Minnesota Press.
Bauman, Z. (1998) *Globalization: The Human Consequences*. Cambridge: Polity.
Bauman, Z. (2007) *Liquid Times: Living in Age of Uncertainty*. Cambridge: Polity.
Beck, U. (1992) *Risk Society: Towards a New Modernity*. Cambridge. Polity.
Beck, U. (1999) *World Risk Society*. Cambridge: Polity.
Beck, U. (2000a) *What Is Globalization?* Cambridge: Polity.
Beck, U. (2000b) 'The Cosmopolitan Perspective: Sociology of the Second Age of Modernity', *The British Journal of Sociology*, 51(1): 79–105.
Bhabha, H. (1994) *The Place of Culture*. London: Routledge.
Bonnano, A. and Constance, H. (2010) *Stories of Globalization: Transnational Corporations, Resistance and the State*. University Park: Penn State University Press.

Bose, A. B. (1992) 'Social Work in India: Developmental Roles for a Helping Profession', in Hokenstad, M. C., Khinduka, S. K. and Midgley, J. (eds.) *Profiles in International Social Work*. Washington: DC: NASW Press, pp. 71–84.

Caragata, L. and Sanchez, M. (2002) 'Globalization and Global Need', *International Social Work*, 45(2): 217–238.

Castells, M. (1996) *The Rise of the Network Society, the Information Age: Economy, Society and Culture*. Vol. 1. Oxford: Blackwell.

Castells, M. (1998) *End of Millennium, the Information Age: Economy, Society and Culture*, Vol. 3. Oxford: Blackwell.

Castells, M. (2000) 'Materials for an Exploratory Theory of the Network Society', *British Journal of Sociology*, 51(1): 5–24.

Castells, M. and Ince, M. (2003) *Conversations with Manuel Castells*. Cambridge: Polity.

Cheung, M. and Liu, M. (2004) 'The Self-Concept of Chinese Women and the Indigenization of Social Work in China', *International Social Work*, 47(1): 109–127.

de Sousa Santos, B. (2014) *Epistemologies of the South: Justice Against Epistemicide*. Oxford: Routledge.

Dicken, P. (2015) *Global Shift: Mapping the Changing Contours of the World Economy*. London: Sage.

Dominelli, L. (2009) *Social Work in a Globalizing World*. Cambridge: Polity Press.

Dominelli, L. (2010) 'Globalization, Contemporary Challenges and Social Work Practice', *International Social Work*, 53(3): 599–612.

Dominelli, L. and Hackett, S. (2005) 'Social Work Responses to the Challenges for Practice in the 21st Century', *International Social Work*, 55(4): 449–453.

Dominelli, L. and Hoogvelt, A. (1996) 'Globalization and the Technocratization of Social Work', *Critical Social Policy*, 47(16): 45–62.

Ferguson, I., Lavalette, M. and Whitmore, E. (2005) *Globalization, Global Justice and Social Work*. London: Routledge.

Friedman, T. (1999) *The Lexus and the Olive Tree*. London: HarperCollins.

Giddens, A. (1990) *The Consequences of Modernity*. Cambridge: Polity.

Giddens, A. (1991) *Modernity and Self Identity: Self and Society in the Late Modern Age*. Cambridge: Polity.

Giddens, A. (2002) *Runaway World: How Globalization is Reshaping Our Lives*. 2nd ed. London: Profile.

Gould, A. (1993) *Capitalist Welfare Systems: A Comparison of Japan, Britain and Sweden*. London: Longman.

Gray, M. (2005) 'Dilemmas of International Social Work: Paradoxical Processes in Indigenisation, Universalism and Imperialism', *International Journal of Social Welfare*, 14(2): 230–237.

Gray, M. and Fook, J. (2004) 'The Quest for a Universal Social Work: Some Issues and Implications', *Social Work Education*, 23(5): 625–644.

Hannerz, U. (1989) 'Notes on the Global Ecumene', *Public Culture*, 1(2): 66–75.

Hardt, M. and Negri, A. (2000) *Empire*. Cambridge, MA: Harvard University Press.

Hare, I. (2004) 'Defining Social Work for the 21st Century: The International Federation of Social Workers' Revised Definition of Social Work', *International Social Work*, 47(3): 407–424.

Harris, J. and Chou, Y. C. (2001) 'Globalization or Glocalization? Community Care in Taiwan and the U.K.', *European Journal of Social Work*, 4(2): 161–172.

Hil, R. (2001) 'Globalisation, Governance and Social Work: Some Implications for Theory and Practice', *Australian Social Work*, 54(4): 63–76.

Hokenstad, M. C. and Midgley, J. (eds.) (1997) *Issues in International Social Work: Global Challenges for a New Century*. Washington, DC: NASW Press.

Hong, P. Y. (2010) 'Glocalization of Social Work Practice: Global and Local Responses to Globalization', *International Social Work*, 53(5): 656–670.

Ietto-Gillies, G. (2002) *Transnational Corporations: Fragmentation Amidst Integration*. Oxford: Routledge.

Ife, J. (1998) 'Globalization, Internationalization and Community Services: Implications for Policy and Practice', *Journal of Applied Social Science*, 23(1): 43–56.

Ife, J. (2001) 'Local and Global Practice: Relocating Social Work as a Human Rights Profession in the New Global Order', *European Journal of Social Work*, 4(1): 5–15.

Ifsw.org. (2017) *International Federation of Social Workers/Resource for social workers to share, discover and learn.* [ONLINE] Available at: http://ifsw.org/ [Accessed 12 March 2017].

Irvine, Z. and Payne, M. (2005) 'Globalisation: Implications for Learning and Teaching', in Burgess, H. and Taylor, I. (eds.) *Effective Learning and Teaching in Social Policy and Social Work.* London: Abingdon Press & Routledge Falmer, pp. 153–169.

Khan, P. and Dominelli, L. (2000) 'The Impact of Globalization on Social Work in the UK', *European Journal of Social Work,* 3(2): 95–108.

Klein, N. (2001) *No Logo.* London: Flamingo.

Lyons, K, (2006) 'Globalization and Social Work: International and Local Implications', *British Journal of Social Work,* 36(3): 365–380.

Midgley, J. (1981) *Professional Imperialism: Social Work in the Third World.* London: Heinemann.

Midgley, J. (1996) 'Social Work and International Social Development: Promoting a Developmental Perspective in the Profession', in Hokenstad, M. C. and Midgley, J. (eds.) *Issues in International Social Work: Global Challenges for a New Century.* Washington, DC: NASW Press, pp. 11–26.

Midgley, J. (2001) 'Issues in International Social Work', *Journal of Social Work,* 1(1): 21–35.

Nagpaul, H. (1993) 'Analysis of Social Work Teaching Material in India: The Need for Indigenous Foundations', *International Social Work,* 36: 207–220.

Nimmagadda, J. and Cowger, C. (1999) 'Cross-Cultural Practice: Social Worker Ingenuity in the Indigenization of Practice Knowledge', *International Social Work,* 42(3): 261–276.

Otis, J. (1986) 'The Transferability of Western Social Work Education across National and Cultural Boundaries: Fact or Fiction?', *Journal of International and Comparative Social Welfare,* 2(1, 2): 37–45.

Otto, H. U. and Lorenz, W. (1998) 'The New Journal for the Social Professions in Europe', *European Journal of Social Work,* 1(1): 1–4.

Patel, L. and Hochfeld, T. (2012) 'Developmental Social Work in South Africa: Translating Policy into Practice', *International Social Work,* 56(5): 1–15.

Payne, M. and Askeland, G. (2008) *Globalization and International Social Work: Postmodern Change and Challenge.* Oxford: Routledge.

Penna, S., Paylor, I. and Washington, J. (2000) 'Globalization, Social Exclusion and the Possibilities for Global Social Work and Welfare', *European Journal of Social Work,* 3(2): 109–122.

Prager, E. (1985) 'American Social Work Imperialism: Consequences for Professional Education in Israel', *Journal of Jewish Communal Service,* 61: 129–138.

Pugh, R. and Gould, N. (2000) 'Globalization, Social Work, and Social Welfare', *European Journal of Social Work,* 3(2): 123–138.

Robertson, R. (1992) *Globalization: Social Theory and Global Culture.* London: Sage.

Robinson, W. (2011) 'Globalization and the Sociology of Immanuel Wallerstein: A Critical Appraisal', *International Sociology,* 26(6): 723–745.

Trevillion, S. (1997) 'The Globalisation of European Social Work', *Social Work in Europe,* 4(1): 1–9.

Tsang, A. K. T. and Yan, M. C. (2001) 'Chinese Corpus, Western Application: The Chinese Strategy of Engagement with Western Social Work Discourse', *International Social Work,* 44(4): 433–545.

Urry, J. (2000a) *Sociology Beyond Societies.* London: Routledge.

Urry, J. (2000b) 'Mobile Sociology', *British Journal of Sociology,* 51(1): 185–203.

Wallerstein, I. (1974) *The Modern World-System I: Capitalist Agriculture and the Origins of the European World-Economy in the Sixteenth Century.* New York: Academic Press.

Wallerstein, I. (2004) *World-Systems Analysis: An Introduction.* Durham: Duke University Press.

Werbner, P. and Modood, T. (eds.) (1997) *Debating Cultural Hybridity.* London: Zed.

10

THE FUTURE OF SOCIAL THEORY AND SOCIAL WORK

Introduction

Throughout this book we have explicated and applied social theoretical ideas and paradigms, using them to cast a powerful and illuminating light on a range of social work practice scenarios, issues and debates. A characteristic feature of these ideas is the divergent perspectives they provide for interrogating a wide range of social and cultural phenomena. In this concluding chapter, we will attempt to pull together the numerous and diverse thematic strands and threads we have unpacked in the previous chapters.

We shall consider three main topics, each of which is crucial for thinking about the nature of the relationship between social theory and social work both now and in the future. The first concerns the question of how useful the ideas of social theory are in relation to social work in a general sense. The intention here is to address how certain core social work values and objectives might be re-evaluated and understood under the conditions of a rapidly globalizing world. How have the most salient changes to and developments in society covered throughout this book impacted on the core values and objectives of social work? With reference to a number of the concepts covered in the previous chapters, we will demonstrate and underscore the important part social theory can play in realizing a number of core social work values in the present day.

The second topic we will address concerns reflexivity. Reflexivity involves actively reflecting on the ways our own socially-shaped perceptions and cultural background inform how we think, feel and act. In the introductory chapter it was suggested that adopting a reflexive stance towards the ideas covered throughout the book would lead to a more transformative relationship with social theory. It is important to reflect on the nature of our engagement with social theoretical ideas, in particular thinking about why we are positively disposed towards certain ideas and perspectives, at the same time as being negatively disposed towards and turning away from others. It is important to exercise a degree of reflexive vigilance when using social theoretical ideas. Doing so allows you to grasp the socially shaped reasons structuring the nature of your own engagement with the world. It enables you to identify and grasp the possibilities and constraints embedded in the ways of thinking that you – the reader – import into your encounter with social theory. In the section on reflexivity, we cast a reflexive eye over the relationship between social work and social theory generally, as well as more specifically the work of Pierre Bourdieu (already covered in Chapter 7).

The third and final topic we will cover concerns the relationship of social theory and social work in the future. Here we will consider how social theory and social work can work to develop a positively enriching and mutually empowering relationship.

Social work values and objectives in a globalizing world

The intellectual debt of modern social theorists to their classical forebears is an extensive one. A useful way of thinking about classical social theory involves seeing it as a series of intellectual provocations. Classical theory raises questions about human social life which subsequent generations of modern theorists have sought to address and answer. Broadly speaking, the influence of classical theory has shaped the thematic concerns of modern social theorists in line with two central concepts: alienation and solidarity. Alienation refers to a situation whereby individuals feel existentially estranged, socially dislocated and culturally disorientated, both from themselves and one another. Solidarity is the flipside of alienation. Solidarity occurs when individuals are socially integrated and culturally bound, as part of wider collectives and forms of communal association. Modernity can be regarded as containing elements of both, in the form of varying degrees of estrangement and disorder, as well as giving rise to expressions of social unity and cultural coherence.

As with social theory, the origins of social work are rooted in the transition to modernity. Also as with social theory, a concern with the themes of alienation and solidarity is central to social work. A core part of social work involves challenging and eradicating discrimination and oppression in society, at the same time as promoting integration and solidarity between individuals and wider collectives. The commitment of social workers to upholding these values is expressed in the moral principles and code of ethics contained within the professional guidelines and policies organising social work practice. These can be found in the ethical statements of professional bodies such as the British Association of Social Workers (BASW), the International Association of Schools of Social Work (IASSW) and the IFSW. In this section of the chapter we consider how the conceptual ideas dealt with throughout this book can be used to try to promote core social work values under the conditions of increasing globalization.

Social work and the redistribution of resources

The task of redistributing welfare resources to those members of society who need them most is the primary social function of social work. The term *resources* refers to a wide range of social work services and forms of assistance. As society has become increasingly complex and differentiated, the range and types of resources social workers are charged with redistributing have steadily increased. The roles played by social workers today are multiple and varied. Social workers can be found across a wide range of social fields, including administration and social policy, child and family social services, community services, education social work, criminal justice, substance abuse, residential childcare, adult health, working with elderly people, mental health and psychiatric services, advocacy and academic social work. As modernity moves into a new stage of global transformation, it is important to consider what this means for the role played by social work in the redistribution of welfare resources.

In the an increasingly global society, the organisation and type of relations conjoining social workers, social work services and service-users are changing. The first point to make here concerns the amount of resources available to social workers. The economic and political dimensions of globalization have impacted negatively on the welfare state. This is often used to justify cuts to spending in the provision of public welfare services. The pressure on national governments to enhance their economic performance in order to remain competitive in the global economic market is increasing. In many nations, this has led to significant cuts to and the increasing marketization of welfare services. The amount of economic expenditure on the welfare state is declining. As the number of people drawing on social work services has increased, the amount of resources available to social work to meet the rising levels of demand is steadily declining.

Globalization exacerbates and accelerates many of the social processes set in motion during earlier stages of modernity. This has impacted significantly on the relationship between social workers and the resources they are charged with redistributing on the one hand, and the relationship they have with the recipients of those resources on the other. Since the 1980s, the relations between social workers and service-users have become increasingly formal, impersonal and indirect. Moreover, the relations of interdependency in which individuals, institutions and entire nations are positioned are extending and stretching ever more across the globe. The distance between social workers and welfare resources is lengthening. Moreover, the relations between social workers and service-users are increasingly likely to include a range of specialist statutory and non-statutory service providers.

As the bureaucratic structures social workers are embedded in have become increasingly complex, stretched and rationalized, the capacity for social workers to directly access welfare resources has diminished. Accessing and making those resources available to service-users require mobilizing and coordinating the actions and interactions of an increasingly wide range of actors social workers are required to try to coordinate the delivery of care services between multiple actors. Positioned across a wide range of fields and networks. These are characterised by their own internal dynamics, interests and power structures. Far from being the gatekeepers they once were, social workers are more likely now to act in the capacity of supervisors and coordinators of care services.

The relationship of social workers to the criteria by which service-users are adjudged to qualify for social work services is less direct than it has ever been (Chapter 6). In the past, the task of allocating resources to service-users was one social workers were integral to (George and Wilding, 1999). Social workers were entrusted to draw on their professional integrity and experience to inform the decisions they made regarding how best to redistribute the resources available to them. The increasing proliferation of ICT within social work has seriously undermined the autonomy of social workers to exercise any agency in this capacity (see Chapter 6). Moreover, while many of the changes associated with the 'e-turn' in social work are justified on the grounds that they lead to greater efficiency and standardization of care services, in actuality many social workers feel increasingly estranged from service-users, the social work relationship and the resources they are charged with redistributing.

The primary social function of social work is to redistribute welfare resources to those members of society experiencing difficulties and hardship. Many of the social processes set in motion in the earlier stages of modernity such as rationalization, marketization, bureaucratization and governmentality have led to social workers becoming increasingly estranged from service-users on the one hand, and the means for distributing and delivering welfare resources on the other. The general consensus within social work is that these changes make it ever more difficult to realize a number of the core values underpinning social work. The theoretical ideas presented in this book have provided us with a vocabulary for identifying and explaining the social reasons informing these processes. Looking to the future, social work needs to reconstruct its relationship with social theory if it is to play a greater hand in maintaining control of and determining the roles and activities social workers are charged with undertaking.

Social work and self-determination

Self-determination is a core social work value. Social workers are committed to ensuring service-users play an active part in shaping the assistance provided to them as well as seeking to empower them more generally, where possible providing them with the skills and tools for regaining control of and determining the course of their own lives. Self-determination is a central concept within social theory. It forms part of the wider set of analytical questions and issues covered by the 'structure versus agency' debate (Chapter 1). Social theory was born of a fundamental concern to develop an in-depth and analytically sophisticated account of the ways human agents are shaped by and are able to shape the social conditions of their lives. This is exactly what the classical social theorists set out to try to understand. Modern social theory elaborates on many of the ideas and concerns of the classical theorists to try to explain how and in what ways human life is determined by the transformations and changes to society in a rapidly globalizing world.

As we saw explicitly in relation to the work of Bourdieu (Chapter 7), the capacity for self-determination relates directly to the concept of autonomy, and the capacity to think and act in ways chosen by oneself as opposed to thinking and acting in ways determined by some external force or authority, whether that be a person, institution or social structure. That is what autonomy means. Throughout this book, we have examined a range of different thinkers and theoretical perspectives, using them to cast light on the ways in which, broadly speaking, social factors impinge on and shape how individuals and groups perceive, think, feel, act and interact. This has meant drawing attention to and demonstrating how the organisation and relations binding individuals and groups enable them to think and act in certain ways while constraining their capacity to think and act in others.

A key point to make here concerns the organisation and structure of modern Western capitalist societies under globalization. In the opening chapter of this book, the question was raised as to why within recent years the value of social theory has steadily diminished within social work. Rather than seeing this as something to do with the nature of social theoretical knowledge per se, the response to this question involved turning our attention to how the relationship between the individual and the social are imagined and represented in a culture of by now, arguably, pathological individualism. A culture of individualism is one in which human agents are understood and understand themselves first and foremost as self-determining and morally autonomous. As we have seen throughout this book that we conceive of ourselves as individuals at all cannot be understood without reference to the social-structural conditions which make it more or less possible for us to think and act in this way.

Perhaps the biggest contribution social theory can make to social work relates directly to the value and realization of self-determination. Social theory provides the conceptual ideas and perspectives needed to be able to grasp the socially constituted nature of social work. Another way of saying this is that social theory brings to light the ways myriad social factors shape the organisation, identity, self-understanding and activities characteristic of social work. Social theory allows us to identify and demonstrates how a range of social factors, structures, processes and dynamics make social work possible at all. Social theory provides the conceptual vocabulary with which to identify and grasp how social workers are enabled by changes to the social contexts in which they are embedded and constrained by them too. In sum, there can be no social work without the 'social', and the 'social' makes possible as well as constrains social work.

A vision of social work without the conceptual means for grasping the socially constituted nature of its own self seems unimaginable, but is becoming increasingly likely. A social work denuded of social theoretical concepts and ways of seeing is one capable of playing only a very impoverished part in determining the nature of its own self-constitution and identity. The capacity of social work to determine the nature of its own identity, its wider social function and the activities of social workers can be only very limited if the means for grasping the social basis of its own constitution are denied. In many ways, the story of the development of social work from the final third of the twentieth century onwards is the story of a profession increasingly denied the means for determining the nature of its own identity, values and activities. This loss of autonomy is likely to continue if social work fails to grasp and explore the social basis of its self-constitution. Now more than ever, social work needs to draw on the penetrating range of insights and ways of thinking characteristic of social theory.

Challenging discrimination

While referring to a number of long-term transformations and transnational processes, globalization has concrete consequences for individuals living in particular local communities. In a rapidly globalizing world, increasing migration and flows of people to and from different countries mean communities are made up of a broadening range of ethnically, religiously and culturally diverse groups. Communities made up of individuals and groups with very diverse, in some cases openly opposing, values and beliefs are brought into contact with and live alongside one another. In many contexts, this has led to rising tensions, hostility and fragmentation both within and between communities as patterns of discrimination and marginalization ordered along various different lines emerge.

In attempting to combat discrimination, social work has drawn extensively on interpersonally oriented forms of social theory such as symbolic interactionist and phenomenologically inspired ideas and concepts. Working with individuals and small groups and in community settings, social workers have appropriated ideas from these theoretical traditions in their efforts to tackle stigma, discrimination and exclusion whenever and wherever they arise. Focussing on individuals and the relationships in which discrimination takes place is important. After all,

discrimination is perpetrated by and against concrete individuals. Viewed from a social theoretical perspective, however, focussing on individuals to the extent that wider social-structural
and relational factors are overlooked is deeply problematic. It heightens the likelihood that discrimination comes to be understood and explained primarily on the basis of individual factors.

At the time of writing, accounts of rising levels of discrimination loom large in the media
and popular consciousness. Stories of hate crimes, racially and religiously aggravated tensions
and discrimination of one form or another appear in the news on an almost daily basis. While
individual factors are part of the explanations behind these deeply troubling incidents, it is
important to retain a focus on the social reasons behind these complex issues. A concern to
explain the social causes of discrimination, hostility and tensions between individuals, groups
and indeed entire nations featured throughout the work of Norbert Elias (Chapter 5). In studies such as *The Established and the Outsiders* (Elias and Scotson 1994 [1965]) and *The Germans*
(1990) Elias wanted to demonstrate and explain that the disposition towards equality, toler-
ance and acceptance of difference – the diametric opposites of discrimination – is only in part
explicable on the basis of individual factors. Just as important for Elias are the wider networks
and figurations of relations of dependency binding human groups.

Discrimination, stigmatization, racism and so on are in part due to personal factors, but even
where this is true, Elias's work identifies the social conditions in which discrimination and
exclusion are more or less likely to occur. Whether or not individuals who engage in stigmatizing and discriminatory practices are ignorant, closed-minded, racist or otherwise is only part
of the story. Elias's work on insider/outsider group relations demonstrates that the figurations
and types of relations in which individuals are situated intimately shape the likelihood that
discrimination and conflict occur at an interpersonal level. As long as attempts to eradicate and
tackle discrimination focus primarily on individual reasons, the likelihood of eradicating the
tensions and hostilities between human groups remains slim.

Elias and Scotson (1994 [1965]) claim the likelihood that discrimination takes place cannot be separated out from the balance, or 'power ratio', of social relationships of dependency
binding members of different groups. Where the relations of dependency between groups are
such that one perceives the other as dependent, as opposed to interdependent, the likelihood
increases that individuals within the more independent group will imagine and represent those
belonging to the dependent group in negative, hostile and caricatured ways. Elias invokes a
vocabulary of 'figurations', 'power ratios', 'relations of dependency', 'social-relational density'
and so on to explain the propensity of individuals and groups to discriminate against one
another. The conceptual ideas and arguments contained within Elias's work which to date
remain virtually untapped by social work provide an invaluable stock of intellectual resources
to carry forward into the post-Brexit era in the U.K. and an increasingly unsettled and precari-
ously poised global society.

As human societies the world over enter a period during which the powerful and divisive
forces of globalization intensify and proliferate, social work needs to expand its theoretical
imagination. Social theory provides ways of thinking capable of grasping the underlying social
processes and dynamics giving rise to hostility and discrimination within and between human
groups. Historically, SI and phenomenological ways of thinking have provided valuable insights
into the socially construction of stigma. As the structural figurations by which whole nations
relate to one another are transformed, social work needs to expand its understanding of the
socially shaped processes feeding into and informing discrimination and prejudice.

Promoting social solidarity

Globalization, as we have seen already, is characterised by a range of contradictory tendencies and tensions. Globalization leads to greater contact and connectivity between human groups and cultures at the same time as giving rise to increasing intolerance and hostility. But this is only half of the story. As part of those same processes, possibilities arise for new types of solidarity, collective associations and forms of identity. Globalization provides the social conditions for new forms of cohesion. In addition to developing a greater awareness of the social causes of discrimination, social work also has an important part to play in promoting new forms of social solidarity. One way this could take place would involve redirecting the delivery of social work services away from an overly narrow concern with individuals, towards more community-based and collective forms of service provision.

As the work of Giddens and Castells (Chapter 9) draws to attention, the increasing proliferation of internet-based technologies intensifies the interconnectedness of people across the globe. Online media and forms of communication give rise to new forms of social network and network-based collectives and communities. Castells regards the radical restructuring of social relations through internet-based communication as a new stage in the development of late modernity. Here he is referring to the transformation in the social-structural basis of social relations away from the relatively static and enduring structures of class, gender, etc. towards multiple proliferating and intersecting networks, some of which are relatively stable and enduring and others more dynamic and fleeting. Understanding changes to the social relations binding people across local, national and transnational contexts forms an important part in the task of promoting new forms of solidarity in a globalizing world.

Combining Castells's focus on networks with Bourdieu's concept of capital provides a conceptual framework for rethinking community-based forms of social work practice aimed at building solidarity between community members at a grass-roots level. In areas and communities divided by inequalities and socio-cultural tensions, the formation of community-based networks instigated and facilitated by social workers could provide an effective method for redistributing different forms of capital within the community (Gilchrist, 2000). Through a combination of face-to-face interactions and internet-based forms of communication such as websites, social media and email, new forms of collective identity and solidarity can develop around issues and themes identified by and relevant to community members. Over time and space, the use of online technologies can increase solidarity between individuals and communities – by developing and building up actual and virtual relationships and exchanges, the means by which a range of socially valuable resources – forms of capital – are able to flow.

The formation of social networks through face-to-face interactions and internet-based technology is relatively inexpensive and cost efficient. Moreover, networks are less likely to give rise to the kinds of top-down hierarchical structures engendered by more formal types of institution and organisation (Gilchrist, 2004). Networks have the advantage of allowing for a freer exchange of capital between individuals and groups, are relatively free of formal bureaucracy and are less likely to reproduce hierarchies and divisions between the wider community and prominent community figures and delegates. As part of their fluid and dynamic nature, networks are able to combine formal and informal elements, statutory and non-statutory elements, individuals and small groups, as well as enabling for the provision of social work services in a range of forms including interactional approaches, neighbourhood work and individual case-management. If community networks are founded on the values of trust and respect for difference, the possibility opens up for the redistribution of forms of capital embedded within the community in a number of ways. Community members with high economic and social capital are able to redistribute their resources towards wider collective initiatives, sponsoring new and innovative community-based initiatives as well as facilitating links between prominent community members and formal organisations (Ennis and West, 2014). The possibility arises too for embedding more isolated members of the community into and across networks, as well as forging links with and reaching out to other communities, either locally, nationally or transnationally.

Reflexivity, social theory and social work

Becoming a social worker involves learning a role which carries certain responsibilities. In many ways the same could be said of social theory. Learning about social theory carries certain responsibilities, particularly in terms of how you use social theoretical knowledge to inform your actions and interactions. Social theory opens up a range of penetrating and often counter-intuitive insights into the nature of human life and society. Those insights can be incredibly empowering for those who take the time to explore and cultivate them. Social theory allows us to think very differently about the social world and by extension ourselves and others. It allows us to grasp the active role we play in shaping situations, and relationships. Social theory is empowering because it provides knowledge which can be used to instigate personal and collective change. Bourdieu (2011: 3) likened social theory to a martial-art: 'basically you can use it to defend yourself, without having the right to use it for unfair attacks.' Perhaps social theory should come with a health warning. Ingesting social theory is liable to change how you think and act in ways you cannot fully anticipate or control. Always consume social theory responsibly!

One of the ways social theory engenders the potential for change involves identifying and raising questions about the nature and use of power. A concern with power is central to social theory and is expressed by the kinds of questions posed by social theorists. What forms does power take? What are the mechanisms by which it is produced? Whose interests are served by organising human groups in particular ways? How does this shape how people think and act? To what extent are they aware of the effects of power? How can power be resisted? It is important to recognise how concerns about power and social theory relate to one another. Just as important is the need to understand how social theoretical knowledge is shaped by and arises out of struggles for power between individuals and groups.

No less than the phenomena they purport to analyse, social theoretical ideas are shot through with relations of power (Thorpe, 2011). As we saw with the work of Foucault (Chapter 6), social theoretical knowledge does not develop in an intellectual vacuum sealed off from wider society. Social theoretical ideas and concepts are produced by individuals either alone or as part of wider collectives. Like any individual, social theorists are possessed of a gender, ethnic identity, social-class position and range of life experiences. Moreover, social theorists are situated in wider struggles for personal, professional and institutional forms of power and advancement. Theoretical ideas are marked by the attributes of the people who create them, the life conditions of the groups they belong to and the professional struggles for power of which they form a part. This is why all social theory is political, even when it claims not to be. As the work of various thinkers featured in this book seeks to demonstrate, the claim that social theory is objective, impartial and purged of the relations of power from which it is forged is a highly ideological one. No less is this true for those who claim it is not, which of course proves the general point!

It is important when you engage with social theory to try to reflect on and grasp as best you can how the socially and culturally shaped dispositions you embody shape the nature of your own engagement with particular theoretical ideas and concepts. Really, the best way to think about your engagement with social theory is to imagine it as like entering a relationship: on the one hand, there is the individual – you; and on the other, social theory – a body of diverse theoretical concepts and ways of thinking about the people and world around you. Adopting a reflexive stance towards the social theoretical ideas you encounter is vital. It provides an opportunity to reflect on the socially shaped dispositions and values you bring to your relationship with social theory. It is in and through relationships that you learn who you are. The more you understand social theory, the more you will understand yourself, and why it is you feel positively inspired by certain ideas, feel indifferent to some and actively come to reject others. You will be able to use the theoretical ideas you have learned to analyse not just yourself, but the socially shaped reasons for the relationship you have towards particular types of social theory.

Questioning the significance of your relationship to certain theoretical ideas is important. The same can be said about the relationship of social work more generally to particular types of social theory. If engaging with social theory is best imagined as entering a relationship, then it is important to consider why the relationship of social work to certain theoretical traditions has flourished e.g. symbolic interactionism (Chapter 4), Foucault and post-structuralism (Chapter 6), and feminist social theory (Chapter 8), while others have been slow to develop e.g. phenomenology (Chapter 3) and globalization theory (Chapter 9), and in some cases have hardly developed at all e.g. Elias (Chapter 5) and Pierre Bourdieu (Chapter 7). In the following section of the chapter, we reflect on what to date might best be described as a relationship of neglect between social work and the conceptual ideas of a thinker who might not be unreasonably referred to as one of the most influential social theorists of the twentieth century.

Bourdieu and social work

It would be hard to over-emphasise Pierre Bourdieu's influence on social theory over the last forty years. In the concepts of habitus, capital and field, Bourdieu devised a systematic and versatile trilogy of theoretical constructs that have been taken up and appropriated by scholars working in a wide range of academic disciplines. Although Bourdieu was regarded as a highly divisive thinker by his contemporaries, there can be little doubt that his intellectual legacy has left a profound mark on the development and direction of modern social theory. Yet in spite of the impact and scale of his work, his ideas have been largely neglected by social work, with the exception of a small number of social work academics. Whereas the work of Foucault, for example, has provided a fertile conceptual terrain for social work academics and professionals, by contrast efforts to engage with and think through the ramifications of Bourdieu's theoretical ideas for social work are conspicuously absent. Given Bourdieu's commitment to the values of social justice, self-determination and empowering those at the sharp end of modern capitalist society, Bourdieu's neglect at the hands of social work is a curious phenomenon indeed. This was a thinker whose work speaks to social work on a number of levels, and yet to date his work has been largely overlooked.

According to Garrett (2007a, 2007b), one of few social work thinkers to engage with the work of Bourdieu, there are a number of reasons why social work has shown so little interest in his ideas. These include the complexity of Bourdieu's prose style, 'the sheer scale of his output' and the 'misleading labels frequently attached to Bourdieu (for example, "Marxist" or "post-modernist")' (Garrett, 2007b: 356). Undoubtedly, these factors carry some degree of explanatory value. But considering the sheer volume of secondary literature devoted to explaining and popularizing Bourdieu's ideas, Garrett's (2007b) reasoning seems far from convincing. This raises a number of important questions in light of what we have said about the kinds of self-knowledge that can be arrived at through developing a relationship to social theory. Of what would a social theoretical explanation of social work's relationship to Bourdieu's work consist? What can this tell us about Bourdieu *as well as* social work?

Rather than regarding the neglect of Bourdieu's ideas within social work as entirely attributable to the failings of the former, a more insightful explanation would involve assuming a relational perspective to consider why the two have never learned to get on. An important point to consider here concerns the various ways Bourdieu's ideas came to be interpreted, framed and caricatured not only during his lifetime, but even more so since his death in 2002. By the final third of the twentieth century, Bourdieu had established his reputation, certainly within European and North American social theory, as a dominant player. Like any other field of human activity, the field of social theory is one characterised by a range of struggles for power, expressed in and through a range of 'distinction games' and 'field strategies' (Chapter 7). Distinction games involve individuals competing with one another to accumulate specific forms of capital. In the distinction games played by social theorists, one of the strategies theorists employ to try to advance their professional reputation involves either siding with or trying to undermine the ideas and arguments of dominant field players.

As Bourdieu's theoretical ideas became increasingly widespread, a number of generic and standardized criticisms steadily began to grow up around them. Over time these formed the basis of an increasingly negative response to Bourdieu's work – in particular the concept of habitus – the wider aim of which formed part of the attempts of social theorists to advance their own positions and reputations within their respective academic fields. As the standardized criticisms of Bourdieu's ideas have entered the wider academy through the pages of journals, critical studies and popular guides and textbooks, they have tended to be simplified and caricatured in ways that go against the spirit in which they were intended to be read. Like so many social theoretical Chinese whispers, the more Bourdieu's ideas have been taken up and spread, the more they have been misconstrued and misrepresented. This is particularly the case with regard to the concept of habitus. The concept of habitus was Bourdieu's attempt to respond to the 'structure versus agency' debate. It concerns how and to what extent individuals are shaped by social structures at the same time as being able to respond creatively to and influence those structures.

Bourdieu's concept of habitus has been subjected to extensive critical scrutiny. Of the numerous charges levied against it, the most recurrent is that it provides an overly deterministic conception of human agents. In this reading, the view is that the social conditions individuals are born and socialized into are more influential for shaping the kind of life(style) they go on to lead than any individual or innate attributes they may or may not possess e.g. strength of character, determination, moral strength, etc. In other words, once the individual is socialized into the habitus of the group, they are typically unable to get out. The (class-based) habitus disposes the individual to see, think and act towards others and the world around them in ways that tend to reaffirm and reproduce the social-shaped dispositions characteristic of the habitus. Furthermore, because the habitus operates at the level of practical consciousness, for the most part individuals tend not to grasp how much of the way they perceive, feel, think and act is shaped by social as opposed to individual factors. In essence, the caricatured version of Bourdieu's concept of habitus likens the individual to a prisoner. The individual is a prisoner of and imprisoned within the class-based habitus of the group with very little chance of ever getting out.

To what extent can this reading of the concept of habitus be considered accurate? Is this how Bourdieu intended it to be interpreted and understood? How does it relate to the neglect of social work scholars and practitioners to engage with Bourdieu's work? Perhaps the most straight-forward point to make is that it directly contradicts Bourdieu's intention for developing the concept. As Bourdieu (1993: 25) himself commented when asked to respond to the charge that his work – typified by the concept of habitus – presented an overly deterministic account of human life, 'the degree to which the social world is *really* determined is not a question of opinion: as a sociologist, it's not for me to be "for determinism" or "for freedom", but to discover necessity, if it exists, in the places where it is.' Throughout his career, Bourdieu argued that *on the whole* modern capitalist society exhibits high levels of class-based domination and reproduction. It is statistically demonstrable in a wide range of ways that individuals with low levels of capital tend to lose the social games they play, and pass this disadvantage on to their children.

The key point to make here is that at no point did Bourdieu claim that being socialized into a particular group habitus *necessarily* leads the individual to reproduce the social position or lifestyle of the wider group they belong to, whether that is a dominated social position characterised by low levels of capital and individual autonomy, or a dominant social position characterised by high levels of capital and autonomy. People from socially dominated forms of group habitus can experience upward social mobility, and people from dominant forms of group habitus can experience downward social mobility. Nonetheless, Bourdieu wanted to identify and explain the social and cultural processes – which the concept of habitus is intended to grasp – for identifying the *tendency*, not necessity, that individuals reproduce the social position and lifestyle of the group into which they were born. The concept of habitus is intended to demonstrate that on the whole socialization into a particular group habitus disposes individuals to perceive, think, feel, act and interact in ways that make it more likely – but not necessary – that they reproduce the class-based lifestyle they were born and socialized into.

The notion that the habitus disposes the individual towards reproducing their social position is not in and of itself a necessarily objectionable one. It quickly assumes a moral gloss when the habitus of the individual is characterised by a range of inequalities and forms of estrangement. In the next section of the chapter, I want to use the concepts of habitus and field to provide a reflexive explanation of the reasons why social work has neglected to take up and engage with Bourdieu, the importance of bringing these to light and the wider implication this has for the relationship between social work and social theory.

Critically thinking the social work habitus

On entering the field of social work, social work graduates are subject to various field-specific processes of socialization, some of which are fully consciously experienced and directed (e.g. through formal procedures, instruction from colleagues and management) and others are only partially consciously experienced (e.g. through informal workplace cultures, discussions with peers). The socialization social work graduates undergo forms part of the process by which they learn to assume the social work habitus. The term *social work habitus* refers to the socially learned and patterned dispositions towards seeing, feeling, thinking and acting characteristic of professional social workers. Because the habitus operates at the level of practical consciousness, over a period of time the individual loses sight of the socially and culturally contingent nature of the practices generated by it e.g. ways of thinking, acting etc.; instead, how they think and act comes to strike them as more or less self-evident and taken-for-granted.

As the social work habitus comes to overwrite and reconfigure the practical consciousness of the trainee social worker, it provides them with the ways of seeing, thinking and acting necessary for doing social work. These are the enabling dimensions of the habitus. If these processes did not take place, individuals would not be able to think and act in the ways necessary for being a social worker. This is the view of the relationship of the individual to habitus as akin to a kind of second nature, as something experienced intuitively as the individual develops a feel for the particular social work games they are involved in playing e.g. child protection, advocacy, etc. As the habitus works to enable the individual, providing them with forms of practice characteristic of social workers, it simultaneously works to constrain them. As social workers are socialized into the 'doxa' of the field – the taken-for-granted and unconscious complex of normative ideals and assumptions, around which the field is organised – so in turn the social worker becomes less aware of the socially, culturally and historically contingent nature of these assumptions and ideals. Again, they experience these as taken-for-granted and natural.

In making this point it is not the intention to suggest that social workers are dupes, or insufficiently reflexive and self-aware. These are generic social processes all individuals undergo as part of the socialization they undertake on entering a particular field of human activity. Rather, the point is that the concepts of habitus and field provide the tools for elevating to a fully conscious level the nature of these collectively shaped processes and how they shape the individual. In doing so, it becomes possible to cast light on the ways the social work habitus disposes individuals towards certain ideas, no less those of Bourdieu(!), and the normative ideas and values contained within them, while at the same time negatively disposing them away from others. In describing the generic socialization processes all social agents undergo as they enter a particular field, Bourdieu draws attention to the contradictory dynamics embedded in the habitus. Social agents are never more constrained by the habitus than when it is working as it should, by enabling the individual to think and act freely, without having to question or reflect on how or why it is they act in the ways they do. The social work habitus is enabling because it provides the patterned ways of perceiving, thinking, feeling and interacting necessary for doing social work. But the more naturalized the habitus becomes the less likely it is that the individual social worker is able to see or grasp how it shapes their subjectivity.

Throughout this book, we have seen that certain social theoretical concepts and forms of reasoning have enjoyed a far more fruitful relationship with social work than others. Why this is the case cannot be fully understood without considering the ontology of human agents contained within particular theoretical ideas and the degree of fit they demonstrate with the conception of human agents arising out of certain core social work values. The conception of human agents as largely self-determining, proactive and capable of self-directed change has led to symbolic interactionist forms of theory having enjoyed a long and productive relationship with social work. The same is true of certain strands of feminist social theory too, particularly in its Marxist-socialist and liberal incarnations. The theoretical concepts of Foucault, in particular the emphasis on unveiling power as realized through a range of powerful forms of discourse, have been well utilised by social work academics and practitioners.

The reluctance of social work to engage with Bourdieu's work speaks of a relationship determined first and foremost by the social work habitus. Confronted with the vision of human agents as determined by the social conditions of their lives in ways that exceed the likelihood they are able to overcome them, social workers generally have been disposed away from developing a relationship with Bourdieu's ideas because of the ontology of social life contained within (the depiction of) his theoretical constructs. Understood from within the social work habitus, Bourdieu's work tends to be imagined as actively going against a number of the fundamental ideals and values on which the social work habitus is premised. But as Bourdieu himself pointed out, a disagreement always presupposes an agreement. Bourdieu's work was intended as a contribution towards trying to realize a great many of the same ideals and values as social work. What is at stake in the relationship between the theoretical ideas of Bourdieu and the social work habitus then is the account of how those values and ideals might be realized, not the values and ideals themselves.

Two important points lead out from this. The first is that Bourdieu's work can be read in a way that *could* lead to a very fruitful encounter with social work. Moreover, it is quite feasible, as has been the case in other disciplines, to draw on certain theoretical concepts while leaving aside and downplaying others. The concept of capital, for example, could quite easily be extrapolated from Bourdieu's wider theoretical edifice to be gainfully adapted for social work. The concept of capital could be used in a number of ways: how and which types of capitals might a service-user need to help them to gain access to a particular field? How could the existing skills and attributes possessed by a service-user be re-appropriated in self-serving ways? How do the types of capital possessed by a service-user decrease the likelihood that they are able to acquire other types of capital? In short, making reference to the concept of capital alone, there are lots of ways in which Bourdieu's theoretical ideas could be harnessed by social work.

The second point concerns a number of more generic points about the failure of social work to develop a relationship with Bourdieu's theoretical legacy. The concepts of habitus and field highlight how the values, beliefs and attitudes of social workers, both individually and collectively, are shaped by the professional culture they are socialized into, and how in turn this disposes them to see, think and act in particular ways.

Bourdieu's work specifically points to a number of the social processes by which individuals and groups come to be estranged from the products of their own activity. This is the definition of alienation depicted by Marx. Alienation refers to a situation whereby individuals and groups are dominated by the ideas, values and actions of previous generations. When this happens, they are far less likely to question them. Instead, they have become normalized, naturalized and are largely taken-for-granted. They no longer strike those dominated by them for what they are – namely, the reified thought products of previous generations, and not, self-evident and timeless truths.

The collective failure of social work other than in a small number of cases to develop a relationship with the work of Bourdieu can be read as testimony to the coercive power of the ideal elements of the social work habitus – the shared values, attitudes and beliefs – to inform and shape the actions of social work academics and professionals. That Bourdieu's work has been largely neglected by social work commentators speaks of the extent to which the normative dimensions of the social work habitus constrain the relationship between social work and particular forms of social theory. In this case, ironically, the social work habitus negatively disposes social work academics and professionals away from developing a relationship with a thinker whose work was underpinned by many of the same core values as social work.

That this is the case is suggestive of a number of things. Social work needs social theory if it is not to become estranged from itself. Social work needs social theory if it is to prevent itself from being dominated by the dead weight of its own past in the form of the ideal, material and normative structures handed down from one generation of social workers to the next. To prevent this from happening, social theory should be part of the education of all social workers. Presently, the marginalization of social theory within the social work curriculum means that it falls to the lot of a small cadre of social work academics to engage with and translate the theoretical ideas that the vast majority of social work practitioners draw on to inform their practice. Such a situation is detrimental to social work – it means that the vast majority of social workers depend upon a very small minority to make decisions about which theoretical ideas social work should draw on and by which it is informed.

A social work habitus infused by a far wider range of social theoretical forms of knowledge and reasoning would improve and enhance the practice of individual social workers as well as the profession, collectively. It would mean that a far greater number of social workers were exposed to the ideas and ways of thinking featured in this book. It would mean that all social workers, rather than a small minority of social work academics, were equipped with the concepts necessary for thinking critically and reflexively about the professional, organisational and relational contexts in which they are positioned. A social work habitus informed by a wide range of social theoretical forms of discourse would assist in the task of trying to claim back a degree of professional autonomy, by raising the collective awareness of the structures and dynamics of power in which social work is situated and how these could be harnessed to advance the professional values and aims of social workers. In summary, social work stands to gain a lot by developing its relationship with social theory, even when those theoretical ideas appear to contradict the ideals and values of the profession.

Social theory and social work: the future of a relationship

This book forms part of a long-standing and at times much closer relationship between social theory and social work. It has provided an overview of the terrain of social theory in the hope that you go on to develop your own relationship with the ideas and thinkers we have covered throughout the book. But really to understand social theory, you have to be prepared to try to develop your own relationship with it, to stick with it even if at first you do not always feel confident about yourself within the relationship. To get the best out of social theory, to find out what it is really like, you will have to form a direct and personal relationship with the original work of the thinkers we have covered. Rather than relying on someone else's interpretation and account of their ideas, you must get to know what they thought and said on the terms used by them. Only then will you be able to make their thinking *your* thinking. Only then will you be able to see the world as they saw it.

As this book has identified, now more than ever in the present day, social workers need to develop a relationship with social theory. Without doing so, it is hard to imagine how it would be possible to grasp the nature of the increasingly fast-paced changes and transformations taking place within human societies across the world. It is hard to imagine how it would be possible to grasp the social processes shaping how service-users see and interact with the people and situations around them. It is hard to imagine how it would be possible to develop a deeper understanding and awareness of the socially constituted nature of your own self and identity. And it is hard to imagine how social work can determine the nature of its own identity and activities in a globalizing world.

This book is intended as an act of communication. It is intended to communicate to current and future generations of social work students and professionals why it is so important to develop a relationship with social theory, why doing so should be considered both a personal and professional obligation – not in a way that becomes oppressive or overly high-minded and serious, but in a way that sharpens up your capacity for thinking critically, and that reveals the subtleties and nuances of human life. For when it has really done its job, social theory will allow you to see the world in ways you will be unable to ignore. At its best, social theory provides ways of thinking and seeing which allow you to express some of the things you may already know but find it difficult to put into words. As a social worker, you will find that the skills social theory can provide you with are invaluable, not only in a professional capacity, when you are working with service-users and colleagues, but in terms of your own self-realization and development too.

References

Bourdieu, P. (1993) *Sociology in Question*. London: Sage.

Bourdieu, P. (2011) *Sociology Is a Martial Art: The Political Writings of Pierre Bourdieu*, Sapiro, G. (ed.). New York: The New Press.

Elias, N. (1990) *The Germans: Power Struggles and the Development of Habitus in the Nineteenth and Twentieth Centuries*. Cambridge: Polity.

Elias, N. and Scotson, J. L. (1994 [1965]) *The Established and the Outsiders: A Sociological Enquiry into Community Problems*. London: Sage.

Ennis, G. and West, G. (2014) 'Community Development and Umbrella Bodies: Networking for Neighbourhood Change', *British Journal of Social Work*, 44: 1582–1601.

Garrett, P. M. (2007a) 'Making Social Work More Bourdieusian: Why the Social Professions Should Critically Engage with the Work of Pierre Bourdieu', *European Journal of Social Work*, 10(2): 225–243.

Garrett, P. M. (2007b) 'The Relevance of Bourdieu for Social Work: A Reflection on Obstacles and Omissions', *Journal of Social Work*, 7(3): 355–379.

George, V. and Wilding, P. (1999) *British Society and Social Welfare: Towards a Sustainable Society*. London: MacMillan Press Limited.

Gilchrist, A. (2000) 'The Well-Connected Community: Networking to the "Edge of Chaos"', *Community Development Journal*, 35(3): 264–275.

Gilchrist, A. (2004) *The Well-Connected Community: A Networking Approach to Community Development*. Bristol: Policy Press.

Thorpe, C. (2011) 'The Dual-Edged Sword of Sociological Theory: Critically Thinking Sociological Theoretical Practice', *Distinktion: Journal of Social Theory*, 12(2): 215–228.

INDEX

Note: Page numbers in italics indicate a table on that page.

acute self-awareness 48–50
Addams, Jane 54
Ahmadi, N. 154
alcohol and drug misuse 24
alienation: concept of 24–5, 25–6; in a global
    world 163; Marx's depiction of 174; social
    exclusion and 28
analysis, defined 43
anomic suicide 20–1
anomic tendencies of modern culture 23
anomie 23
anti-social behaviour, identity and 85–6
anxiety disorders 24
archaeological method, Foucault's 92
association, collective forms of 58–59
association and stability, traditional forms of 23
Asylums (Goffman) 60
Austin, J. L. 131
autonomy 120–1

Bagilhole, B. 137
Bailey, Roy 27
'base' metaphor, Marx's 25
Beck, Ulrich 144, 147–8, 154
Becker, Howard 59–61; *Outsiders* (1963) 61
Bentham, Jeremy 94
Berger, P.L. 40–1, *41*
Bernstein, Basil 41–2, *42*
Blumer, Herbert 57–8, *58, 64*
bodily conduct and self-regulation 74
body–mind power shift 94
body–subject concept 43–4, 48–50

Bourdieu, Pierre: concept of habitus 9; *Distinction*
    114; on fuzzy logic 118; Garrett on 171; on
    habitus and capital 108–11; influence on social
    work theory 170–2; on the notion of choice
    117–19; 'relational' perspective on social life 11;
    on self-exclusion 117–19; social unconscious
    and 121; on social work 119–21; social work
    as socio-analysis 115–17; social work habitus,
    critical reflection on 173–5; socio-analysis and
    115–17; on symbolic violence 107–8
Brake, Mike 27
British Association of Social Workers
    (BASW) 163
bureaucracy 30–1, 83
Butler, Judith 131, 132
Byrne, D. 28
Bywaters, P. 65

Calvinist religious ideals and values 29
canalisation (socialization process) 127
capital: fields and 120–1; habitus and 109–11;
    online technologies and 168
capitalist culture 116–17
capitalist society: Calvinist religious ideals and
    values 29; pathological individualism and 23;
    women and workforce exploitation 128
capitalist world system, Wallerstein's concept of
    145–6
'care *versus* control' debate 89–90
Castells, M. 148–50, *150, 157–8,* 168
Central Council for Education and Training in
    Social Work (CCETSW) 103

change, dialectical nature of 24–5
Charity Organisation Society (COS) 101–2
Charlesworth, Simon 46–7
childhood: discursively shaped category 97–8;
    as emotional and behavioural training 79–80;
    modern schooling and meritocratic values
    112–13; shame and embarrassment and 75–6;
    socialization 18, 79–80
child–labour, exploitation of 153
choice, Bourdieu on the notion of 117–19
Civilization and Its Discontents (Freud) 77
civilizing process (CP) *76*; bureaucratic
    relations and 83–4; childhood as emotional
    and behavioural training 79–80; emotions,
    rationality, and self-restraint 73–6; identity
    and anti-social behaviour 85–6; introduction
    71–3; nature of social relationships in the
    West 73–6, *76*; social habitus 76–8, *77,*
    83–5; social habitus A 78–9; social habitus
    B 80–3
The Civilizing Process (Elias) 71, 73
class: as preeminent social fact 116; service-user
    differences 137
class-based habitus 108, 172
class-based inequalities 114
classical pragmatism 54
classical social theory 163
class struggles 111–15
client/consumer/service-user evolution 98
The Client Speaks (Mayer and Timms) 64
code, language as a form of 41–2
Cohen, Stanley 61–2
collective associations 65–6
collective conscience 18–19
collective disunity 23–4
collective identity and self-image 116
collective phenomena 59, 65–6
collective representations 18
communication: linguistic habitus 110;
    local dialect, habitus and 113; social work
    relationship nd 64–5
conflict: in social work relationships 71; in society
    24–5; world 152–3
Connell, Raewyn 132, 137
consciousness 37, 43–4
consumer goods and services 28
consumer practices 28
contemporary social work, organisational basis
    of 83
Cooley, Charles Horton 58–9, *59*
core states 145
Council for Training in Social Work 2
court society, emergence of 75
Cross, S. 137
cultural capital: prestige and 109–10; self-identity
    and 116–17; socially dominant groups and 114

cultural homogenization thesis 151
cultural imperialism 151, 157
cultural myths 90
cultural power, symbolic violence and 113–15
cultural tastes and preferences 114
'cultural turn' feminism. *see* post-modernist
    feminism
culture: in capitalist society 116; coercive power
    of 23–4; socialization and 17–18
culture of control 95
culture of insecurity 154

dataveillance 95–6, 99
defamiliarization of the familiar 8
dependency 19
de Swaan, A. 72
deviance: Becker on 61; construction of selfhood
    60; stigma and 66–8; symbolic interactionism
    and 61; tendency towards 23–4
Dewey, John 54
diachronic perspective 91
dialect, habitus and 113
dialectic of milieu and action 44
dialectics, notion of 24–5
dialogical conception of the self 54–5
Discipline and Punish (Foucault) 92
discourse 90, 91–2, *92*
discrimination, challenging 166–7
discursive consciousness 38
disposable income 28
dispositions *vs.* traits 85
Distinction (Bourdieu) 114
distinction games 113–15, 114–15, *115,* 171
division of labour 19, 158
divorce statistics 24
dominance, social capital and 112
doxa (doxic ways of thinking) 109, 112
dramaturgical model (Goffman) *60*
Durkheim, Emile: control and consensus 17–21;
    functional perspective to social work 17; homo
    duplex 22; on rising individuality characteristic
    of modern society 3; structuralism and 12, 90;
    summary *20*

economic capital 109–10, 114
economic factors, conflict in society and 24–5
economic globalization 145
education system, social inequalities and 112–13
ego 77
egoistic suicide 20
elaborate code 41–2
electronic databases 99–100
electronic panopticon 95–6
Elias, N.: *The Civilizing Process* 71, 73; *The
    Established and the Outsiders* 167; *The Germans*
    167; influences on 73; notion of 'process'

72; 'processual' view of social reality 72; on
socialization 22, 28
embodied capital 109–10, 120
embodiment and experience 48–50
emotional and corporeal restraint 76
emotions, rationality, and self-restraint: childhood
as emotional and behavioural training 79–80;
the civilizing process 73–6; introduction 71–3;
social habitus 76–8; social habitus, identity, and
anti-social behaviour 85–6; social habitus A
78–9; social habitus B 80–4
employment opportunities 24
Engels, Friedrich 128; *The Origin of the Family,
Private Property and the State* (Engels) 128
epistemology 10–11, 37
Erasmus programme 157
The Established and the Outsiders (Elias) 167
etiquette books and manuals 73
e-turn (electronic turn) 99
exclusion 107–8, 117–19
existential phenomenology 42–3
expert by experience 98
exploitation of child–labour 153

family relationships 65–6
Family Systems Theory 66
female service-users 135–6
female space 45
feminism 124, 125–33
feminist social theory: in-house tensions 138–9;
introduction 124–5; liberal feminism 126–7;
Marxist/socialist feminism 127–30; Oakley on
126–7; past and present 125–33; post-modernist
feminism 131–3; radical feminism 130–1; social
work knowledge and values and 133–40
feminist social work origins 103, 124
feminist social work practice 135
field of power 121
fields, games, and distinctions 111–12, *112,* 120–1
first-order categories 38–9, 45–6
first-wave feminism 125
Folk Devils and Moral Panics (Cohen) 61–2
'forms of sociation' 55
Forte, J. A. 65
Foucault, Michel: on discourse 91–2; post-
structuralism in France 90; on socialization 22;
social work and professional power 89–104
Freud, Sigmund 5, 73, 77
Friedman, Milton 145
functional solidarity 82
fuzzy logic, Bourdieu on 118

game playing 56–7, 111–12, 120–1
games, social life as a series of 118
Garland, D. 95
Garrett, P. M. 171

gender advantages in social work 120
gender and socialization 126–7
gender-based identity 135–6
gender bias 124, 128
gender blind social work practice 135
gender imbalance 139
gender inequalities 124, 127–8
gender order 132
gender performativity 131–2
gender–social position relationship 129–30
gender stereotypes 139
genealogical approach, Foucault's 92
General Agreement on Tariffs and Trade
(GATT) 146
generalized other concept 56–7, 63
General Social Care Council (GSSC) 103, 138–9
The Germans (Elias) 167
Giddens, Anthony 147, 148–50, 168
globality 150–1, 154
globalization: Beck and 147–8; challenging
discrimination 166–7; concrete consequences
for individuals 166–7; cultural dimensions
of *152;* culture and 150–2; defined 147;
economic dimensions of 145–6; Giddens
and Castells 148–50; overview 143–4;
paradoxical effects of 147; perceived effects of
147; political dimensions of 146–7; positive
social change and 155; prominence within
social sciences and humanities 144–5; social
dynamics of 147; social solidarity and 168–9;
social work consciousness of 154–5; social
work objectives and values 163–9; social
work theories and 152–4; uncertainty and
unpredictability 24; universal social work and
155–9
global risk society 147–8
global social work body 156
glocalization 151
Goffman, Erving 59, *60*
governmentality: concept of 90; Foucault's ideas
about 92–3; social work and 100–4; summary
of *95;* in surveillance society 95–6, *96*
Greek economy, collapse of 146
group habitus 108, 116

habitualized interactions 40
habitus: Bourdieu's concept of 9; capital and
109–11; capital and field trilogy 170–2;
class-based 108; critical commentary on
122; defined 108; extensive critical scrutiny
171; group habitus 108; ideal elements of
108; individual 116; linguistic 110; material
elements of 108; paradoxical nature of 174;
practices and 109, 115–16; social-class 110;
summary of *109;* types of practices and 109
habitus and capital, Bourdieu on 108–11

Health and Care Professions Council 103
Hegel, Georg 24–5
hegemonic masculinity 132, 137
Heidegger, Martin 42–3
hermeneutics 29
Hil, R. 152
Hokenstad, M. C. 158
homo duplex 17, 22
hospital admissions 24
Hull House 54
human behaviour standards 73–4
human experience, embodied nature of 48–50
human history, 'materialist' theory of 24–5
human labour (work), transformation of 26
human mind, nature of 37
human nature, duality of 22
human psyche, Freud's model of 5, 77
human sciences, rise of 93–4
human trafficking 153
Huppatz, K. 140
Husserl, Edmund 37

the 'I' and the 'Me' 56–7, 61, 63
id 77
ideal elements of habitus 108
ideal factors of society 29, 30
identity and anti-social behaviour 85–6
identity and social institutions 58–9, *59*
ideological individualism 4
The Ideological Practice of Sociology (Smith) 129
ideology 128
'illusio' 111
impression management 60
inclusion and exclusion 107–8, 117–19
India 158
indigenous social work models 157
individual actors 59
individual autonomy, suicide and 19–21
individual failings, lack of success and 116
individual habitus 116
individualism 3–4, 158
individuals, group habitus and 108
individual self as social entity 55
Information Age 148–50
informationalism 149
information and communications technology
    (ICT) 99
information technologies, surveillance society and
    95–6
insecurity, uncertainty, and anxiety, culture of 154
institutions: conception of 59; 'panoptic' principles
    and 94; within SI thinking 65–6
inter-group hostilities 23–4
internalization 40
International Association of Schools of Social
    Work (IASSW) 163

International Federation of Social Workers
    (IFSW) 155–6
international trade laws 146
internet-based technologies 149
interpersonal conduct, shame and embarrassment
    and 75
interpersonal crimes 23–4
interpersonal dynamics 65, 66–8
interpretative traditions 11–12

James, William 54
job stability 24
Jones, C. 102

Kant, Immanuel 18, 37
knowledge exchange 157

Labelling Theory 61
language: and development of selfhood 62–3;
    in development of selfhood 58; as a form of
    code 41–2; habitus and 113; selfhood and
    interpersonal communication and 55–6; as type
    of code 110
language, discourse, and power 90–2
language–meaning relationship 91
Levi-Strauss, Claude 90
liberal feminism 125–6, 126–7, 139
life, uncertainty and unpredictability of 24
'lifeworld' 36, 37–9, 45–6, 46–7
'line-of-fault' concept 128–9
linguistic capital 110
linguistic habitus 110
local dialect, habitus and 113
London School of Economics 101–2
long-term unemployment 28
'looking-glass self' 58
Luckmann, T. 40–1, *41*

male service-users 135–6, 137
manipulation (socialization process) 127
marijuana use metaphor 61
Marx, Karl 1–2; 'base/superstructure' model 25;
    conflict and capitalism 24–6; on development
    of modern society 40; influence on social work
    thinking and practice 27; modes of production
    128; on philosophy 2; on social structures 17;
    structuralist thinking of 12; 'structure *versus*
    agency' debate 12–13; summary of *26*
Marxist/socialist feminism 125–6, 127–30,
    130, 139
masculinities 132
masculinity, identity based on 81–2
'masters of discourse' 93–4
material elements of habitus 108
material factors of society 29, 30
materialist theory of human history 24–5

Mayer, J. 64
the 'Me' 56–7
Mead, George Herbert 55–7, *57*
Mead, G. H. 55
meaning: interpersonal dynamics and 65; multiple, overlapping, mutually reinforcing systems of 91; negotiated character of 64–5; social order and 57, *58*
meaning–action relationship 29
mechanical solidarity 19, 82
medieval period behaviours 73–5
men, feminist social work practice and 135
mental health problems, service-users and 68
mental health research 24
mental illness 94–5
meritocratic values, modern schooling and 112–13
Merleau-Ponty, Maurice 43–4, *44*, 47, 48–50
middle-class groups: behaviours 75; education and habitus 113
Midgley, J. 158
Mind (UK charity) 24
Mind, Self and Society (Mead) 55
mind–body distinction 43
misrecognition 112, 118–19
modernity: origins of 13; social work, social theory, and 163–4; unintended consequences of 147
modern society: complex nature of 5–6; Panopticon power metaphor 95; as a prison 94
modern work, transient nature of 23
modes of production, Marx and 128
moral entrepreneurs 61, 62, 67
moral panics 61–2, 67
moral values and normative ideals 158
Moss, P. 98
multi-agency teams 65
myth, discourses embedded in 92

narrative-based approach 99
natural attitude 38
network society, Information Age as 148–50
normalizing judgements 93
normative codes and values 23
normative expectations, service-users and 63
notion of 'choice' 117–19
'noumena,' Kant's world of 37, 39

Oakley, Anne: *Sex, Gender and Society* 127; on sex and gender 126–7; *The Sociology of Housework* 127
onanism 1
online world 150
ontology 10–11
opposing forces 24–5
organic solidarity 19

The Origin of the Family, Private Property and the State (Engels) 128
Outsiders (Becker) 61

Panopticon 94, 95
parental influence (socialization process) 127
parental supervision 81
pathological individualism 3, 19, 23, 24
patriarchal society 128–9
patriarchy 124, 130
Pease, R. 136, 140
performativity 131–2
peripheral states 145
personal data systems 96
personal identity: distinction games and 114–15; relationships and 53
personality, concept of 53–4
person-centred planning 36
Petrie, P. 98
'phenomena,' Kant's world of 37
phenomena–noumena distinction 37
phenomenological sociology 37–8
phenomenology 11; defined 36; existential 42–4; overview 35–6; philosophical origins of 37–42; Smith and 128; social theory and 35–51; social work and 44–50
philosophy, Marx on 2
Pierce, C. S. 54
political autonomy, threats to 146
political field 121
'poor relief' origins 72
positions, within a field 120
positivism 11–12
post-modernist feminism 125–6, 131–3
power: empowerment and 7–8; exclusion from mainstream society and 117–19; external relations of 120–1; nature and use of 169; panoptic principles of 94; relationship to social work in society 119; structural changes over time 121; uneven distribution and wielding of 107–8
power and autonomy, Bourdieu on 120–1
power dynamics 98
practical consciousness 38, 48
practices, habitus and 109, 115–16
primary socialization 18, 22
Pringle, K. 140
processual view of social reality 72
proletariat 25
'pro-social' dispositions 81
The Protestant Ethic and the Spirit of Capitalism (Weber) 29
psychoanalysis, socio-analysis as collective counterpart to 115
psychoanalytic thinking 103
'psycho-genesis' concept 72
psychological discourse 91

psychologization, capacity for 79
psychology, changing discourse of 93

radical feminism 125–6, 130–1, *131,* 139
Radical Social Work (Bailey and Brake) 27
radical social work movement 2, 27
rationalization, bureaucracy and 29–31
reality: as a product of discourse 92; social
    construction of 40–1
redistribution of resources 163–5
reflexive awareness 9–10
reflexivity 162–3
reflexivity, social theory, and social work 169–70
relationships, selfhood and identity and 53–4
resources, redistribution of 163–5
restraint, emotional and corporeal 76
restricted code 41–2, 46–8
risk and prevention, surveillance and 96
Robertson, Roland 150–1
role distance 60
roles, bureaucratic 30–1
ruling class 25

Saussure, Ferdinand de 90–1
school, as first-order category 45
School of Sociology (London) 2, 101–2
Schutz, Alfred 37–8, *40*
scientific discourse 101
scientific methods 93
Scotson, J. L. 167
secondary socialization 22
second-order categories 38–9, 46
second-wave feminism 125
segmental solidarity 82
Seidler, V. J. 136
selective attention 54–5
self-awareness 48–50
self-determination 107–8, 158, 165–7
self-exclusion 117–19
'self-feeling' 58
selfhood: distinction games and 114–15; emergent
    properties of 55; formation of 28; identity and
    53–4
'self-idea' concept 58, *59*
self-identity: practices and habitus and 115–16;
    social exclusion and 28
self-indication 57–8, 64
self-objectification, achieved through talk 63
self-realization 158
self-regulation, 'panoptic' principles and 94
self-restraint: emotional and corporeal 76;
    regulation and 74
semi-peripheral states 145
sensory information about the world 37
service-users: as a discursive construct 97;
    embodiment and experience 48–50; emotional

stress and self-regulation 83–4; evolution of
    terminology 98; formation of selfhood 28;
    fraud and 67; gender differences 135; lifeworld
    of 44–6; mental health problems and 68;
    notion of 'choice' and 118–19; self-exclusion
    and 117–19; self-image at the job centre 35–6,
    50; social habitus and 83; socially marginalized
    backgrounds of 27; social work relationship 62;
    stigma and 66–8; 'talking therapies' and models
    62–3; terminologies and categories used to
    classify 99; unemployment impact on 46–7
Sex, Gender and Society (Oakley) 127
sex and gender inequalities 124–5, 126–7
sex–gender distinction 131
sexual exploitation 153
shame and embarrassment 73–4, 75
shared moral values, lack of 23
shared normative ideals and values 40
'shunting' 153
Simmel, Georg 54, 55, 73
Skeggs, Beverley 129, 136
Smith, Dorothy 128
social action, hermeneutic method to the study
    of 29
social capital 110
social care services, morally ambiguous nature of
    67
social class and social exclusion 27
social-class habitus 110
The Social Construction of Reality (Berger and
    Luckmann) 40
social dominance, cultural capital and 114
social dynamics, stigma and 66–8
social exclusion and alienation 28
social habitus 76–8, *77*
social habitus, identity, and anti-social behaviour
    85–6
social habitus A 78–9
social habitus B 80–4, 86
social–individual relationship 3–4
social inequalities, education system and 112–13
social institutions 65–6
social interactions, rules underpinning 59–60
socialist feminism 126, 127–30
socialization 17–18, 21–4
socialization process, key elements of 127
social life: class and ideal and symbolic dimensions
    of 108; Durkheim's functionalist approach to
    17–21; as a series of games 118
social media sites 150
social networks, online 168
social order 25
social pathology 19–21, 23
social position–gender relationship 129–30
social reality 11; Foucault's conception of 91; as a
    process 55; women's experience of 128

social relations: of biological reproduction 128; changing attitudes over time 73; changing attitudes toward the poor 72; dependency 19; in medieval behaviours 73–5
social solidarity 168–9
social structuralism 11
social structures: coercive power of 17; declining power to regulate 23
social theoretical knowledge: composition of *12*; origins of 169–70
social theory: anatomy of 10–12; classical 163; defamiliarization 8; defined 5–6; epistemological orientation of 11–12; Freud's influence on 5; as a martial art 169; Marx and 1–2; modern–classical distinction 31–2; myths dispelled 6–7; past, present, and future 13; perceived value of 2; phenomenology and 35–51; power and empowerment 7–8; private–public connection 8–9; reflexive awareness and 9–10; reflexivity and social work 169–70; rise of individualism 3; shift in thinking and practice 2–3; structure and agency 12–13
social theory, classical: conflict and capitalism 24–6; control and consensus 17–21; culture and socialization 17–18; Durkheim on 19–21; exclusion and alienation 28–9; Marx and 24–6, *26*, 27–9; overview 16; rationalization and bureaucracy 30; social class and social exclusion 27–9; socialization 21–4; social pathologies and individual problems 23–4; social pathology 21; social work, bureaucracy, and alienation 31–2; solidarity and integration 18–19; Verstehen 31; Weber and rationality 29–31; Weber and social work 31–2
social theory–social work relationship 175–6
social unconscious, Bourdieu on 121
the social 'whole' 17, 21
social work: Bourdieu on 119–21; bureaucracy and alienation and 31–2; changes over time 89–90; as a charitable activity 102; as a class-based activity 27; defined 2; discrimination and 166–7; feminism and 138–9; gender advantages 120; gender bias in 124–5; gender imbalance in 139; gender stereotypes in 139; globalization and 143–59; governmentality and 100–4; knowledge and values 133–40; as a locality-based profession 154; primary goal of 21; primary social function of 165; professional authority and control 32; professionalization of 121; redistribution of resources and 163–5; reflexivity and social theory 169–70; self-determination and 165–6; as a socially conservative form of activity 21; as socio-analysis 115–17; as socio-analysis, Bourdieu on 115–17; surveillance and 99–100; values and

ethics 124; vocabulary of habitus, capital, and field 119–21; welfare state and 121
social work curriculum 96–7
social work education 101–3
social workers, as carriers of discourse 97
social worker–service-user relationship 96
social work habitus, critical reflection on 173–5
social work relationship: changing nature of 62; electronic databases and 99–100; with families 65–6; a fixed and self-affirming resource 63; negotiating meaning in 64–5
'social work self' 62
social work services, information and communications technology (ICT) 99
social work service-users. *see* service-users
social work–social theory relationship 1–13, 175–6
social work theory: Bourdieu influence on 170–2; impartial, objective, and value-free 129
sociation, forms of 55
society: defined 144; social-structural development of 158
socio-analysis, Bourdieu and 115–17
'socio-genesis' concept 72
sociological discourse 91, 102–3
sociology, established as a discipline 2
The Sociology of Housework (Oakley) 127
sociology–social theory relationship 5
solidarity: classical social work theory and 163; and integration 18–19; segmental and functional forms of 82
South Africa 156
'space of flows' 150
Spectator Theory of Knowledge 54
'speech acts' 131
spending money, as a social activity 28
stakes (forms of capital) 111
standard English 113
standardized modes of conduct 75
state power, exercise of 92–3
statistical methods 93
statist welfare model 153
stigma 60–1, *60*, 66–8
Stigma (Goffman) 60
stress levels, of social workers 32
structural autonomy 121
structural differentiation of society 79
structuralism 90–1
'structure *versus* agency' debate 12–13, 117–19, 171
substance misuse 24
suicide 19–21, 23
Suicide (Durkheim) 19
superego 77
'superstructure' metaphor, Marx's 25
surveillance, social work and 99–100

surveillance discourse and practice 90
surveillance society, governmentality in 95–6, *96*
Swaan, A. de 72
Sweden 153
symbolic capital, uneven distribution of 114–15
symbolic interactionism 11; applied to social
   work 62–4; Becker, Howard 61; Blumer,
   Herbert 57–8; Cooley, Charles Horton 58–9;
   development of 59–61; foundations of 54–5;
   Mead, George Herbert 55–7; moral panics
   61–2; negotiating meaning in the social work
   relationship 64–5; social reality as a process
   55; the social work self and service-user
   empowerment 62–4; stigma and service-users
   66–8; working with families 65–6
symbolic interactionist (SI) conceptions of
   selfhood 53–4
symbolic power, social capital and 114
symbolic violence: Bourdieu on 107–8; self-
   exclusion and 117–19
synchronic perspective 91

Taft, Jesse 54
'talking therapies' and models 62–3
taste dispositions 114–15
technologies, internet-based 149
terrorism, threat of 24
Thatcher, Margaret 103
third-wave feminism 125–6
time orientation 78–9
Timms, N. 64
Toyota 146
trafficking of women and children 153
traits 85
transnational corporations (TNCs) 146
transnational social work 156
transparency in the surveillance society 100
typifications, first-order categories and 38–9, 45

unemployment 28, 46
unintended consequences 9, 30, 72, 103, 139–40,
   143, 147

universalization debate 156, 157
universal social work 155–6
upper-class groups, symbolic power
   and 114
upper-middle-class groups linguistic
   habitus 110

value-oriented behaviour 30
verbal appellations (socialization process) 127
verstehen 29, 31
visual field 43–4

Wacquant, L. 115, 120
Wallerstein, Immanuel 145, *146*
watcher–watched relationship 95–6
Webb, S. 36
Weber, Max 29, *31*; *Protestant Ethic and the Spirit of*
   Capitalism 29
welfare services, marketization of 153
welfare state 102, 121
Western culture 151
winners and losers 111
Wollstonecraft, Mary 125
women. *see also* feminist social theory: as a
   category 125–6; exploitation of 128
women's rights 125
work, in a capitalist society 26
workforce exploitation 128
working-class groups: education and habitus
   113; linguistic habitus and 110; Marx on
   25; service-user differences 136; symbolic
   power and 114; women and economic
   exploitation 128
World Bank metaphor 59
world risk society 157–8
world-systems 145, *146*
World Universities Network (WUN) 157

Younghusband, Eileen 2
Younghusband Report (1957) 2

'zero-sum' games 111